Spirit Whirled

The Deaf Phoenicians

by

Dylan Michael Saccoccio

DEDICATION

My Creator and the living souls, sols, suns, sons, the sovereign inhabitants of the Earth, the Heart. I am here to raise the dead and cast away the undead. I am the Great Tide of Truth. I give all thanks, glory, and honor to God, whose light reveals that which is secret and occulted, whose power accomplishes all miracles of creation and establishes the Natural Law that governs it. One cannot make contact with that which he hath no power to attract. If my guardians have guided you to this book, you have been made a watchman, and must rise to the occasion. Failure to do so will result in dissolution of your soul. To defeat the Satanic cult of human-trafficking pedophile mass murdering parasites, knowledge is required. Keep this in goodness, and as you face the legionaries of Hell, call down the watery fire from Heaven, in service to our Creator, and burn their paper sea.

"Whoever acknowledges me before men, I will also acknowledge him before my Father in heaven. But whoever disowns me before men, I will disown him before my Father in heaven. Do not suppose that I have come to bring peace to the earth, but a sword. For I have come to turn a man against his father, a daughter against her mother, a daughter-in-law against her mother-in-law. A man's enemies will be the members of his own household. Anyone who loves his father or mother more than me is not worthy of me; anyone who loves his son or daughter more than me is not worthy of me; and anyone who does not take up his cross and follow me is not worthy of me. Whosoever finds his life will lose it, and whoever loses his life for my sake will find it." – *Jesus, the Lord Fish, son of the Pure Sea*

ACKNOWLEDGMENTS

Chris Duane, Mark Passio, Santos Bonacci, James Bomar, Chiron Last, for teaching me this skillset, the Angels that guided me to this information, all living souls who have the courage to stand in Truth, and most importantly, our Creator.

I inquired about the nature of humanity's existence and was shown the **Sword** of the Magus. The deeper you go, the more you will know. The more you know, the less you will believe, and the less you believe, the less you will fear.

"If you seek Truth, you will not seek to gain a victory by every possible means; and when you have found Truth, you need not fear being defeated." - *Epictetus*

"He who will hold another down in the mud must stay in the mud to keep him down." - *Chinua Achebe*

"No one accepts Truth until he has been forced to do so by means of experience gained through suffering. Until humanity as a whole turns its attention to the science of attaining and preserving health, it will indeed be difficult for any great number to be interested in anything but opinions. Indeed, a great deal of time will actually be spent in arguing against facts."
- *Inez Eudora Perry*

"Language, is the instrument of spirit, has a life of its own—even though it is only a reflection of the universal idea." - *Fulcanelli*

"The illiterate of the 21st century will not be those who cannot read and write, but those who cannot learn, unlearn, and relearn." – *Alvin Toffler*

"Human sickness is so severe that few can bear to look at it. But those who do will become well." - *Vernon Howard*

"Many a single word also is itself a concentrated poem, having stories of poetical thought and imagery laid up in it. Examine it and it will be found to rest on some deep analogy of things natural and things spiritual, bringing those to illustrate and to give an abiding form and body to these. For certainly in itself there is no study which may be made at once more instructive and entertaining than the study of the use, origin, and distinction of words." - *Richard Chenevix Trench*

'And He saith to me, "Go in, and see the evil abominations that they are doing there." And I go in, and look, and lo, every form of creeping thing, and detestable beast – and all the Idols of the house of Israel – graved on the wall, all round about.' – *Ezekiel 8:9-10*

CONTENTS

	Acknowledgments	i
1	You Are Nowhere	Pg 1
2	The Selfish	Pg 6
3	Creatures of Creation	Pg 21
4	Birds of a Feather	Pg 34
5	The Seven Say Ten	Pg 48
6	A Play or a Plea?	Pg 79
7	The Price of Passage	Pg 90
8	Jesus, the Rock Star	Pg 95
9	Sara's Money	Pg 112
10	The Sea of Divided Souls	Pg 118
11	Diction of Aries	Pg 123
12	The Great Enucleation	Pg 131
13	The Vault of Heaven	Pg 142
14	Caput All	Pg 151
15	The Death Pledge	Pg 159
16	Dispelling the Hex of Revelation	Pg 169
17	The Mars Covenant	Pg 195
18	Natura Naturata	Pg 216
19	Sal Duplicatum	Pg 225
20	Re-Sun to Live	Pg 236

1 YOU ARE NOWHERE

How did it get to this? Why must our babies be born into slavery? Why must we register our property? Why must we obtain licenses to do what we wish? Why is the fruit of our labor stolen from us? Why are we forced to use a currency that is nothing more than an **IOU** note, backed by nothing and inflated into worthlessness so that we can never create generational wealth with it? Why must our elderly pay taxes on property they've "paid" off? Why must we pay taxes on any transactions? What happened in the 19th and 20th centuries that created the human slavery of the 21st century? Why do people who produce so little take so much? How were 62 people able to accumulate as much wealth as half the world's population in 2016?

To acquire the answer to these inquiries, we must look to different ages, because the solutions to the 21st century's problems are not found in the 21st century mindset. The 21st century mindset accepts authority as Truth instead of Truth as authority. It mistakes the whims of man for the laws of nature. Its imagination has been led to the slaughter under the dins of different laughter. For those that read this in the following centuries, as I write these words, an estimated 9.5 million people are playing a "hybrid reality" game on their smartphones where they chase fictional videogame characters in the real world simulation using their device's location services. Ironically, the game was developed by a CIA-funded software front group that had its hand in other social media

1

platforms, creating the most pervasive network of surveillance the world has ever known. If you are reading this in the future, may you live prosperously without ever encountering such abominations. While hordes of people are stuck in a construct within a construct, a digital simulation, the world is on the brink of World War III, Venezuelans are crossing borders and killing pets to feed themselves, the insolvent banks have transferred their burdens onto nations, and countries are collapsing. As I write you, the most popular news stories are the Republican National Convention of the United States presidential reality show and a feud between two musicians whose lawyers are getting ready to do battle over leaked phone conversations being recorded and publicized without consent. Meanwhile, the government has been spying on Americans, and people all over the world, and recording them without their consent for decades with almost zero outrage.

This book is not meant to find the people of my generation, although those who do find it will benefit from it if they take it seriously. The current race is quite literally considered lost at sea, the dead, corpses known as legal fiction corporations. They are incessantly mocked with zombie movies and television shows, alluding to them, but like walking dead zombies, they mindlessly consume the mockery and love it. It is their substance. This book is meant to find you, reader, so that you can know what happened leading up to and during the most significant event of human history. I imagine most records will have been destroyed and edited by the time you get this, leaving no paper trail of what was done to your ancestors. However, to know the way the game is played, we must learn how language is used as a tool to protect those that control this paradigm from those who maintain it, or in other terms, to prevent the seven-chakra hue-mans, the pawns, from reaching the eighth square on the grand chessboard, the next octave in the seven-color spectrum, and turning into something else.

First, let us look at the definition of a **Deaf** Phoenician, provided by Chiron Last: "One who stops at the status quo's interpretation of a word, ignoring etymology and phonics."

Did you see the wordplay? Phonetically, a definition is a Deaf Phoenician. Words like phonics, phonetics, phonemes, phonology, phone, phony, etc. come from the Phoenicians, the architects of the oldest verified alphabet, derived from Egyptian hieroglyphics, containing 22 letters: 11:11. We'll get into the esoteric meanings of 11:11 later.

In order to master the use of language, one cannot not stop at the status quo's interpretation of a word. One cannot accept any authority's claim of what a word means, but rather consider it along with the other possibilities and potentials with which that word may be used. There is also a spiritual intent infused in a word's creation that may only benefit the creator(s) of it, lest that intent be known to others who speak that very word, so that it is precisely projected into the ocean of energy that exists, between bodies, with the original intent for which it was formed. One must consider various physical world elements relating to the word and then contemplate the spiritual significance of how the words are being applied, not merely by intent and action, but also by syncromysticism, physical senses, and soul senses.

To avoid confusion, the seven physical senses are **touch, taste, smell, sight, hearing, intuition,** and **thought transference.** Someone might scoff at the ludicrous claim that words could be tasted or smelled. But when something *leaves a bad taste in one's mouth,* the idiom indicates that something made one feel like something was amiss, wrong, unfair, or ill-willed. When something "smells fishy," it indicates one sensing dishonesty or something to be suspicious of. Words have all kinds of effects on people, and just because one cannot appreciate another's experience, it does not disprove or invalidate that experience.

The seven soul senses are **the power to psychometrize** (to know an object's or thing's history by touching it), **the power to absorb and enjoy the finer essence of the life wave, the power to distinguish the spiritual aromas of nature,** the lucid state called **clairvoyance** (the ability to discern objects not present to the senses or perceive matters beyond the range of one's seemingly ordinary perception), the ability to perceive the ethereal vibrations termed **clairaudience, the capacity to receive true inspiration,** and **the power to converse with spiritual intelligences at will.** We will get to the correspondences of the seven physical and spiritual senses with the seven notes of music, seven colors of the spectrum, seven chakras, seven planets, etc. soon enough.

Let me be unmistakably clear. If you have not been tampered with, you have these abilities. It is up to you to cultivate them. Most of us have been tampered with unfortunately, which is why there are so many defects in our genome. However, through epigenetics, you are not your DNA, and thus you can change yourself through the biology of your thoughts and overcome the setbacks that epieugenicists have inflicted upon you.

As one develops his or her physical and spiritual senses, many words will reveal their soul, their **sol**, to him or her through syncromysticism, defined by Jake Kotze as "the art of re alizing meaningful coincidence in the seemingly mundane with mystical or esoteric significance."

If the various options for discovering the science of the sounds of speech and the nature of one's reality become overwhelming, try experimenting with one sense or method at a time. Trying to do everything at once will cause imbalance and discord, both internally and externally. Clear your mind, speak your intent, and ask for assistance. If you are sincere, it will come to you, and like a beautiful flower, it will sprout from its seemingly dark surroundings in the soil and blossom into a higher level of consciousness.

Now, to teach you the skillset that Chiron Last taught me, let us state the primary methods of dissecting and knowing the wholeness of a word:

1. Study the different definitions throughout history. Their meanings may change with the whims of man and the evolutions or devolutions of vernaculars.
2. Explore etymologies, and remember, some scholars' guesses, though educated, are merely guesses. This is when you must tap into other senses to assist you in comprehending a word's **history** (high story) and power. Under no circumstances are you to use black magick to attain this sacred knowledge. We'll get into that, but to avoid digression we must press on.
3. Experiment with phonics and phonetics to unlock and learn the Language of the Birds, also known as Green Language, a

secret and perfect language that is the key to perfect knowledge and the evolution of human consciousness. It is the phonetic law of the spoken Kabbalah that frees the spirit of the word, allowing it to mingle with you, the living soul.

4. Play with word-splitting, the art of finding concealed meanings of words by dividing them and rearranging them into a different sequence. For example: 'Understand' can be rearranged to mean "stand under," which is why judges ask you if you understand the charges against you. They are *not* asking you if you are competent enough to comprehend the charges. We'll get into that later.

5. Anagrams, i.e. 'earth' equals 'heart' when its letters are rearranged, and the Earth functions in the seven-planet solar system the exact same way that the heart functions in the body and the heart chakra functions in the seven-chakra system. They also correspond to the green in the seven-color spectrum, which is why Nature produces green in abundance and why the Language of the Birds is called Green Language. Do you have ears to hear? Move the 's' in ears to the front of the word and you get 'sear,' "to burn or char the surface" or "to mark with a branding iron." But phonetically, 'sear' can be 'seer,' "a person blessed with profound moral and spiritual knowledge," "one who sees," or "one who prophesies the future." Are you a seer, a prophet? Do you have eyes to see? Will your life be profitable?

Before we jump into the rabbit hole, let us conclude this chapter with one of the most powerful words in the English language: 'nowhere.' Do you know where you are? You are now here because you can be nowhere else.

2 THE SELFISH

There are two primary forces in nature that are constantly in conflict to create the sine wave energy field that makes up our construct. Whether looked at metaphorically or literally, these forces could be titled syntropy and entropy, growth and decay, life and death, light and shadow, good and evil, etc.

However, in the divine idea of **Absolute** Truth, there cannot be more than one absolute. Truth is **absolute**. Freedom is **absolute**. The polarities of good and evil have a symbiotic relationship, and since everything came from one source, whether that was a big bang, a Creator or some other phenomena, all evil can be reconciled with absolute good because it all descends from the Divine Spark, the Will of Creation, whether intelligent or not.

Polarity is an observable phenomenon, or mechanism, of natural law where everything is dual and opposites are identical in nature though seemingly different in degree. But as the Truth is absolute, all paradoxes can be unified. Such is the case with good and evil, light and shadow, syntropy and entropy, spiritual and material, animalistic and angelic nature, etc. These are nothing more than the dualistic nature of the sine wave, the natural, ethereal energy that composes all matter. The moment resistance is removed from the plane of effects is the moment the wave, and thus the construct, collapses. This is the way out. As Chiron Last teaches, "Resistance is assistance."

If you're reading this, I imagine you're still in the construct, though I've written this as a ritual to honor those who have transcended it. This was my trial: to seek Truth and then to help others by sharing it. In this mundane reality, there are various states of consciousness and various stages of evolution and involution. Animal nature, what some may term as evil, darkness, ignorance, materialism, etc., revolves around one principle above all else: preservation of self.

When one witnesses an animal kill something, whether that be a bear mauling a deer or a lion mauling a zebra, though appalling as it may be, most people will dismiss it as animal nature. Very few people would state that the bear or lion is evil.

However, if a man uses a gun to shoot and then a bow and arrow to kill a lion named Cecil in Zimbabwe, there is international outrage over it. He is considered by many to be evil. As someone who observes the laws of morality, there is no question that since this man's actions involved the theft of another being's life, it was indeed an immoral act, and thus wrong, or as some might say, evil. This is because it is not animal nature to pay $55,000 for the right to kill an endangered animal. Animals don't pay to kill others. That's the business of man. So under these terms, man is not an animal, since if he were, his actions would be dismissible as animal nature. Since he is not an animal, he has the ability to know the difference between right and wrong, thus his murderous behavior is immoral. The future readers will not have a reference point for this illusory price of worthless currency, so to make it easy to conceptualize in the tangible world, the purchasing power of $55,000 in 2016 is equivalent to what foolish people valued 41 ounces of gold at (approximately $1,300 USD per ounce), not including premiums.

When inquiring about why this human murderer's actions are evil, some might say because lions are endangered. They are rare. Our apologies to all of the cows, chickens, lambs, and pigs in America, because farmed animals are not rare, so their lives are not as valuable or meaningful as Cecil's life was. Since the enslavement, torture, rape, and eventual murder of farmed animals is not a tourist attraction, few living souls care about them. Under these circumstances, the enslavement, torture, rape, and murder of animals is considered moral by man because man is thought to be an omnivore, and must engage in this behavior so he or she can eat meat and survive. Therefore man is an animal, and under these conditions, man has no choice but to murder in order to survive, thus his murderous behavior is moral.

If someone were to murder children in a terror attack, that person is demonized as a terrorist. However, if the President of the United States has a drone program in which many of the casualties are innocent civilians, well, he's a champion for freedom and deserving of a Nobel Peace Prize. If someone were to kill a U.S. Government official, it would be an act of war. However, when the U.S. Government kills the officials of other nations, it's to fight terrorism. It's business as usual.

As I write this in July of 2016, an estimated 1,884 - 2,411 people were murdered by drone strikes in Afghanistan alone from 2015 till now, about 100 of which were civilians and children. There is no public outrage because they are not American. However, if an Islamic person kills people, it's all we see on every media outlet around the world, followed by the warnings of the threats that radical Islam poses. I agree that all radical movements pose a threat to sovereign inhabitants, but is it not radical to invade a nation like Iraq and kill 1.5 million of its citizens under the pretext of its government having weapons of mass destruction, later to be declared that it obviously did not? At no point am I justifying *any* immoral behavior or taking sides with *any* collective. I am merely stating the obvious.

In summary, when man lures a lion to a place where he can murder it, he is immoral and has committed a wrong because he is not an animal and is competent enough to know his actions are immoral, which is why there was international outrage over it. However, if he kills other animals for the sake of food, it is moral because he is an animal that needs to engage in consuming flesh to survive. If he kills innocent people under the guise of war or fighting terrorism, he is righteous, for human beings are animals and the cycles of nations and mobs correspond to the kill or be killed nature of the animal kingdom. Like the wilderness, survival of the fittest and the ability to adapt determine which species live on. But if he fights back against his oppressors, the fittest, he is a terrorist.

Law Enforcement Officers have killed 639 people in the year 2016 as of July 18th. According to mainstream media research, 869 people were killed in "mass shootings" in America since 1966. We are only halfway through 2016 and police have killed almost as many Americans as all of the mass shootings in America over 50 years combined. But right now, there is a political movement called "gun-control" being perpetrated by government officials to disarm and then dissolve the rights of Americans that don't commit crimes rather than a political movement to end the system of Uniform Commercial Code (UCC) that Law Enforcement Officers (LEOs) operate under and presumably derive their authority. The irony is that LEOs cannot enforce UCC without guns.

Why was this brief digression necessary? To illustrate the dualistic nature of subjects who are victims of black magick. They suffer from cognitive dissonance, the stress inflicted on an individual from holding contradictory beliefs or views. They know murder is wrong, but ignore how their way of life results in the murder of hundreds of billions of beings every year. They are under mind-control and have been deceived into practicing moral relativism, and erroneously believing that the Truth is relative, or that there is no such thing as Truth, and then suppose that there can be no such thing as right, or wrong. This is not the case. The Truth is singular, observable, objective, discoverable, and knowable, regardless of our perception of it, or lack thereof. Do you think this is an outrageous claim, to be under mind-control? Well, using the skills that were just taught, you don't have to dig very deep to prove it.

Under the second skillset of the last chapter, we encouraged you to explore etymologies of words. If you take the word 'government,' you will see that it comes from the Latin verb 'gubernare,' which is "to control," combined with the Latin noun 'mente,' which is "mind." Simply put, 'gubernare' + 'mente' = "To control mind." 'Government' quite literally is "mind-control." Are you or are you not living under a system of government? If you are, you are living under mind-control. If you're not, please tell me where you are so I can move there.

Moral relativism is a product of self-preservation, the idea that all behavior is right, thus justified, so long as it is right for the individual engaging in that behavior. Does that mean moral relativists are evil people? No. As we've established, Truth, like morality, is absolute. All polarities and paradoxes may be reconciled. Relativism may be harmonized into absolutism. Moral relativism may be harmonized into moral absolutism. Relative evil is merely undeveloped goodness. Morality is absolute. Something is either wrong or it is right. There is no in-between, sort of right, or kind of wrong in the natural world. Something is either right (causes no harm) or it is wrong (harms another), absolutely so. Therefore selfishness is merely undeveloped selflessness, and the paradoxical nature of this is that the key to preserving the higher, spiritual world Self is to stop serving the animal nature of the material world's lowercase self. Less is indeed more.

The nature of the animal soul is merely concerned with its own self-preservation, for it is at a point in its evolutionary process where all it knows is survival. This does not mean it is evil, but rather it is adjusting to its existence in a realm of undeveloped good, a realm that is governed by laws of lower animal nature where beings cannot discuss morality. Animals do not have the capacity to converse about their behavior amongst themselves, or with other species, and whether or not the nature of their survival is moral. They exist in a realm where they must do whatever they can to stay alive.

It was necessary to establish this information because it is from the highest forms of guile and intellect in the animal plane that black magick is derived. Spiritual entities exist everywhere, both on the astral plane and the physical one. They are neither elementals (Cosmic, Animal, Planetary) nor elementaries (animal souls of wicked mortals that sank beneath the human plane through their depravity and separated themselves from the divine source).

These spiritual beings are much more powerful than humankind, ruling dark territories of the astral plane and then manifesting their evil desires on the physical plane through their various fraternities and schools of sorcery run by their physical correspondences known as the Black Magi, the Inversive Brethren. They are easily identifiable and do not conceal who they are. They represent it well. But if you cannot comprehend their symbols, then you cannot decipher their messages.

Not only do these people know that you are a spiritual being, they enjoy informing you that they know you are a spiritual being, through mockery, and then inverting your worldviews by tricking you to believe you're on an insignificant speck of dust drifting through an infinite universe that came from nothing and is as common as a grain of sand on a coastal beach. They delight in it. 'De-' is a prefix that means, "to remove or negate." To 'de-light' in something is "to remove or negate its light." The absence of light is darkness; therefore to 'de-light' is "to envelope in darkness," which is why psychopaths get duper's delight, euphoria that comes from deceiving others.

All of the world's ills and conditions of slavery can trace their origins to the deceptions of these entities on the plane of causality that then manifest on the plane of effects through the behaviors of their willfully ignorant prey, also referred to as their *dogs* or *pets*. Have you never wondered why they give *dog tags* to their *pets* in the military and police forces? Not only do they trick these victims to absorb the karmic consequences of their black magick, but they also mock them for it.

The Inversive Brethren mold the tactics of their sorcery to suit the mental faculty of the times, corrupting the minds of the current race and eventually poisoning the souls of their victims through subtle possession, till they are unconsciously whirling the world through the words of the deceivers and creating the boundaries of their self-imposed slavery. The only way out of this is for the initiate to conquer the self and transcend the need to preserve it.

The selfish, the 'gotten,' stay silent in the face of evil. The selfish are responsible for every breed of evil in this realm, for they do nothing as it runs amok. The best way to induce self-preservation, which leads to self-destruction, is through the perversion and obfuscation of Truth. If they can trick you into espousing the ideologies of solipsism, moral relativism, social Darwinism, collectivism, and all other erroneous dogma, they can brainwash you into not knowing who you are, what you are, or where you are. Their ultimate goal is to thwart the triumph of your soul.

Why would they do this? Because this is the only way they can sustain themselves. There are only two states of existence: mortality and immortality. Mortal bodies may be dissolved, but immortal bodies are incorruptible and eternal. This is the source of the conflict. The upper and lower realms are fighting over your body. That is the prize.

Man is the microcosm of perfection and imperfection coexisting in the same place where spirit is in union with matter, but they cannot coexist forever, and the essences of mortality and immortality will both eventually ebb to the sources whence they came. If he chooses the lower nature, mortality, his soul will be disembodied and he will lose his connection to Source, his Creator. If he chooses the higher nature, he will evolve to the spiritual realms of immortality that will eventually return him to his missing half, the soul mate, where he can unite with it and gain immortality.

However, while one is in this earthen crossroads of the soul, it will serve him or her well to know that non-humans exist in the form of humans and operate, nay, control the world, but they do not possess the inherent qualities that define humans. They must learn to feign those qualities in order to appear human and survive amongst them. Science recognizes this non-human entity as the psychopath. Once humans expose these parasites, they can create an environment that stops feeding them, and like a rope worm or another intestinal parasite, they will detach from the host and be expelled from the body. But to rip them off through violence will cause internal damage to the body, which can be fatal. This is why violent revolt will not work against them.

There are several ways in which a human body can be hijacked by a Black Mage, sorceress, or one of their spiritual counterparts. The most observable instances of this type of theft occur in the entertainment industry, the media, and the political arena, though it is prevalent everywhere, from religions to government and science. Ah, but I repeat myself.

The first type of victim is one with a strong magnetism for being a medium. He or she possesses a beautiful mind that has no inclination towards another type of social group, but unfortunately suffers from a weak constitution and an amoral personality. These individuals are humans, or at least they start off that way, but due to the subtle yet overt penetration of their psyche, they lose control of their vessel to what initiates of the Occult term "disembodied earthbound spirits," but even worse, and in some regions more frequently, they are made into slaves by the animal souls of wicked mortals who sank beneath the physical plane, also known as elementaries. The soul was aborted, usually from a young age or even infancy, through some sort of ritual abuse or trauma. There are some instances of the living soul vanquishing its occupier(s) and reclaiming its body, but these instances are extremely rare. The struggles, especially in the entertainment industry, can be seen in public spectacles. However, since agents of the elementaries control the media, these events are often depicted as celebrities having mental or emotional meltdowns, and the behavior is largely dismissed by the ignorant, clueless public, and then forgotten once the next distraction is presented to them.

The second type of human victim, that will fail to inherit immortality by virtue of his or her humanity, falls prey to what occultists term as '**premeditated obsession**.' While this may be sufficient for the initiated, I coined an alternative term to describe the nature of this victim based on my own experience: '**willful desire**.

'**Willful desire**' was chosen specifically to convey, "the negation or removal of one's sovereign creative power through his or her free will."

Without digressing too much, I took the word '**willful**' and used the techniques established previously.

1)   '**Will**': "the promise to do something in the future through determination, expectation, or requirement" (auxiliary verb) or "de**sire**; to wish" (verb) + '**full**': "the condition of something having been, or being, **filled**" (adjective) = "the act of ful**filling** a promise, agreement, de**sire**, wish, or obligation **full**y (completely, entirely) through one's own volition (free **will**)" (verb).

2)   '**W**': "Double You" (phonetically; noun) + '**ill**': "diseased, sick, infirm" or "evil, cross, wrong" (adj.) or "misfortune, suffering, misery" (n.) + '**full**': "complete, entire" (adj.) = "**Dua**lity (double you) causes complete **dis**-ease, evil, misfortune, and suffering, or simply put, causes one to be ill-full." And as seen in the word '**wish**' (**w-i-sh**), which comes from one of the definitions of **will**, the double you (**w**) silences (**sh**) the self/eye/I/one (**i**), which is the single you. We could summarize, "Duality closes the harmonious single eye of light, the unity consciousness, thus creating

discord or chaos."

Why have I given you different meanings of the same word? To illustrate the polarities that words have, the paradoxes contained within them, and how the same word can mean entirely different things, thus creating different thought forms based on the intent of he or she who *casts* that word into the ether through speech. Also, once created, they can be manipulated and changed by the will of the mage or any other who chooses to participate in the creation of his or her environment. However, these seemingly different meanings can be reconciled in two ways.

Any time an individual takes action to fulfill the **obligations** of another, if not aligned with his or her own will and the higher will, the Will of Creation, then he or she is putting himself or herself into a state of duality, which causes discord and disease, thus he or she becomes a slave. Contrarily, if the individual takes action to fulfill the **determination** of his or her own volition, then he or she is thinking, feeling, and acting in unison with his or her conscience, spirit (the higher Will), mind, body, and the laws of Nature, thus the mage is in a state of unity. This is the state of absolute Truth, the law of one (singularity), not two (duality). As a side note, this singularity is not the same as the manufactured artificial intelligence being forced on humanity to merge it with technology. Artificial singularity is a product of willful desire, and it will fail. It may fail gracefully, without horrible consequences, if humanity becomes aware of what the Inversive Brethren are doing with AI, or it will fail at the expense of humanity's existence should they continue to remain ignorant of this immoral shortcut to immortality. Either way, the end result is the same. The Black Magi will fail because it's all that they can do. They are nothing but a spiritual Ponzi scheme that collapses the moment there are no more victims foolish enough to feed them.

Thus, the basis on which one judges the meaning of the word 'willful' must be decided by whether the context of it is through **obligation** (slavery) or **determination** (freedom). These are the polarities of the word that are reconciled under absolute Truth, for when no one violates the Truth, which is that **every living soul of flesh and blood is inherently free in its creation or manifestation**, sovereignty can never be undone, even while experiencing temporary enslavement, violence, coercion, or other means of theft. The absolute Truth is that all are free. Anyone who teaches moral relativism, solipsism, relativity, or any other false ideologies is at best under mind-control, but under most circumstances he or she is a **willful desirer**, to which death (spiritual dissolution) is the punishment, and that's the next word that we will look at to complete our understanding of this potent combination of words.

'**Desire**,' as a verb, is "to wish or long for, to want." As a noun, it is "a sexual urge, an expressed craving or wish." However, these dictionary definitions that I paraphrase are merely the airy dictions of a dictator, designed to be a locked gate to thwart Deaf Phoenicians. You will not be one for much longer. You are a living soul, a sovereign inhabitant, and I create as I speak that you will be resired to your sovereign creative powers henceforth for perpetual remembrance thereof, never to be severed from the source of Creation unless it is through your own knowledgeable volition.

1) '**De-**' (prefix): "removal of or from something specified, reversal of something, departure from, the reduction or degradation of something."

2) '**Sire**' (noun): "A lord, a sovereign."

3) '**Sire**' (verb): "to procreate as the father."

Therefore, to '**desire**' (de-sire) something is "to remove, reverse, reduce, degrade, or force it to depart from its sovereign creative power."

I offered the alternative **sword**, 'willful desire,' to the occult designation of the condition in which the second type of human will not naturally realize immortality, '**premeditated obsession**,' to something that would help convey its meaning to the occultists and magi of the present time. Let it be known that a human being may lose his or her immortality to '**willful desire**,' "the act of removing oneself from his or her sovereign creative power, inherently granted by his or her Creator, through his or her own free will."

Thus, the noun '**willful desirer**' is "one who causes willful desire" and the 'willfully desired' is "the victim of willful desire."

However, here is the paradox of the word that reconciles its polarities. Both the victim and the perpetrator are one in the same because they each engage in willful desire through their own volition. This is seen in the word 'perpetrator,' where the prefix 'per-' means "for each," and then it is combined with 'pet,' a "domesticated animal" (a slave), and '-trator,' which phonetically is 'traitor,' "one who betrays."

A 'perpetrator' is not only "one who commits a crime or violation," but also "one who makes himself a slave by betraying another." In a master-slave relationship, the master becomes the slave because without slaves, he or she cannot be a master, so the master is a slave to his or her immoral perpetrations based on his or her dependency on them existing, and once the slaves, the sustenance, cease to exist, the master is delivered unto spiritual dissolution: death. This is why the elemental spirits and elementaries must dupe their victims into betraying the laws of Nature so that they can feed off of their victims' soul energy and prolong their own existence. There is ultimately one absolute Truth, and in regards to willful desire, it is this: sovereignty is removed through the conscious premeditated betrayal of the Will of Creation. As a side note, it's important that the reader comprehends that I am completely impartial to how you conceptualize the Will of Creation. Some find it easier to personify it and give it a name, others prefer to call it the Big Bang. It's the source of all that is. In context to this book, my intent is not to alienate atheists or religious people, though I am confident I will offend you all before this is done. Be that as it may, it is not my intent to do so, but rather to encourage and help the reader embrace the diversity of Nature and our differences while harmonizing with one another under Natural Law.

This second type of human, who will not naturally inherit immortality, has a magnetic temperament that is normal for a hue-man. However, the absence of spiritual righteousness or allegiance to morality and Truth causes it to be the perfect victim of willful desire, premeditated obsession. These people are strong spiritual mediums, but they are amoral. Even though they have no moral principles or standards, they are not necessarily mean-spirited people, though there are no restrictive beliefs to limit them should they decide to do evil. They tend to be the sons and daughters of people with great wealth and resources that can create an environment for their children that panders to their whims, allowing them to experience everything and get bored of everything, but also to be insulated from consequences. The lack of resistance or challenges in their lives cultivates an environment of spiritual and material apathy.

The awful irony of the situation, that this second class is born into, is that since money is black magick, which requires one's belief in it to exist, the people with the most money generally have the most Black Magi and sorceresses in their lives to make sure they do not do anything that would disrupt the strength of the hexes. So when the Inversive Brethren detect strong mediumistic vessels without the spiritual fortitude to defend the Kingdom of Self, the elementaries and their physical counterparts have no difficulty whatsoever aborting the soul of their victims. The friends and family of the victims will most certainly notice the change in their loved one, but very few will suspect the fate that has befallen them.

If the reader is not mature enough to consider that this world is utterly different from the way he or she has been brainwashed to believe it works, then the reader is not mature enough to learn how to do anything about the immense suffering and the condition of human slavery that has undoubtedly been imposed upon the world, and that blood will be upon his or her hands.

Let us return our attention to the psychopath. This is the third class of "hue-man" that will not inherit immortality naturally unless it avoids falling prey to the Inversive Brethren and lives its life within the boundaries of morality. The psychopath is a combination of all the physical qualities of a human, as well as the most intense, powerful condition of selfishness and pride that Nature can manifest, but they do not possess the inherent qualities of humans such as empathy and compassion. The ones with low IQs are the types that slaughter animals for a living or steal freedom for a paycheck. Their favorite excuses are, "I was just following orders" and "I've got a family to feed." They're automatons. The dark work they do will also turn a normal human into a secondary psychopath if exposed to it long enough. They will eventually get what they deserve, but the amount of people that suffer because of their behavior will be determined by how long you sit on your ass and do nothing with the knowledge you've been given. The ones with high IQs usually possess stunning intellect, an ungodly powerful will, and those that are strong mediums become the perfect vessel for a Black Mage. These intellectuals are generally attracted to the study of psychology, the knowledge of Self, and of Natural Law, the way this world works. I'm telling you this as someone who has been initiated, and raised by someone who was initiated, that this is the most occulted knowledge there is, and why the psychopath is the most dangerous entity there is, because they have the drive, intellect, willpower, ambition, patience, devotion, ambition, lust for power, desire to be God, and the magnetic temperament to interact with the astral entities and their physical world counterparts. The psychopath is so ambitious that he or she is willing to sign a contract and sacrifice immortality for temporary gains. The psychopath is willing to perform the ritual sacrifice of children, regularly, to satisfy the demands of his infernal masters. He is willing to do whatever is necessary to orchestrate mass ritual sacrifice, otherwise known as war, including the murder of thousands of innocent people in staged terror events and then blaming it on other groups to stir the masses into a racist frenzy. Do you know why? We live in a quantum universe. Though it may not be made up of particles, it is made up of torus fields, and there is a required amount of energy that must be met in order for a shift in consciousness to occur. In order to manifest one's designs, a certain amount of co-creators must be persuaded to create it. If those numbers are not met, then the desired reality cannot be manifested. The universe was made as such to benefit all life forms, not just humans. That's why there is such an intense war occurring for your soul. Humans, though a completely programmable species, are the apex of physical evolution. We are the union of the spiritual and material world. Why do you think the Black Magi have to control the media, governments, religions, schools, universities, industries, etc.? They must successfully program you or their paradigm could collapse by tomorrow morning.

If you have parasites in your body, you don't keep feeding them if you seek health. Correspondingly, you don't keep living an immoral life and engaging in awful behavior that feeds these astral parasites if you seek freedom. Freedom and morality are directly proportional to each other, and no amount of selfish moral relativism, solipsism, or ignorance will change that. Get used to it.

Contracts are black magick. Debt is black magick. Uniform Commercial Code and all courts and legal systems within that system are black magick. Government is black magick. Religion is black magick. The mnemonic programming in the mass media is black magick. The projection of symbols and other thought forms into the recesses of subconscious minds by way of the entertainment industry is black magick. You think it's coincidence that mnemonic rhymes with demonic?

None of this spiritual wickedness is binding without consent. It's all illusory black magick. The problem is that the majority of co-creators (humans) in this world are the ones who participate in this depravity and enforce it, thus are the ones generating this paradigm of slavery and suffering, and until they understand what is being done to them, they cannot solve the problems on the plane of causality and will remain powerless to do anything about it. This understanding of the Black Magi will be useful in the second part of this book. The **selfish** are the **cell fish**, the batteries in this ocean of dark energy. The wood of a holly tree was made to craft the wands of the Druids.

The Druids of the West are the Priests of Apollo, so when a black magick cult names its missions to the Moon after Apollo, or builds its particle colliders in towns that are named after Apollo, it should tell you everything you need to know about the cult. This gives an inclination as to the type of magick that those who created Hollywood were fond of. Holly wood is not the preferred choice for wands for the White Magi of the Hermetic Brotherhood, who adhere to the tradition of the Hermetica. The Druids of the West are the Jews (the Jew-ids, Lords of the Day, the solar cult; 'ids' is an anagram for 'Dis,' hence Hollywood's obsession with Jew-Dis: Judas), the Magi of Persia, and the priests of Hindoostan and Egypt.

It's not "Jews" that control Hollywood, but the Druids, the solar cult of Apollo. Sure, they may use race baiting to play the victim and character assassinate those who expose them, but this conspiracy is much more complex and pervasive than any ethnicity, and I would

Dylan Michael Saccoccio

encourage people to not take their frustration out on any one race, no matter how many of them seem to be involved in different aspects of this grand conspiracy. These orders have wandered the earth for millennia, using the same systems of magick to enslave each new race that manifests here. The minute details of this subject are not the primary focus of this book, nor do I consider them interesting, but they are very much connected to what's occurring and thus necessary for my readers to consider. In no way am I speaking of real Jews, Christians, Muslims, Hindus, Buddhists, Taoists, etc., who have no idea what's really controlling their cults. I'm speaking of the satanic pedophile human trafficking murderers who have hijacked the natural systems of this world.

20

3 CREATURES OF CREATION

Perhaps the most ignorant genre of Deaf Phoenicians is the believer. The believer, by definition, believes. He does not know. He believes he knows. But one who knows something does so regardless of his beliefs. To believe is a choice. To know is not a choice. One either knows or does not know something. The only choice he has is to forget it. That which occurred may not be undone, just as words cannot be unsaid after they have been said nor unheard once they have been heard. This is the power of language. This is precisely why Truth is not relative and all assertions of such are erroneous.

Let's play with the word 'believer,' which equals 'be' + 'lie' + 'ver.' The word 'be' indicates or describes "the identity, quality, or condition of a person or thing." A 'lie' is an "intentional untruth, falsehood," or "a statement that is intentionally made to deceive." The word 'ver' in Mediterranean languages like Portuguese and Spanish is associated with sight, "to live through, to behold or witness something, a view or an opinion of something," etc. But in French, 'ver' is a 'worm,' which is "a spineless, boneless, creature without legs or arms, that moves through tight spaces," usually earth or water, which is why in English the verb 'worm' is "to move through a tight space." But a 'worm' is also a "bad person, someone who is not liked or respected, a wretch, a snake or serpent," or in technology, a 'worm' is a "computer program that performs a destructive action."

In Icelandic, 'ver' is a "cover made of cloth," which is the same meaning of 'ver' in Norwegian, 'var' in Swedish, and 'vår' in Danish.

In Latin, 'ver' is the root word of "Truth," hence another word for Truth is 'veritas,' which is why the goddess of Truth is Veritas, the daughter of Saturn, El, Dagon, God, which will support the hidden identity of Jesus later on.

Phonetically, in Latin, the word 'vēr' is the season of spring, hence the word 'vernal,' as in Vernal Equinox, and can also be used as an adjective to describe something as "youthful, fresh, or new." This is also where Venus comes from, which is the Roman goddess of love, beauty, fertility, sex, prosperity, and victory. Venus is also the planet that rules Taurus, which represents matter in its most spiritual state, an Earthy sign, a requirement for the manifestation of intelligence, hence it is a servant of Spirit, which is why Venus is the element of love in Nature. It is for this reason that Taurus, the body of the Bull, Isis, is encoded in the Riddle of the Sphinx.

Phonetically, in English, 'ver' could be made to sound like 'veer,' which is "a change in course or direction" as a noun, but also "to change course or direction" as a verb.

In the word 'be-lie-ver,' a person is in a state (be) where a lie is intentionally concealing the truth (ver) from him or her, as evidenced in the word 'concealing,' where the truth is sealed (the correct spelling of the phonetic sound of ceal) by a con, "a trick or scam" (n.), but also "to swindle" (v.). This corresponds to the Icelandic/Norwegian noun 'ver,' which is "a cover made of cloth," which by definition conceals something, as well as to the English verb 'veer,' the phonetic option of 'ver,' because to 'con' is "to direct the steering or course of a vessel," i.e. "to control, conduct, or conduce a thing."

The phonetic correspondence of 'er' in believ-er is 'err,' which means "to be led astray in thought or belief." And 'liev' equals 'leave' phonetically, which, as a verb is "to forsake or abandon."

A 'be-leave-err' is "a living soul who, through trickery or ignorance, has been led astray in thought or belief due to the intentional concealment of Truth."

If this were not the case, the individual would not be a 'believer,' but a 'knower,' one who "perceives Truth directly, with clarity, certainty, and without doubt."

The Truth cannot be concealed from he or she who knows it, thus a 'knower' cannot be led astray in thought or belief, for he or she is anchored by Truth, and though he or she may plunge into the murky depths of information and speculation, he or she will ultimately return to Truth. This is the difference between a 'knower' and a 'believer.' The latter is literally and legally incompetent and lost at sea, for he or she cannot compete or see. Unfortunately, the majority of the population in this world has been swindled into becoming 'believers' from a very early age by those who know, and to think this does not correspond to the Black Magi is an erroneous belief, a leaf that will be turned, folded, and removed at the whim of he or she who holds it.

Which sea is the 'believer' lost in? The Holy See (Sea), the Ecclesiastical See (Sea), the Law of the Sea. These are the laws of current-sea (currency), commerce, Uniform Commercial Code, Maritime Admiralty Law.

The irony in the term 'Holy See' is found in its correspondence to the word 'divide.' 'Di' in Latin means "god," and 'vide' in Latin means "see," thus 'Di' (god) + 'vide' (see) = 'Divide' (God See). God is holy, thus the word 'Divide' is the same as the 'Holy See.' This is because if one looks for God anywhere outside of himself, he is divided by trying to see God. Thus the 'individual' (in + divide + dual) is "one who is 'in' a 'dual' state, phonetically a 'duel' state of contest or combat, created by the schism of trying to see God (Di-vide), and thus mistakenly being caught in the futility of trying to separate himself from God."

The creations are reflections of the creators, so in order to see the creative spark that manifests life, one must look within, to the creative source of his own spirit. The kingdom of heaven is within the hearts of men.

The Spanish words for 'the sea' is 'el mar.' 'El' is the word for 'God' in the Canaanite religion and the Hebrew Bible, found in many languages with the same etymological origin (cognates) of the word, such as Phoenician, Ugaritic, Syriac, Arabic, and Akkadian.

Mars is the Roman god of war. In Ptolemy's table of Essential Dignities (astrology), Mars is the only planet that rules all three water triplicities (Cancer, Scorpio, Pisces) during both the day and night. This is because Mars rules the oceans, the seas, Rome, and thus Roman **Mar**itime Admiralty Law, the Law of the Sea: commerce. This is where **mars**hal (martial) law comes from. Hence, '**el mar**' in Spanish has an occult meaning of '**God Mars**,' in addition to '**the sea**.' Rome merely stole all its gods and laws from ancient Greece, which is why Maritime Law also has Rhodian influences.

The word '**maritime**' simply means "of or pertaining to the sea." In Latin, '**mare**' means "**sea**," which corresponds to '**mare**' in English, "the dark plains on the Moon," because astronomers originally thought they were oceans. '**Mare**' is also a female horse in English. Bad dreams are called '**nightmares**.'

In Old English, the letter 'i' was written as 'y,' so '**maritime**' could also be '**marytyme**' or '**Mary-Time**' with no stretch of the imagination. Since Mary is Isis, which is the Moon, and Time is Kronos/Cronus, which is Chronos, where '**chrono**logical' is derived, which is Saturn, the occult symbol of which is the Crown, it is no stretch of the imagination that '**Mary-Time**' has the occult meaning of a symbiotic relationship between the Moon and Saturn: '**Moon-Saturn**' or '**Isis-El**' or '**Moon-Crown**.'

This same occult meaning is seen in the word '**mindset**,' with '**mind**' coming from the lunar god '**Min**,' and '**Set**' being not only an aspect of light in the '**setting**' Sun, but also a symbol for '**Saturn**,' or '**Satan**' in astro-theology, hence the branch of the dark occult titled the Temple of **Set**. This is where we get the words '**minutes**' and '**hours**.' '**Minutes**' represents the Moon (Min) while '**hours**' is an anagram for '**Horus**,' which represents the Sun, the Egyptian Sun-god. Horus is the Sun at sunrise, hence the origin of the word '**horizon**,' which is a combination of '**Horus**' and '**On**,' the city of the Sun. In the Zodiac, Horus corresponds to Aquarius, which is why some occultists refer to the Age of Aquarius as the Age of Horus. This is encoded in the head of the Sphinx, which is the head of man, the Water Bearer, as Aquarius is the Age of Man. It is also encoded in the Bible in Luke 22:10, "And he said to them, 'Lo, in your entering into the city, there you shall meet a man (Aquarius), bearing a pitcher of water, follow him to the house where he doth go in."

From Noon (Nun, which is the 14ᵗʰ letter of the Hebrew alphabet and the mother of Joshua/Jesus, which, like 'sus,' also means "fish") till sunset, the Sun is known as 'Ra,' hence the term 'rays' of light. This corresponds to the period from Cancer through Libra on the Zodiac, which is why Leo is the Sun's House of Rulership.

If you add the Sun into the occult meaning of maritime, the word becomes 'Moon-Sun-Saturn,' otherwise known as 'Isis-Ra-El,' which when truncated becomes 'IsRaEl' = 'Israel.' This is why everyone, who knows anything about the mystery tradition that the modern desert sky-god religions plagiarize, knows that Israel is in the sky. Solomon's starry temple is not to be found as a physical place on the earth. All claims that Israel and the Temple of Solomon are physical locations are erroneous, blasphemous, and immoral due to their intentionally deceptive nature. All members of the human family are Israelites. Everyone is included as God's chosen people. The physical location named Israel is not the real Israel, nor will it ever be, and by their fruit you shall know them.

"Go ye in through the straight gate, because wide is the gate, and broad the way that is leading to the destruction, and many are those going in through it. How straight is the gate, and compressed the way that is leading to the life, and few are those finding it! But, take heed of the false prophets, who come unto you in sheep's clothing, and inwardly ravening wolves. From their fruits ye shall know them; do men gather from thorns grapes? Or from thistles figs? So every good tree doth yield good fruits, but the bad tree doth yield evil fruits. A good tree is not able to yield evil fruits, nor a bad tree to yield good fruits. Every tree not yielding good fruit is cut down and cast to fire, therefore from their fruits ye shall know them. Not everyone who is saying to me Lord, lord, shall come into the reign of the heavens; but he who is doing the will of my Father who is in the heavens. Many will say to me in that day, Lord, lord, have we not in thy name prophesied, and in thy name cast out demons, and in thy name done many mighty things? And I will acknowledge to them that – I never knew you. Depart from me ye who are working lawlessness." – *Matthew 7:13-23*

The fruits of Christianity, Judaism, and Islam are bloodshed and slavery. They are a perversion of the science of the stars and soul that comes from ancient Egypt, which may also go all the way back to Hindoostan. There are no retorts or defenses to this statement that can stand in Truth. Anyone who says otherwise is an absolute shill, because Truth is absolute. While the macrobes may forgive one's nescience, he or she will not be saved should the laws of Nature be ignored. The same can be said for those who unknowingly blaspheme the Creator with their man-made religions.

This is why Jesus ('Je' means "I" in French + 'sus' means "fish" in Latin) is the son of Mary, the son/Sun of the Moon (the element of Water, the sacred Feminine), the same way Horus is the son of Isis, the Sun of the Moon: Solomon, the Soul of Man (Aquarius). 'Virgin' also means "pure, first, undefiled, without alloy or modification, not previously exploited, cultivated, or used," and we've already established that 'Mary' also means "sea" through the Latin word 'mare.' Therefore, 'Virgin Mary' also means "Original or Pure Sea." Jesus is symbolic to a fish because they are the fruits of the sea. Go with him and he will make you fishers of men (Pisces). Jesus, the I-Fish, or Eye-Fish, is the sacred geometry of the Vesica Piscis, indicating those born in Time (Saturn) must die in Time, which is why he is the offspring of David (El, Dagon, Saturn), which makes him Ba'al, the Sun. Do you see? These stories are not historical accounts. They are personifications of occulted knowledge.

The reason these allegories/metaphors have so many commonalities is because they were stolen from the same story of the stars, and the Zodiac, from ancient Egypt. This is why Monday is the Moon's day, Sunday is the Sun's day, and Saturday is Saturn's day. We'll delve deeper into this later, once the Deaf Phoenicians have been filtered, because they will never be able to know the black magick that is being performed on them. They'll roam and ravage the earth as the dead, lost at sea, the sea of Moon-Time (maritime), till their souls are dissolved into more useful creations. But the Deaf Phoenicians who allow themselves to be raised from their coffins will again know their sovereignty and their Creator, and stop participating in these criminally phony systems.

The prefix 'mon-' can mean "one" (a variant of 'mono-' before a vowel) as in monoacid, or it can mean "moon," an anagram of 'mono,' as in Monday, monster (moon-star), or demon (deity of the moon or divided-one). Both meanings, 'mono' and 'moon,' are incorporated into the word 'money,' which is the current-sea governed by maritime admiralty law, the law of commerce: money. This is also exposed in the word 'lunacy,' phonetically 'Luna' (Moon) + 'sea' (Moon-sea), which is "sporadic fits of insanity originally believed to be caused by phases of the Moon." Lunacy is something one may feel as he or she discovers all the occult meanings and powers of words, and then their correlations to the religion of Money. But as the research is done, the feeling will subside through the validity of the empirical information one comes across.

Exploring the second part of 'maritime,' Cronus is the Titan of the Harvest, whose symbol is the sickle or scythe, but also the snake. This corresponds to the nature of the cycles of time as depicted in the Ouroboros, the snake devouring its own tail. It is a representation of the beginning and end, specifically, that there is no beginning and there is no end, that the end is the beginning and the beginning is the end, and the All is one.

'Ouroboros' can be split into 'Our-O-Bor-Os,' which phonetically can be 'Our-O-Bore-Us' or 'Our-O-Bore-Oz.' If one takes 'O' to be a symbol of a cycle, circle, completion, or wholeness, a symbol of the Ouroboros, the Zodiac, or even the number zero, one can see that hidden in the word is the meaning, "our wholeness bore us, our zero bore us," or "hour zero bore us," because this is the point at which we manifest into this construct of Time that governs us, and to transcend to higher states of consciousness, we must transcend the Ouroboros and escape Father Time, who is Saturn, who is Satan. Previously, we've divulged that hours is an anagram for Horus, the Sun, which alludes to the spiritual Sun that bore us, but this is also the Divine Spark within us (the Christ), the point of which some may refer to as 'nothingness,' which supports why the Kabbalistic Tree of Life is called the Ten Sephirot of Nothingness. This is why the solution to the Riddle of the Universe is taught by some occultists to be $0 = 2$, in that all that is, no matter how complex, comes from zero, which is why the 'nothingness' that the *Sefer Yetzirah* (Book of Creation) refers to is meant to be of an indescribable heavenly nature, unspeakable.

Ironically, the word 'one' starts with 'O,' but is pronounced as though it starts with 'W' ('double you' means from your perspective, you'd refer to yourself as a 'double I,' which is 'I, I' or 'Eye, Eye,' as in 'Aye aye, Captain'). In astrology, the symbol for the Twin Souls of Gemini is II because they come from the Creator, Zero, the ineffable, O = II, the divine oneness from which all is descended, which is why during the soul's involution from the Creator, it separates in two at Gemini, and then makes the journey to complete the cycle at Pisces, eventually reconnecting with the soul mate and gaining immortality. This cycle corresponds to man and his material destiny during the first round of the Cycle of Necessity, which is why in Freemasonry they borrow this concept: **Man must build his temple with his own hands.** The keystone of its arch is **Will**, and its foundation is love. The Temple of Solomon is the Temple of the Soul-of-Man, and each man must build his own, just like the 32 Paths of Wisdom in Kabbalah are private paths that must be walked individually. In terms of the Zodiac corresponding to this spiritual journey, the highest point of the arch is Cancer and the lowest point of crystallization is Capricorn. In the physical world, this is observable in the heavens, which is why all the primitive Sun-Gods are born in Capricorn, just after the winter solstice.

'Oz' in Hebrew means "strength, courage, powerful," so the second meaning of Ouroboros ('Our-O-Bore-Oz') could be taken as "our oneness bore strength, courage, and power," hence the meaning of the title, *The Wizard of Oz*.

'Oz' is also the abbreviation for ounces, units of weight that quantify the heaviness or mass of matter. The anagram for 'Oz' is 'Zo,' which means "zoo," which is the hidden meaning of the Zodiac and further illustrates the 'O' being a symbol for the Zodiac (more to come on this). 'O' is also the shape of the Sun and the Full Moon, but also an egg.

The possibilities, though not endless, provide many different ways of understanding and using words. For an exercise, reader, you must look up the different meanings of 'bore,' whether that be the verb or the past tense of 'bear,' and complete your understanding of 'our O bore us/oz.' It is not right for me to rob you of the experience of discovering Truth for yourself.

Continuing our exploration of 'maritime,' Cronus was absorbed by the Romans and named Saturn, which is Satan (the adversary to the Sun), which is why the Grim Reaper, Father Time, reaps the souls (sols/suns/sons) with a scythe and why they say he devours his own children, because those who are born in time must die in time. In alchemy, lead corresponds to Saturn because it swallows all light, hence the scientific use of it to block radiation in the physical world.

The 'lunar sea' (lunacy) could be the **'Moon See'** because 'maritime' is also **'Mar-Eye-Time,'** and the reason they put the all-seeing eye on the world's reserve current-sea is because the one eye (mono-eye) keeps tabs on its user, thus binding him or her to maritime law every time he exchanges it, because it is imprinted as a seal on a bill (bill is Green Language for Ba'al, the Sun) that people mistakenly call money (moon-eye), which binds everything to the Law of the Sea, the Law of the See (Holy See). This is Chaos Sorcery, which is why in Tarot, the Moon Trump XVIII symbolizes sorcery, for it puts the symbol of spiritual enlightenment, the Eye of Providence, the spiritual Sun, on an illusory debt note that tricks people to equate possession of these fraudulent instruments as "wealth," and they color it green to trick your subconscious mind into thinking you'll have balance, harmony, happiness, etc. by slaving your life away for it.

Phonetically, 'holy' is 'wholly,' as in "full," like the Moon gets. 'Holy' and 'wholly' are also phonetically 'holey,' which is to be "full of holes."

There's a saying that the Moon is made of cheese, presumably due to its yellow-white glow and visible craters, because it looks like it is full of holes when it is wholly full. This is why another term for making moon-eye (money) is "making cheddar," which is also the same as "making money, honey."

Moon-honey is symbolic to **money**, a blending of the words, which is why after people get married, they go on a **honeymoon**, to produce a **bay-bee** (water bee) that they will raise to replenish their generation in making **moon-honey** for the **Queen Bee**, the Whore of **Bay-bee-El-On** (Babylon; 'El' = God; 'On' = City of the Sun).

When one has moon-honey (money), **current-sea**, he has **cash flow** and **liquid assets**, but when an asset has gone under its book value in worth, it is said to be **underwater**. The Law of the Sea is the law of money, because money is liquid, hence the reason one has a marriage ceremony (**sera-moon-ey/money**), 'sera' being plural for '**serum**,' which is a "watery fluid."

Maritime Admiralty Law comes from Rome. Rome was founded by Remus and Romulus, begotten by a Vestal Virgin named Rhea Silvia, who was allegedly raped by **Mars**. **Mars**, the god of war, sees over the seas, oceans, and thus controls **Commer**ce and **Mar**itime Admiralty Law. A 'law' is a 'rule,' which is in the term '**martial law**,' a wartime condition in which the military takes over and rules a government. Therefore, '**marshal law**' is also '**marshal rule**,' which phonetically reveals "Mars shall rule," hence the wartime circumstances when this condition is implemented.

Returning to the word '**mare**' in Latin, which means "sea," it has the exact spelling of '**mare**,' a "female horse" in English, which is phonetically the first sound in both '**mar**riage' and '**mar**itime.'

A '**carriage**' is a wheeled vehicle, as in one that is drawn by horses. Does that mean a '**marriage**' is essentially a business vehicle drawn by the female? If '**marriage**' isn't a business, why do people need marriage licenses? Why do couples call their spouses their '**partners**?' Why is the male called the '**groom**' during a marriage ceremony? A '**groom**' is one who is in charge of horses or the stable, "one who grooms horses," who bridles the '**bride**' with a '**bridle**,' a headstall, bit, and reins of a harness that restrains the mare as she draws the carriage. Rome is the groom that bridles the sea, the mare, the female horse, with its admiralty law that enslaves the world.

But what is the carriage? The first sound in '**carriage**' is '**car**,' which may or may not be linked to the root word '**carn**,' which is "flesh." This is where words like '**carne**,' '**carnal**,' '**carn**ivorous,' 'in**carn**ate,' 'rein**carn**ation,' '**carn**ival,' etc. are derived.

Understandably, the word '**car**' probably has its origins from the Latin word '**carrus**,' which is a wagon. However, the word '**carrion**' also shares '**car**' as its first phonetic sound, and is not bound by the 'n' in '**carn**,' but '**carrion**' is by definition "rotting or dead flesh." '**Carriage**' and '**carrion**,' two completely different words, both share the majority of their form in the prefix 'carri-,' which is linked to wagon. Since there doesn't seem to be clearly defined rules, it doesn't require imagination to see that 'carrion' proves a word can incorporate "flesh" or "meat" into its meaning merely by inclusion of the prefix 'car-.' So with that understanding, though it may be a stretch to those trained to operate within rigid boundaries, let us suppose that 'car-' can mean "flesh, meat."

If we split 'carriage,' we get 'car-i-age,' or 'flesh/meat-I-age.' To age meat is to preserve it. The word 'eed' is Dutch for "oath." Thus, when combining the Latin and Dutch words, to be 'mare-eed' is to take a 'sea-oath,' an oath to the Moon (mary-eed), or an oath to the See (Holy See). They are all one in the same once reconciled under Absolute Truth. **Mary, Isis, Diana**, the **Moon**, is the universal mother, the source of all manifestation. She is encoded in the body of the bull, in the riddle of the Sphinx, because the bull is Taurus, which is symbolic of earth and fertility, hence it is ruled by Venus, the goddess of love and beauty. The earth is known as Terra, which comes from the goddess Taaraa, another representation of the Sacred Feminine aspect of consciousness. This is why you hear dark occultists waging a **War on Terra** (the occult phonetics of War on Terror), and why they named their enemy **Isis**. Venus is **Lucifer**, the morning star. The story in the Bible is an allegory for Venus' path in the heavens. It is the brightest star in the predawn sky. It "announces" the Sun of the morning. Once the Sun appears, Venus competes with it to be the "most high," but due to its path, it sinks below the horizon, or is "cast out of heaven." It stays below the horizon, or in the "underworld," till the time of the year when it rises again in the evening as Vesper, Lord of the Night. Never has it been, nor will it ever be, a masculine energy. It is why they added it to the Bible as a representation of evil, to reinforce this war on the Sacred Feminine aspect of consciousness, and the reason they get away with this immoral behavior is because the majority of the female population (and male population) remains ignorant of this knowledge, or if they do know, they remain silent about it. The reason I assign the responsibility to the female population is not out of blame or any other bigoted reasons, but merely because it is quite observable that they are the emotionally superior of the species, and were they to use their will and cut off these male dominators, the situation would change within a decade. The majority of men who bring the resultant harm into manifestation are behaving in a way that they believe will attract women. When they are no longer rewarded for their behavior by the companionship of females, and are shunned by females for their actions, they will no longer participate in the system that suppresses females and perpetuates human slavery.

The Sacred Feminine corresponds to **Care**, the Generative Principle, responsible for creating the quality of our experience here. This is why the physical correspondents of the Black Magi perform the Cremation of **Care** ritual at Bohemian Grove every year. It is a ritual to destroy the Sacred Feminine aspect of consciousness and absolve themselves from their atrocities, because the goddess Isis represents the thoughts of God being put into form.

Who is their god? **El** = Dagon = Saturn = Time = Set = Satan, hence the term **el**ites, the name the servants of the Black Magi chose for themselves. Saturn corresponds to lead, which is an earthy element that blocks light. The Earth is responsible for the procreative process that is seeded in the moisture of the element Water and developed in love and action, which is Mars. Capricorn is an Earth sign, which is why its ruler is Saturn, and an occulted symbol for Capricorn is the **unicorn**, which is conveyed on the Royal Arms because the Crown is also a symbol for Saturn. This is the occult meaning of 'maritime,' ruled by the **mars**hal power of Rome, the head of which is the vital energy of God, the Sun. Unfortunately, as we'll delve into it during the second half of this book, the energy controlling Roman Maritime Admiralty Law, Commerce, the law of money, has nothing to do with God.

Since marriage is a business, does that indicate its function is to preserve the flesh of the parties through the creation of liquid assets called **bay-bees**? Are **bay-bees** not **birth**ed through their mother's **birth canal** after her **water** breaks? Do **ship**s not sit in their **berth**s at port? Are you not given citizen**ship** through means of a **birth** certificate? Is a **matrix** not a **womb**? Are we not **birth**ed from a **matrix**? And are we not **berth**ed in a **matrix**? Is Earth the **womb**, or is it a wharf in which our citizen**ship** is **berth**ed? Since 'earth' is an anagram for 'heart,' can a 'heart' be a 'womb?' Is a woman just a man with a womb, a **womb-man**?

The immature Deaf Phoenician will mock, ridicule, and dismiss such questions due to the out-of-control ego that imprisons him or her. But perhaps there is some curiosity left in his soul that will allow him to break free from his Stockholm syndrome and see the world anew, through the eyes of himself rather than the eyes of others. The goal of this work is not to impose a worldview upon the reader, but help the Neophyte develop his or her own.

A 'language' ('Lan' + 'Gu' + 'Age') is "a creature of creation and destruction that impersonally guards those who command them throughout the Aeons."

Using word-splitting and etymology, this is seen in both the Chinese and Vietnamese word 'lan,' which is an "orchid" in the feminine tense and, in the masculine tense, it becomes "mountain mist" in Chinese and "unicorn" (coincidence?) in Vietnamese.

The creature that is born from this is the 'kỳ lân' in Vietnamese, which is related to the 'qilin' in Chinese, a **mystical** creature that appears to protect the noble ones.

Think about 'mystical,' which using the Language of the Birds and phonetics is 'mist' + 'I' + 'see' + 'all' (myst + i + c + al) = "in the mist I see all," or "I see all in the mist." This is the talent of the mystics, to pierce the veil.

'Gu' is the Dahomey god of war, smiths, and craftsmen. This corresponds to **Mars,** whose action leads to creation.

An 'age' is an "aeon," a long period of time, and as related to the Zodiac, the ages retrograde and each one lasts for 2160 years.

Historically, outside of secret orders of the initiated, it has only been the elites that wielded the power of words and constructing paradigms with them, because they've had the time, attention, and resources to invest into learning the occult science of languages. Meanwhile, the masses occupy themselves with games, entertainment, recreational drugs, false saviors, erroneous dogmas, and other distractions that further compound their ignorance and incompetence.

Hopefully, after experiencing this work, you will play with the words you see and hear in the silence of the golden god, 'audio' ('Au' (the symbol for gold) + 'Dio' ("god" in Italian)). One of the axioms of black magick is that **silence is golden,** for they presume it to be **consent.**

4 BIRDS OF A FEATHER

Perhaps the most famous of all mythical creatures, from the dim mists of civilization till now, is the phoenix. The Japanese, Chinese, Arabian, Egyptian, Greek, Roman, Russian, Native American cultures, etc., all had their own versions of this fiery bird that was often a symbol of nobility and a symbolic allegory for the nature of the Sun.

The Deaf Phoenicians see the phoenix symbolism everywhere, especially during their sports rituals, and never think of its implications or origins. They see the markings of the Inversive Brethren everywhere yet still don't know whose territory they stand in. It is the equivalent of a foreigner unwittingly crossing the forbidden boundaries of a criminal gang's territory, marked by their graffiti, gang signs and logos, and then losing his life due to his ignorance of those logos.

It's utterly pitiful that someone could look at the word 'phoenix' and not see its origin and connection to **Phoenicia** or their phonics and phonetics. However, this is the majority of the current race due to their traumatic, **Phoenician** black magick ritual abuse that has indoctrinated them and their ancestors for at least the past ten millennia.

The meanings of the phoenix are similar to the meanings of the Ouroboros. Words, just like symbols, also have their polarities and are made of multiple layers. Since one can get the Deaf **Phoenician** definition of 'phoenix' anywhere, we'll focus on the esoteric meanings.

The phoenix gets its name from the Latin word '**phoeniceus**,' which is the color "purple-red." Why did the Romans/Venetians/**Phoeni**cians call purple-red '**phoeni**ceus?' Because the Phoenicians are the ones who invented purple dyes, getting the ingredients from conch shells and other sea snails, hence the name **Phoenicia**: "land of purple." This is where the color Tyrian purple originates, and part of the reason why royalty wears it, because they are all in some way involved with the Phoenicians, whether through descent or servitude.

The more esoteric meaning behind the color purple is that it is made by balancing, or blending, the colors blue and red. Colors are frequencies and therefore energy. Blue is the frequency of love, water, the Moon, nurture, procreation, acceptance, and passivity, while red is the frequency of fear, fire, the Sun, infinite wisdom, the eternal source of life, defiance, and activity. The balance of these sacred elements of the Feminine (Blue; negative) and Masculine (Red; positive) creates the harmoniously neutral, yet powerful, frequency of Purple. Red and blue are the polarities of purple. To divide the spiritually royal purple is to create people who identify with blue or red.

In America, we have Democrats (blue) and Republicans (red). This is because they are people who are divided, or dualistic. The Democrats have issues with their mothers, which is why they seek government to be their nanny and caretaker, thus identifying with blue (feminine; negative), while the Republicans are the polarity that corresponds to people who have issues with their fathers, which is why they seek government to be their protector and provide a strong military/police state presence, thus identifying with the color red (masculine; positive).

These divided people seek what they have been spiritually deprived (internally) through government (externally). The problem with this, aside from the obvious duality and discord it creates, is that '**government**' means "mind-control" in Latin, which is exactly what both sides put themselves under by consenting to government = '**gubernare**' (to control) + '**mente**' (mind).

In an oversimplification, blue corresponds to the right hemisphere of the brain, while red corresponds to the left hemisphere of the brain. The right hemisphere tends to be spiritually oriented, artistic, and intuitive, while the left hemisphere tends to be scientific, pragmatic, and materially oriented. Both are absolutely necessary to a healthy mind. Both sides are absolutely destructive if unbalanced. Both sides, when in discord, tend to produce outcomes that are one and the same: collective institutions, hive-mind cults, and the destruction of sovereignty based on the presumptions of ignorant, malicious people. This explains why religion and government, though seemingly opposite, are not only one in the same, but are controlled by the same groups of people. They are symptoms (effects) of people whose minds are unbalanced (cause), which is why many mystery traditions, in their pure form, revolve around balancing the mind and the seemingly opposite aspects of consciousness, which, under Absolute Truth, may be reconciled into one. The allegory of balancing the Sun (male; positive; Fire) and the Moon (female; negative; Water) teaches this. It is how the initiated erect the temple of the Sun and Moon (Solomon) within themselves and become enlightened, hence the Green Language of the Ionic (Eye-On-I-C) Pillar. With the "Eye on, I see." This is why the representation of the unity consciousness is one all-seeing eye, or a 'mono-eye': *money*, because as the Bibles states, "If thine eye is single/perfect, thy body will be full of light" (enlightened; illuminated).

Police 'sirens' are alternating lights that flash red and blue frequencies at those they pursue to cause discord, or chaos, from which they know how to bring order. What is a 'siren?' It is a sea-chanter, a mer-chant, a water nymph that lures mariners to their destruction with the attractive sounds of its voice. Mariners are bound by maritime law because they are a product of the sea (el mar; God of the Sea), mare, Mary, the Queen Bee, Isis, the Moon, as seen in the word 'marine.' This also displays whom the marines serve and operate under, whether they know it or not. We'll delve into this later on, but in terms of the sirens, the alternating current of red and blue energy causes duality upon its intended targets, creating a submissive, obedient subjects (blue), or provoking a defiant reaction from the subjects (red) that will give the LEOs an excuse to persecute them under Uniform Commercial Code and profit off of their victims' enslavement.

This is why they are called 'police' (pole-ice). They are the 'ice' on the 'pole' of consciousness that thwarts all who try to ascend it, and by doing so they thwart their own spiritual evolution, because in order to remain 'pole ice,' one must remain frozen on the pole.

To be frozen is to remain at 32 degrees or less, which is why the degree of illumination in Freemasonry is 33 degrees, because this is the degree at which frozen water (ice) thaws and becomes liquid. This is why many people who hold 'office' (off-ice) are in positions of power and control, and may **freeze** bank accounts at their leisure, because they have gotten themselves 'off ice' and have become liquid, like water. This is why they have cash flow and liquidity at everyone else's expense, because off-icers are paycheck players that conduct the system on behalf of the masters above them. But have no fear, because the adjustment of the universe is perfect, and the 'officer' is an 'off-eye-seer,' even though he is 'off ice,' because the master is the slave, and he is as dualistic and condemnable as the ones he pretends to rule, hence he is a **seer** with his **eye** turned **off**, and of no use except to the Black Magi that know how to harness the chaos created by the officers, and then convert it into sorcery that they will use to bring even more of the world and its living souls under the slavery of their paradigm.

This duality is seen everywhere in corporate logos, but it is perhaps most prevalent in the flags of nations all over the world. Pay attention to those with red and blue in them, usually separated by another color such as white or gold. The red and blue duality is similar to the white and black duality on the chessboard. At the very least, they are exposing you to this duality, just like the game chess. When one agrees to participate, he is automatically making an opponent out of the other player. This is the microcosm for the dynamic of nations and flags. By dividing the world with imaginary boundaries and different man-made rules, it puts the whole race of humanity into duality, and then eventually into a position of hating each other for their petty differences, which creates the precise amount of resistance necessary to conduct chaos sorcery. Without the intense resistance of the co-creators, there is no sine wave of energy. The more the energy can be excited, the greater the wave of change can be manifested. This is the causal factor for why terrorist organizations are funded by the Black Magi that run this world, because nothing inspires change like the emotion of fear, and nothing inspires fear like the probability of unexpected, violent death. But since the casters of the hexes know the Truth, they can maintain balance of their thoughts, emotions, and actions, a state of unity consciousness. This is the power of purple. It is the balance of love and fear, negative and positive, feminine and masculine, and most importantly, matter and spirit.

For a physical description of this mythological creature, perhaps the best one comes from Pliny the Elder in the 1ˢᵗ century CE, who wrote, "The **phoenix**, of which there is only **one** in the world, is the size of an **eagle**. It is **gold** around the neck, its body is **purple**, and its tail is **blue** with some **rose**-colored feathers."

But what happens after the red and blue are balanced into purple? What is beyond blue? Green. What does nature produce the most of? Green. What is the color of the heart chakra? Green. What is the color that balances the spectrum? Green. What do the dark occultists color the world's reserve currency in, the most universally recognized **one**-dollar bill? Green. So you see, the fire in the sky seeds the water below, and out of the earth blossoms the eternal balance of Nature in all its green glory. Green is the color of the Language of the Birds. It is a frequency that your subconscious mind understands well, which is why the selfish capitalize on it.

You must know what was to know what is and what will be. Using our new skills, we see that **Phoenician**, **phoenix**, **phony**, **phonic**s, poly**phonic**, and **phone**tics all share the root 'phoeni' through the use of anagrams, Green Language, or phonetics. Do not be discouraged if you don't see it.

This word has been extremely occulted, so let's look at the most basic definition of '**phony**,' which is an adjective to describe someone or something as being "not real, fake, counterfeit, deceiving, concocted, insincere, or pretentious." It is important to remember this about anything related to the Black Magi, because it sums up the epitome of their character, power, and their paradigms. However, if their victims can be tricked into buying the lies, the phoniness, the subjects can be made to use their sovereign creative powers to feed and sustain the paradigm, even though it doesn't benefit them.

The first **phone**tic sound of **phon**y is the same **phone**tic sound in **Phoen**ician. This is why the anagram for 'phoen' is 'phone,' the very sound being referenced. '**Phone**' is related to the sound of speech, but as a verb, it means "to speak to or summon someone by telephone, to send a message to someone by telephone."

To 'summon' someone is "to **call** upon, for, or notify him or her." This is why people '**call**' each other on the phone. By addition or omission of a simple comma, the speaker could be commanding the subject to call him or her the name '**baby**,' as evidenced in "Call me baby," or the speaker could be calling the subject '**baby**' while commanding him or her to call the speaker by telephone in, "Call me, baby."

We take these little subtleties for granted every day, and supposed that language developed by chance through a slow evolutionary process, not realizing that there is real magick in the way words and phonetics are structured, and that none of it was by accident, just like the word '**curse**' is phonetically clear in the word '**cursive**.' If the '**spell**' is '**spelled**' incorrectly, the '**rite**' will not have been written the '**right**' way by the '**writer**.' The Deaf Phoenicians cannot see that languages are the poly**phon**ic machinations of Black Magi, because the ignorant masses are too lazy to take control of the languages for their own benefit. But you can change that.

'**IX**' is the Roman numeral for the number '**nine**.' An anagram for '**IX**' is '**XI**,' the Roman numeral for '**eleven**.' Therefore, through the use of anagrams, the word '**phoenix**' is also '**phone-nine**' (phone-ix) or '**phone-eleven**' (phone-xi). This is the occult meaning behind the emergency service '**911**,' in which people '**call**' (phone) '**nine-one-one**' (nine-eleven) to summon assistance or help.

To '**call**' is to "convoke, summon, shout, command, request, invite, waken," or in a more spiritual application, to '**call**' is to "invoke." If one needs assistance, he or she may '**call 911**,' but if Black Magicians need assistance, they '**phoenix**,' or '**invoke Nine-Eleven, 9/11**.'

To understand the significance of Nine-Eleven, we must look to 1:4 of the *Sefer Yetzirah*, which, in the context of teaching the use of the Kabbalistic Tree of Life, specifically warns, "Ten and not nine. Ten and not eleven."

There are ten Sephirot on the Tree of Life. The closest word that the ancients could surmise to describe God was pure 'Will.' The problem this presented was that Keter, the first of the Sephirot on the Tree of life, is also 'Will.' Since God created Keter, along with the other Sephirot, all of the Sephirot are inferior to God, thus if God is Keter, then it logically follows that only **nine** Sephirot could remain. If God were to be included in the Tree of Life, in addition to Keter, then there would be **eleven** Sephirot.

"Ten and not **eleven**" warns the mystic that as he or she penetrates the Sephirot, he or she may fancy himself or herself becoming God. Though ascension towards the infinite being is probable, the mystic can never obtain the infinite by becoming the Creator. The invocation of **nine-eleven**, the **phoenix**, is the Black Magician's attempt to become God by eliminating the Divine Will from the equation or degrade it to a sublunary level.

> "They have a king over them, the angel of the **abyss**. His name in Hebrew is Abaddon, and in the Greek, he has the name Apollyon." – *Revelation 9:11*

Is it any wonder that NASA titled their "missions" to the Moon under the name **Apollo**, or that CERN is located in Saint-Genus-Poilly? '**Poilly**' comes from the Latin word '**Appolliacum**,' which is named after **Apollo** because the people that lived there believed it to be a gateway to the **abyss**.

"The **phoenix**, of which there is only **one** in the world, is the size of an **eagle**." Pliny the Elder is not the only one who describes the phoenix in the image of an eagle. In the 5th Century BCE, Herodotus described the phoenix as "the general make and size are almost exactly that of the eagle."

What is the official animal symbol of the United States? The eagle. What is written on the ribbon in the eagle's mouth on the back of the US one-dollar bill, as well as on the back of all the US coinage?

'E PLURIBUS UNUM'

In Latin, this translates to '**OUT OF MANY, ONE**,' or

'FROM MANY, ONE.' This is also seen in the English word 'monopoly,' which is the combination of the words 'mono' (one) and 'poly' (many). The literal meaning of 'monopoly' is "one many," but through word-splitting it can be arranged into "many one," as in "out of many, one." A 'monopoly' is "exclusive control or possession of something."

What do the Black Magi have a monopoly on? The world's reserve currency, which is the US one-dollar bill. What is the occulted phoenix facing opposite of on the back of the one-dollar bill? The Great Seal. What is inscribed on the banner beneath the pyramid ('pyr-' + 'amid'; 'fire in the middle')?

'NOVUS ORDO SECLORUM'

In Latin, this translates to 'NEW WORLD ORDER.' What caps the fire in the middle, the 'pyramid'? The all-seeing eye, the one-eye, the mono-eye. The mon-ey, the Moon-eye or moon-honey, is imprinted on the most used money in the world. Between the Great Seal and the occulted phoenix is the word 'ONE' in all capital (CAP-IT-ALL) letters. The meaning of that black magick will be revealed in the second half of the book. What is written above 'ONE,' in all capital letters, yet in smaller font?

'IN GOD WE TRUST'

Who is the god they trust? Apollo (Ba'al), the son of Zeus, which is why they named the Suez Canal as such. 'Suez' is an anagram for 'Zeus.' This is how they work. What is written on the each side of the all-seeing eye?

'ANNUIT COEPTUS'

In Latin, this translates as, 'HE APPROVES OUR UNDERTAKINGS.'

What are their undertakings? How many times must they openly tell you before you get it? It's a sincere question. If you don't know by now, then that is a great self-assessment of where you're at mentally and spiritually. Not only is the answer on the Great Seal, but also it directly corresponds to 'nine-eleven' and Keter. Keter is the first of the Sephirot. 'First' pertains to 'one' and Keter means "crown" (Kronos, Cronus, Saturn) and is the topmost of the Sephirot. Saturn is the Lord of the Rings, and as J.R.R. Tolkien wrote, "One ring to rule them all." Keter is the primordial ether of nothingness, the origin of pure Will, which is why it is above Wisdom and Understanding. This is what the Black Magi seek to replace, bypass, or commandeer with their own will, so that they can be the rulers of all.

In 1972, Richard Nixon said, "Each of us has the hope to build a **New World Order**."

In 1987, Mikhail Gorbachev said, "We are moving toward a **New World Order**, the world of communism."

In 1991, George H.W. Bush said, "We have before us the opportunity to forge, for ourselves and for the future generations, a **New World Order**," and "The world can therefore seize this opportunity to fulfill the long-held promise of a **New World Order**."

In 1994, David Rockefeller said, "All we need is the right major crisis and the nations will accept the **New World Order**."

In 2008, in regards to President Obama, Henry Kissinger said, "I think that his task will be to develop an overall strategy for America in this period, when really a **New World Order** can be created."

In 2013, vice-president Joe Biden said, "The affirmative task before us is to create a **New World Order**."

What is the **New World Order**? It is a one-world government, with a one-world banking system, and a one-world military. Out of many, one. How did they catalyze their agenda? By summoning the phoenix, invoking 'nine-eleven.' The New World Order is Communism, which is really Satanism, hence the reason they share the same holiday: May 1ˢᵗ, May Day, Walpurgisnacht, **Bel**tane. Who is Bel? If you don't know, you'll soon learn. Keep in mind that this merely marks the halfway point between the Spring Equinox and Summer Solstice, and the day itself isn't evil. What dark occultists do on this day has nothing to do with its true nature.

On September 11, 2001, an event referred to as 'nine-eleven' because of its correspondence to the date 9/11, several towers in the World Trade Center were destroyed. The key focus of the event was the destruction of the Twin Towers, also foreshadowed by the title "The Lord of the Rings: The Two Towers."

However, the Twin Towers, or pillars, or hands, are based off of much older mystery traditions, whereby the towers represented both the masculine and feminine aspect of consciousness (Jachin and Boaz in Freemasonry, and the Five Loves and Five Strengths in Kabbalah), as evidenced by the phallic antenna on top of the male tower of the World Trade Center.

After the Twin Towers were destroyed, one tower was erected in its place and named the *Freedom Tower*. This is a perverted representation of the old Jewish scripture, "And they twain shall be one flesh." It might as well be the *Tower of Free Doom*, because that's all you'll get from it. But who was the driving force behind the creation of the Twin Towers? David Rockefeller. But don't worry about that. It's probably just coincidence. The Deaf Phoenicians are the world's foremost authority on coincidence theories. Everything is coincidence to them. The idea of people working together towards a common goal is preposterous to the Deaf Phoenicians.

The question you must ask yourself is, "What is the right major crisis that will make the nations accept the **New World Order**?"

To know the invisible, you must first see the visible. There are no shortcuts. There is no actual number of one. Where is there only one of anything in Nature? Zero is the real one. Zero means the totality, connectedness, wholeness, fullness, and completion of everything. Recall the connection that was made between the Holy See and the Holey Moon made of cheese. It pretends to be full, yet is never balanced, just like the Whore of Babalon (the whore of the Father Sun-being) it represents: Virgo, for she is the whore of Leo and the Moon is the whore of the Sun. Do you see the disgusting worldview that the dark occult imposes upon people?

One is the 'King,' the 'I,' the 'me.' It's the only one that claims it is exclusively sovereign, has a divine right to rule, and is holier than thou. But as we've already established, sovereign means to be "above rulership" ('sovereign' is from the Latin words 'super' + 'regnum'), and so if something cannot be ruled, it cannot rule either because to rule is to be ruled, for in any slavery relationship, the master is a slave. The King, just like the Moon pretending to be full, is also full of holes. So phonetically, perhaps he is 'holier' than thou in the sense that his title has more holes in it than Swiss cheese.

'One' wants to be zero. If this were not the case, it would not be spelled with an 'O,' which looks like a hole because it is whole. 'One' sounds like it should be spelled with a 'W,' a 'double you,' like 'wonder.' The 'O' is both holy, because it is whole, and it is holey because it has a hole. There is no beginning or end. You are one with the world, and in order to see it properly, you must see it through yourself, not a program. But take special care that you do not succumb to a solipsistic worldview.

As long as you are 'chasing that paper' to 'make that cheddar,' you will not be whole or holy, but you will be 'de-sired,' 'de-lighted,' 'de-fined,' and full of holes, or in another word, 'in-complete.'

'One' is the selfish, childish notion, the carnal desire, that man can become God, and it is the path to Hell. That's what 'nine-eleven' is. Think about that before you celebrate one of their holey days.

Where do the Deaf Phoenicians find their definitions? Texts. A definition is someone's action of defining something. In the case of words, definitions are defined in dictionaries, the diction of Aries. 'Diction' is 'airy' because it is a style of speaking, which is dependent on the choice of words/wards the caster speaks through the air. To write (rite) them down in text is to dictate them, which is to prescribe or lay down authoritatively, with authority, as the author, the creator. 'Dictate' comes from the Latin verb 'dictare,' which is "to say repeatedly, or to order."

This is why dictators must repeat themselves over and over to get the masses to believe them. When Deaf Phoenicians get their definitions through the airy diction of dictators, they are accepting, and by definition consenting, to that dictator's authority. However, this is still a belief, and not a legitimate claim that can be observed or proven in nature.

Since all authority is illegitimate in the case of an individual, then it follows logically that the individual cannot acquire a power that he does not inherently possess merely by forming a group of individuals, even if every person in the group can be fooled into believing that such behavior can manifest powers as a collective that they do not inherently possess as individuals. Therefore, since the individual has no inherent authority over another sovereign, a group of individuals may not possess inherent authority over another sovereign either, and all such claims, especially under the pretext of government, are thus equally illegitimate, harmful, and wrong.

A Deaf Phoenician will see 'government' as a form or system that directs the affairs of a state or community. But as we've shown through word-splitting, it has a deeper etymology that means "to control mind," or "mind-control." This is because we live in a mental universe, hence the reason that Hermeticists teach that we live in the All, and the All is Mind, and since 'government' is "to control mind," it also is "to control all, the All."

So what is the solution? It's simple, but the Deaf Phoenician is so helplessly imprisoned by his ego, false beliefs, and poisoned worldview that he has a difficult time coming to terms with it. Most people are so crossed that they actually believe they are heroes while their behavior enslaves the world. They see the worst in everyone because they themselves are the worst. They think that without man-made laws there would be chaos, but they've no understanding of Natural Law or that seeking control is what creates chaos on the plane of effects. Apparently they haven't looked at the world for the last few thousand years. The Deaf Phoenicians work tirelessly, often unwittingly, to create man-made scarcity at the behest of their masters, all the while imagining they live in freedom, the pinnacle of civilization. But if you try to develop your own system, watch out. They'll free the shit out of you with summary executions, staged coups, and drone strikes, and then laugh about it on 'television,' where the Black Magi 'tell a vision,' their vision.

Deaf Phoenicians love to make asinine statements such as "there's no such thing as Natural Law," and believe that if we don't have men claiming to be our rulers and governing us, the world will go to shit. They love to say "there's no such thing as truth," so that they can feel comfortable with doing whatever they want, regardless of how it affects others, since in that solipsistic worldview they get to decide what's right and wrong based on their whims. The best thing any sovereign inhabitant can do is to shun people who espouse this ideology so that they starve until they learn the laws of Nature through experience and meet their end through their own behavior without taking the rest of the world with them on their descent to the spiritual rock bottom punishment of death. Perhaps they can reverse their course, like many have done, and become a beacon of Truth.

The solution to 'government' is the greatest fear of the Deaf Phoenician. In fact, if sovereign inhabitants want to remain free and healthy, all they have to do is take action in a manner that is exactly opposite of what Deaf Phoenicians tell them is good for them. If the Deaf Phoenicians say chemotherapy cures cancer, then don't get chemotherapy. If they say vaccines cure disease, don't get vaccines. If they say genetically modified food is safe to eat, only eat organic, non-genetically modified food. If they say you need to consume the dead flesh of other beings to survive, don't eat meat. If they say cannabis oil doesn't heal the body, then use it. Whatever they make illegal is the best for you. Whatever they ascribe the least value to is actually the most valuable. He who disobeys the Deaf Phoenicians will profit both spiritually and physically, in this world and the next.

What is the opposite consciousness of government, the greatest fear of the Deaf Phoenicians? Anarchy. Deaf Phoenicians love to pervert this word more than any other word in existence. It is derived from the Greek prefix 'an-,' which translates as "the absence of; to be without" and the Greek noun 'archon,' which means "ruler, master, lord."

Simply put, 'anarchy' means "no rulers, masters, or lords," also known as "freedom." That's why they pervert this word, through the holey, airy authority of their dictionary dictators, as though mankind will experience nothing but disorder without rulers.

Rest easy brothers and sisters, for it matters not if the entire race of humanity becomes lemmings and succumbs to slavery. The Truth can never be destroyed. Without masters, there can be no slaves. Therefore 'anarchy' is the only way humanity will ever know freedom, and one who cannot understand this cannot understand freedom or ever experience it. There is no other way, and anyone who attempts to say otherwise is a fool at best, and a spiritual enemy of the gravest kind at worse. Without slavery, there can only be one state: freedom. Anarchy is the domain of the free. Like Truth, freedom is absolute. There is no such thing as a semi-free human. All beings are born with absolute freedom granted to them by the divine Will of Creation.

We do not manifest with natural masters. This is observable to even the most sublunary idiot. The man-made, scarcity-based mindset that breeds slavery is only possible through violence and theft. Those who attack anarchy and all works that support anarchy, which is nothing more than voluntarism, identify themselves as Deaf Phoenicians. They are the automatons that program human slavery, and as such, should be permanently shunned.

One does not have to reach the pinnacle of intellect to understand the obvious axiom, that in order to have independence, one must not be dependent. This is easily observed in the microcosm and the macrocosm, from learning to grow one's own food to learning to build one's own house to learning to create a paradigm outside of the system of government. Americans may have become independent of a monarchy in a quantum amount, but they never became independent of government in a quantum amount, and this is how they erred in their ways.

5 THE SEVEN SAY TEN

What whirled this world of words? What spun the sacred geometry of all things into a self-similar weave of correspondences across all scales of microcosms and macrocosms? What is the significance of the number seven in this reality, and what role do the seven planets play in it? The Deaf Phoenicians tend to have answers for all questions, but the answers strand their souls in a spiritual wasteland that is predicated on infinite possibilities of accidental manifestation rather than intelligent creative Will.

Everything, before it exists in the physical world, must first exist as some sort of frequency or energy on the plane of causality. The easiest way this can be conceptualized for most people is through thought. Thoughts manifest emotions, which manifest actions. Using the Law of Correspondences, "As it is above, so it is below; as it is on Earth, so it is in the sky," we see that man is the microcosm of the universe. So if man manifests action through the catalyst of his thoughts, then there must be some sort of equivalent of that on the grand scales of the solar system, galaxies, and so on until we escape the physical world and enter the spiritual one where the living souls, energy, can trace back to their origins.

Words also reflect the Law of Correspondence as above, and so below. There is a hidden history, a hidden energy or soul, sol (sun; light), in all words that cannot be destroyed, and thus reveal the past. Never is this more apparent than in the first day of the week, the Sun's day, or as we say in English, '**Sunday**.' But what do other languages call this day? In Spanish, they say 'domingo.' In Italian, they call it 'domenica.' In Romanian they call it 'duminică,' which means "Sunday; Sabbath."

These correspond to the Latin word 'dominica,' which means "lordly; of the lord; Sunday" in Latin but is also present in many other languages, because as you will learn, Latin never died. The Republic of Dominica, the Dominican Republic, was named after this, which clearly showcases its lordly nature of the Sun. This is because all of these words share the common phonetic sound of 'Domini,' which means "masters; owners," specifically of slaves, in Latin, which corresponds to 'archons' in Greek. It is plural for 'Dominus.'

'Domini' corresponds to the Hebrew 'Adonai' and the Greek 'Kyrios.' 'Adonai' means "lords; masters; owners," the plural of 'adon,' which comes from the Ugaritic word 'ad,' meaning "father." 'Kyrios' also means "lord; master, owner," and is typically how Greek slaves referred to their masters, but it also refers to the head of a household. In the New Testament, 'Kyrios' is usually a reference to Jesus Christ, the Christian God, the lord and savior, the Sun/Son of God.

Most dictionaries and other resources will define 'anno Domini' as an abbreviation for 'anno Domini Nostri Jesu Christi,' meaning "in the year of our Lord Jesus Christ."

Since 'Domini' can also be plural for 'Dominus,' it's worth considering that the 'anno Domini' may mean "in the year of our Lords, Masters, Owners." This would make it a collective order or society. Which order or society pertains to Jesus Christ? Christianity, or more specifically, the Society of Jesus: the Jesuits. This is evidenced through Christopher Columbus' naming of the Dominican Republic as such. The Knights of Columbus, though not founded till the 20th century, are a Jesuit order. The current Pope is the first Jesuit to hold that position.

Clearly, there is some sort of connection between Jesus, Christianity, Roman Catholicism, the Jesuits, the Sun, and their Sabbath, the Sun's day: Sunday, which we've already exposed as priestcraft sorcery that goes all the way back to Hindoostan.

Many Christians will go to their grave attempting to debunk this, for they erroneously believe the Bible was originally written in

Greek, never suspecting the deception that the Diegesis of Egypt was brought to the priests of Europe and translated into Latin, and then, as a way of obstructing sincere scholars from learning the sinister Truth, it was put out in Greek as though the original language was Greek. The name Jesus in Greek (Ἰησοῦς) is bad Greek, and it evidences that it was adapted to Greek from Latin, not from Greek into Latin. You will find different versions of the story in India, Persia, Egypt, and Greece, thousands of years earlier than it was supposed to have occurred in Palestine. This is the priestcraft sorcery of the phony Phoenicians, who are guided by the much older order of the Black Magi, and it is the primary reason why most people are in possession of negative knowledge, spreading their plague to anyone who listens to them. They would be better off knowing nothing and saying nothing than their current state of black magick infection that's eager to contaminate anyone who is willing to suffer episodes of being verbally vomited on. Shun them.

Since the word 'sun' is phonetically equivalent to the word 'son,' it's not a coincidence that Jesus is referred to as the son of God while the relationship that the 'Sun' has with the creator is equivalent to being God's sun, whatever we fancy the idea of God to be. This is the same relationship that Ba'al, the Sun, has to El (God, Dagon, Saturn), which is evidenced by all of the cube and hexagram symbolism found in the major religions. It is also seen in the word 'Xmas,' which is a common abbreviation of 'Christmas' because 'X' is a symbol of the Sun, the Son of God, and 'X' was the symbol of Osiris in ancient Egypt, the Sun, and then also of Tammuz, known as the Cross of Tammuz. This is what Christians are really putting on their foreheads on Ash Wednesday, for it is marking them on the most important part of their body: the Eye Single.

Anyone who attempts claim that Jesus is not the Sun, and that Christianity is not a solar cult based on sun worship, exposes themselves as woefully ignorant at best, or at worst, an enemy of Truth, the real Will of Creation that we call God, the punishment of which is dissolution of the soul. To be unmistakably clear, the beautiful science that these stories pervert is God's gift to you, the most beautiful map ever made, the story in the firmament that cannot be corrupted by mankind's depraved hands. This is the divine cartography to help all who descend into this sublunary plane thrive while they're here and eventually find their way back to the Creator. However, to read these allegories as though they were historical accounts is a fool's errand, and perhaps there is no surer path away from God.

Everything in Christianity, and all other religions, was plagiarized from much older traditions, and then perverted, not from lack of imagination, but rather because those who kept this knowledge in their orders and bloodlines, namely the priest classes and the royalty, have used these same tricks, the same black magick mechanism, upon unwitting populations for millennia in order to keep them waiting for external saviors to fix internal problems, thus remaining unchanged, enslaved, waiting for what never was nor will ever be.

For whatever reason, there is a trait in the human being that can be exploited by those who recognize it, and that is the nature of the psyche and ego of the self. This mechanism, if left uninhibited, will eventually lead to self-actualization, the fulfillment of one's highest and best version of himself, and also self-realization, the discovery of the knowledge of oneself, to know who we are and what our origins are. The occultation of this information is the causal factor of humanity's self-loathing. Humanity, by and large, has not discovered its own origins, and has been intentionally deceived by those who do know our origins into thinking that the human race was spawned by its evolution from mundane planes of existence rather than its involution from higher spheres of life.

The dark occultists of this world know that the human being is a spiritual being. They love to let others know that they know the human being is a spiritual being. Furthermore, they experience duper's delight by peddling erroneous information onto the masses and thriving from the chaos that is created by humanity dividing itself through its false dogmas. Even the most symbol illiterate dunces can verify this for themselves by looking at the symbol of Satanism: the pentagram (the inverted five-pointed star). The apex of the pentagram is the bottommost part of the symbol. This is an emblem of the Inversive Brethren, albeit their entry-level filtration process, as seen by its identical yet inverse resemblance to the pentacle (the upright five-pointed star).

Both the pentagram and the pentacle share the word 'penta-,' which is a Greek prefix meaning "five." Both symbols are composed of the same meanings, yet they are the polar opposites of each other. The two legs and two arms represent the four physical elements of creation: **Air** (oxygen), **Fire** (carbon), **Water** (hydrogen), and **Earth** (nitrogen), and the apex of the five-pointed star is the quintessence, the quinta essentia (the **fifth** element): **Spirit.**

In the penta**cle**, the upright five-pointed star, the Spirit is toward the heavens and higher celestial spheres of existence. The suffix "**-cle**" comes from "**-ulus**" in Latin, which in '**grammar,**' pertains to diminutive (tiny) nouns. This is because the pentacle is a representation of the human (two legs + two arms + head), who stands upright as the apex of physical evolution, where the material world unites with the spiritual world, co-creating the world around him, within the boundaries of natural law, with his thoughts, emotions, and actions. He is a microcosm of God.

The penta**gram** is an inversion of human spirit, encouraging people to invert the pentacle and turn to the dark side, Satan, Saturn, Winter. This is the occult meaning behind one of the most popular book and televisions series' slogans, "Winter is Coming," but also because we have entered the Age of Aquarius, ruled by Saturn and Uranus, and then in another 2160 years it will be the Age of Capricorn, also ruled by Saturn. These signs correspond to the months of February and January, retrograding towards December, which are the months of Winter, which is why they are ruled by Saturn, Father Time, hence the return of the King. They're really telling you that **Satan** is coming, or like in *The Lord of the Rings: The Return of the King,* **Saturn,** the lord of the rings, is returning.

The word '**pentagram**' can be split into '**penta-g-ram,**' which is '**penta-**' + '**gee**' + '**ram**' through Green Language. '**Gee**' is a verb that means "to turn to the right side," which is more mockery because the left-hand path can never be righteous, for it is the path of nine-eleven, the path of the Black Magi, thus it is immoral.

The '**ram**' is not only a symbol of the uterus, fallopian tubes, cervix, and vagina, but also a symbol of Aries (the constellation of Mars), the cardinal **fire** sign, the first of the twelve signs of the Zodiac, the cerebrum, and a male goat. Aries is symbolic to Moses (because the Age of Aries is when the story of Moses takes place) and the Vernal Equinox, where Jesus is crucified and Christ (the Sun) is resurrected to give renewal to all life in the season of spring. This is why Freemasons refer to Jesus Christ as Christ Jesus, because Christ rises and Jesus dies.

Moses, just like Jesus, is born in the sign of Capricorn (the fish-goat). He was named Moses by Pharaoh's daughter because, according to Exodus 2:10, she "drew him out of the **water**." This is also why Je-sus literally means "I-fish," the king or lord fish. *J* is also the shape of a fishhook. God asks Job, "Canst thou draw out leviathan with a hook?"

In Kabbalah, the sea is Binah, Understanding. The serpent (Tanniyn) is sexual power. This is why the sign of Scorpio is symbolic to sex, the victory of Satan (Winter) over Summer, as it lures the Sun of God out of the Garden of Eden and into the Fall (Autumn) of Man. The House of Scorpio is the House of Death, the kiss of death, because the balanced being recognizes sex as the law, the foundation of all, the door to a new legacy and regeneration. By inverting the pentacle to make it a pentagram, Satanists are luring people to lower their spiritual, creative, sexual energy towards base desires and an animal nature rather than raising it to regions where it will beget power and magnetism, love, and enthusiasm. They are **de-siring** them. According to the Tablets of Aeth, "sex gives vigor to whatever region it is raised to, but if lowered, to be spent with no returns, it debases and renders life a desert of dry bones."

What element does Scorpio correspond to? **Water**. This is why the law of money, the Law of the Sea, Maritime Admiralty Law, is the law of Commerce. 'Commerce' is by definition "sexual intercourse," and since Aries is the constellation of Mars (action), it only makes sense that the anti-freedom, anti-human laws of the sea are ruled by the **mar**tial law of **Mars**, the father of Romulus and Remus: Rome. That's why Uniform Commercial Code is Roman Civil Law.

The five Hebrew letters that surround the Mendes goat's head, starting at the left ear, spell out the name 'לִוְיָתָן.' This is 'Leviathan,' the master of all fishes, the serpent who will be killed at the end of all time in Isaiah 27:1, "In that day, Yahweh with his hard and great and strong sword will punish leviathan, the fleeing serpent, and leviathan the crooked serpent; and he will kill the dragon that is in the sea."

This is why the Goat of Mendes emblem, the Sigil of Baphomet, of the Sabbatic Goat, and symbol of Pan, fits perfectly into the pentagram. 'Gram' represents occult magick, as seen in 'gramarye,' which is connected to the Old French word 'gramaire,' meaning "grammar, book of magick." This is where 'grammar' comes from, which is not only linked to magick, it is magick. Through etymology, we see that 'pentagram' literally means "Five-magick; magick of five; magick book of five."

In Norse mythology, 'Gram' is the sword that Sigurd used to kill Fafnir, a dragon. This comes from the Old Norse word 'gramr,' which means "wrath, king, or warrior." Through the Language of the Birds and phonetics, 'gramr' is also 'grammar,' which when expanding upon its meaning of "occult magick," adds an angry (wrath), selfish (king), or righteous (warrior) depth to it.

After Fafnir is killed by Sigurd, Sigurd and his foster father **Reginn** take the treasures that Fafnir guarded. Note that a 'jinn' is an Arabic word for "spirit," and phonetically is 'gin,' an alcoholic "spirit" in English. 'Spirit' comes from the Latin word 'spiritus,' meaning "breath." Since 'Re/Ra' is a Sun-god, Reginn's name (Re-jinn) has the occult meaning of "Sun-spirit." We'll touch upon this later when we delve into Commerce and 'profit margins.'

Sigurd, after tasting Fafnir's blood while cooking his heart, acquired a new skill: the knowledge of the speech of birds. But I'm sure that has nothing to do with Green Language, the Language of the Birds. None of this is related according to the beliefs of the Deaf Phoenicians, for they have eyes but see not, and ears, but alas, hear not.

Upon learning the speech of birds, Sigurd hears that Reginn plotted to kill him, so Sigurd used 'Gram' to kill Reginn, the occult Sun-spirit. This is an allegory for how water (Gram) must put out fire (Reginn; Fafnir: dragons are associated with fire) or, if not, the exposure to heat (treachery) will dry water out (death). A 'gram' is connected to the element of **Water** because its original definition was "the absolute weight of a volume of pure **water** equal to the cube of the hundredth part of a metre, and at the temperature of melting ice." One gram incidentally equals **five** carats, which connects it to 'penta-.'

Gram of Denmark is a mythological king that was based on Thor, who is an allegory for Jove, which is Jupiter, the Godfather, the father of all gods, hence Thursday is Thor's day, Jupiter's day.

Jupiter comes from 'Iuppiter.' *I* was the same sound as *J* in Latin, as there is no letter *J*. 'Iuppiter' is composed of 'Iou' (*Jew' Peter;* "Jove" in Old Latin) and 'piter,' which comes from 'pater,' meaning "father" in Latin.

In Old English it became 'fæder,' which became 'father' in English. It unearths a whole new meaning of 'Fæderal Government,' meaning "Father Mind-Control."

In Proto-Indo-European, 'dyew-,' which is phonetically 'Iu,' means "to be bright; day sky, heaven." It comes from the Proto-Indo-European word 'diu,' which means "bright, to shine." In Proto-Italic, 'djous' also meant "day, sky," which shares the origin of the Latin word 'diēs,' meaning "day."

In Ancient Greek, 'Zeû páter' means "o father Zeus." This corresponds to the Sanskrit words 'Dyaus pitar,' which means "heavenly father." After combining all of these meanings, this is why Jupiter means "Jove, god of the sky and chief/father of the gods." Now you know whom God the Father is, of The Church of Jesus Christ of Latter-day Saints (the Mormons): **Jupiter, Jove, Zeus**. All the sun worship corresponds to that of the spiritual sun that the ancients imagined physical life to evolve from. All of the desert sky-god religions are perversions of the science of the stars that comes from Ancient Egypt. Jupiter is merely a creation of the Creator, and just like those who tread the path of nine-eleven, Jupiter can never be God. Those who do not wish to cut themselves off from God had better abandon their covens of sorcerers that peddle black magick onto unsuspecting living souls.

Jupiter is the son of God/El/Dagon/Time/Kronos/**Saturn**/Satan/Set. He fathered **Mercury** (the messenger of the gods), **Venus** (the goddess of Love; Lucifer, the morning star), Diana (the goddess of the **Moon**; Isis), and Apollo (god of the **Sun**; Osiris, Horus, Ra, Ba'al, and Jesus, whose name is an occulted blend of Jupiter and Zeus).

Monday is the Moon's day. Another word for 'moon' is 'luna,' or 'luni' in Romanian, which is where the word 'lunatic' is derived.

Tuesday is derived from the West Germanic Mars equivalent: Tiw, hence phonetically, we have Tiw's day. Wednesday is Woden's day. Woden is Mercury in Roman mythology, so Wednesday is Mercury's Day. Friday belongs to the goddess of love. It's Frigg's day, Freya's day, Venus' day, or Lucifer's day. Most Muslims will say this book is the work of the Dajjal, their version of the antichrist, but hilarity ensues when the Quran 62:9 states, "O you who believe! When the call to prayer is proclaimed on Friday hasten earnestly to the remembrance of God, and leave aside business. That is best for you if you but knew."

The Islamic symbol is a depiction of an astronomical event called Venus Occultation, where Isis (the Moon) hides Lucifer (Venus). Both are feminine planetary bodies. Islam's Sabbath day is on Lucifer's Day: Friday. Note that I see the beauty in Lucifer, for it is a Latin word in reference to Venus, that was not added to the Bible till the 4th Century AD. Lucifer (Venus, Love) has nothing to do with the Devil or masculine energy at all. However, like all good things, it has been perverted by Black Magi to mean something else, something "evil." Nevertheless, Muslims take Lucifer's Day as their Sabbath, and there's no getting around that in the perverted paradigm of the desert sky-god religions. From their fruit you shall know them, and what is the fruit of Christianity (Sun, Christ), Islam (Venus, Lucifer), and Judaism (Saturn, El)? Bloodshed, suffering, and slavery.

The Jews chose Saturn's Day, Saturday, as their Sabbath: "one ring to rule them all, and in the darkness bind them." This is why the Pope, the cardinals, and the Jews all wear skullcaps. It represents Saturn. The sacred black cube of Islam, the Kaaba in Mecca, is a symbol for Saturn. The Tefillin, the black cube worn by religious Jews while praying, is a symbol of Saturn. The Cross, worn by Christians, is an unfolded cube, and when folded back up is a perfect cube, thus it is an occulted symbol of Saturn.

Now you know who the savior that the Christians wait for is: Apollyon, the angel of the Abyss, Jesus, Ba'al, who rises from the underworld in the morning as Horus (the progeny of Isis and Osiris), then becomes Ra as the most high at noon, and as the Sun dies (sets), because he is murdered by Set (Saturn; Satan) and cut into pieces, he is sent back into the underworld as Osiris. As the

Sun rises and sets over the water, it can be seen to "walk" on it. All of this is just an allegory for the aspects of the Sun's light during its four crucial angels of the twelve-hour day, right? Or is it something else? The joke is that Jupiter overthrew Saturn, his father, and became the god of the cosmos. Saturn then fled to Italy, hint, hint. The Black Magi have concocted these stories to mock you. They are the phony Phoenicians that trace their priestcraft sorcery all the way back to Hindoostan. The irony of someone pretending to be Christian while waiting for the progeny of Saturn to save him from himself is hilarious to them. The same goes for the Muslims, Jews, Buddhists, Hindus, and all other religions. They're all the same false gods, concocted by the religious and ruling classes that have controlled the world by keeping this knowledge in their secret orders and families.

'X' is the symbol of the Sun. 'X' marks the spot on a treasure map where the gold is hidden, and where you sign your name on the dotted line. 'X' is "ten" in Roman numerals. Say ten. Obama's slogan was "Yes we can." If you reverse it, through the occult laws of reversal, "Yes we can" becomes "Thank you, Satan." This is why Black Magi love anagrams, and back-words/back-wards, because they literally are protection spells: wards. X-press yourself. Press the mark of the beast on yourself. Sign on the dotted line. Mark it. Say-ten. This is what the Black Magi have done to you through their systems of religions.

Deaf Phoenicians may experience some sort of emotional mind-control reaction after reading this, but I'm not here to serve false gods of the Inversive Brethren of the Dark Satellite. I'm here to serve the One, the Divine Spark of the Will of Creation, and usher in the real Christ energy. And I'm not saying that all of these religions should be discarded completely. But it's important to have the skill-set to sift through the deception when studying them. Christ has nothing to do with external saviors. The Cristos, the anointed one, is within you. You are the one you've been waiting for. If not now, then never. If not you, then no one.

How many days of the week are there? Seven. How many planets? Seven. There should be eight, but there's no day to honor

Earth, the most important environment to you. Is this because Earth is not a planet? Right now the Deaf Phoenician is scoffing or snickering in his self-imposed egotistical prison cell, for all Deaf Phoenicians are cell fish. They're laughing at this, sitting in property they don't own, because they don't have real money to pay for it. Instead of converting real assets for their temporary possessions, they discharged debt to someone else in the form of a promise to pay that they accrued by participating in a paradigm of debt and death, and are thus temporary tenants of whatever fleeting property they erroneously believe they own, which is why they don't have Allodial title and must pay taxes on their "property." They're so blinded by their own ignorance that they cannot even entertain questions, or information contrary to their beliefs, without having an emotional reaction. If you don't have Allodial title to your assets, or don't know what that means without looking it up, sit still, shut the fuck up, and learn something, because left to your own devices, you are a self-destructive cog in a wheel that was designed to eradicate you after siphoning your spiritual currencies from your short, miserable, and now defunct sovereign existence. Why is there no day of the week to honor the Earth that we inhabit? What is different about Earth from the rest of the wandering stars, i.e. the Sun, the Moon, Mars, Mercury, Jupiter, Venus, and Saturn?

Why is the vector, an occulted seven (the same seven on the palm of your right hand), NASA's logo? Why isn't it eight, to include the Earth? Look up the origins of NASA on your own. The five founders are Jack Parsons (occultist, rocket scientist), Aleister Crowley (occultist, spy for British Intelligence), L. Ron Hubbard (occultist, creator of the Church of Scientology Cult), Wernher von Braun (Nazi rocket scientist), and Walt Disney (occultist, Hollywood Mogul; in the Druidic system, magick wands are made of the wood of a holly tree, hence the name Hollywood, the epicenter of movie magick, where the casts of films (actors) report to Set (Saturn, Satan) to cast their black magick upon unsuspecting populations through captivating performances (rituals). They don't call it Mass (an act of worship) Media for nothing. As we've already covered, the Druids of the West are the Priests of Apollo. Get it? Must I make it any clearer?

There are far too many topics to get into regarding these men, but Disney is responsible for the 'hero programming' in young men, which teaches them that women are damsels in distress and need to be saved by acts of heroism and valor, and also 'princess programming' in young women, which teaches them that they are helpless princesses that need to wait for a strong male archetype to save them. Do you think the story of *Beauty and the Beast* is a coincidence? What is the number of the beast? You can see it in the Walt Disney logo. 666. The first six is in the *W*, the second six is in the dot of the *i*, and the third six is in the *y*. Behold it yourself. Don't believe anything.

What was Aleister Crowley known as? The "wickedest man alive" and "the Beast." Perhaps the biggest influence Crowley had on the occult orders of today is the art of doing things backwards and in reverse. The art of inversion is a defining characteristic of the Black Magi, the Inversive Brethren. From their fruit you shall know them, and so even though Crowley made extraordinary contributions, those who are initiated into mystery traditions that hold his work in high regard cannot see the forest for the trees, and thus will unwittingly invoke upon themselves the Second Death. The reader is encouraged to research this subject further. As someone who is initiated into the same orders as he, I can tell you that he lost his way primarily through sex magick. Among all the violations of Natural Law, sex magick is what ruins the most promising of neophytes early on. Some of the orders he belonged to warn against this, but he clearly left those behind early on and willfully chose, as many do, the left-hand path. His work reflects his life: beautiful, chaotic, inspiring, and deceiving. He played with the infernal laws that govern animal nature, and taught people how to use black magick. This information didn't serve Truth, and as a result, the work attracted and fell into the hands of those who were most feared to get ahold of it. This unfettered service to ego is the primary tenet of Satanism: service to self, which is why Anton LaVey was tasked with founding the Church of Satan. He even writes that Satan is merely the Ego, the number of which is nine, for even when the most complicated numbers are multiplied by nine, through Gematria, they always return to nine in the final equation, the allegory of which is that no matter how complex something is, when you increase the influence of Ego, all that is returned is more Ego. It never transforms into something else. Ego always returns to itself, so it serves the neophyte to learn to omit Ego in the processes of practicing High Magick, else he will be visited by what he puts out.

One may wonder why Satanism is full of so many pitfalls yet attracts so much talent. The Church of Satan is pretty much the lowest entry level of the dark occult. Like Freemasonry, they'll take anyone. It's not meant to groom talented magicians. It's meant to uncover the most psychopathic individuals and groom them to be the most useful tools. If you don't know this about your order, I congratulate you, for you're not psychopathic enough to advance. This is a good thing, and it is for you that I write this. All collective orders serve this purpose, which is why it is advised that everyone who seeks Truth should walk the path alone. Those meant to be in your life will walk it with you while allowing you to discover the indestructible Truth for yourself. Listen to everyone, learn from everything, but follow no one, especially me. I'm here to provide you information that I am qualified both spiritually and genetically to do, but I am not the arbiter of Truth. The price I paid to acquire some of this knowledge was an unbearable inner cost.

There are so many things I'd like to write, but these topics have been thoroughly vetted in other works, so there's no need to digress on L. Ron Hubbard, Jack Parsons, etc., but suffice to say, NASA was founded by cult members who were adept at mind-control and black magick. This cannot be denied. Combined with Hollywood technology and thorough indoctrination, they have created a perfect system to obfuscate Truth in all matters. Any time one is dealing with relativity, he or she is dealing with Satanic deception. There is nothing relative about Truth. It is what occurred that manifested what is. It happened regardless of human perception or ignorance of it. Truth is independent of our beliefs, and it exists even if no one is aware of it. Truth doesn't require the attention of our narrow, limited minds in order for it to exist. It is objective, observable, discoverable, and knowable by all who penetrate it. This is not an opinion. It is a statement of fact that, like Truth, can never be destroyed. This book would not have been the same without the work of Aleister Crowley, so it is not my intention to deride those who are cited in my work, however, I will not hesitate to use someone as an example for the purpose of education. I happen to admire some of Aleister's work as much as I would condemn other parts of it. Under the absolute Truth, all is good and all returns to the One. But immortality is not guaranteed. Enough violations of Natural Law will ensure that the identity is lost as the soul is dissolved and its parts are scattered into more useful creations. However, pertaining to the question of why Earth is not part of the seven weekdays, you can be confident that the members of the Cult of Scientism knew the Truth. But if you think NASA choosing the name Apollo from Apollyon in Revelation 9:11 for their missions to the Moon is merely a coincidence, not only is the joke on you, but you are the joke. It's because you have no knowledge. Without knowledge, you cannot gain understanding, and without understanding, you cannot gain wisdom. Without wisdom, you cannot guide passion.

In death, Wernher Magnus Maximilian von Braun gave all the Truth as to why there is no day in the week to honor the planet Earth. It's in his name. '**Magnus**' is a Latin word meaning "great." '**Maximilian**' comes from the Latin word '**maximus**,' meaning "greatest." But great at what? '**Mag**' comes from an old Akkadian word, '**imga**,' meaning "wise, holy, and learned." The races succeeding the Akkadians, which became the Chaldeans, turned '**imga**' into '**mag**,' which became '**magi**' in Latin and '**magos**' in Greek. This is where the term '**magick**' is derived from. But to the blind, this is all coincidence.

A '**magus**' is both '**magnus**' and '**maximus**' because he is initiated into occult knowledge. This allows him to be a mage or a sorcerer, depending on whether he chooses the right-hand path or the left-hand path. Either way, he will be highly sought after, and if not a servant of Truth and the Creator, will no doubt be absorbed into the priest class that colludes with the ruling class to enslave humanity.

So what did this magnus magus give us upon his death? A message on his grave. All it says is "Wernher von Braun, 1912 – 1977, Psalms 19:1." The curious mind will look up Psalms 19:1 and behold, "The heavens declare the glory of **God**; and the **firmament** showeth the work of His hands."

The '**firmament**' is "a **vault** of the heavens." A '**vault**,' as a noun, is "a type of **arch** that supports a ceiling," or in a bank, a 'vault' is "a room that is used to seal and store tangible valuables." As a verb, 'vault' means "to jump over something or to be moved to a higher, more important position."

Do you see what you're in yet? Do you see what the Sun does in relation to it? Do you know what you must do to get out of it? If not, don't panic. Resisting them will only be assisting them. Breathe. Inspire the ether, and then expire the waste that doesn't serve you. Now, in the words of Aleister Crowley, you will be initiated into the nature of the construct. Are you ready?

"The Universe unfoldeth itself as a **Rose**, and shutteth itself up as the **Cross** that is bent into the **Cube**. And this is the comedy of Pan that is played at night in the thick forest. And this is the mystery of Dionysus Zagreus that is celebrated upon the holy mountain of Kithairon. And this is the secret of the brothers of the Rosy Cross; and this is the heart of the ritual that is accomplished in the **Vault** of the Adepts that is hidden in the Mountain of the Caverns, even the Holy Mountain Abiegnus. And this is the meaning of the Supper of the Passover, the spilling of the blood of the Lamb being a ritual of the **Dark Brothers**, for they have sealed up the Pylon with blood, lest the Angel of Death should enter therein. Thus do they shut themselves off from the company of the saints. Thus do they keep themselves from compassion and from understanding. Accursed are they, for they shut up their blood in their heart. They keep themselves from the kisses of my Mother Babylon, and in their lonely fortresses they pray to the false moon. And they bind themselves together, and they have power, and mastery, and in their cauldrons do they brew the harsh wine of delusion, mingled with the poison of their selfishness. Thus they make war upon the Holy One, sending forth their delusion upon men, and upon everything that liveth so that their false compassion is called compassion, and their false understanding is called understanding, for **this is their most potent spell.** Yet of their own poison do they perish, and in their lonely fortresses shall they be eaten up by **Time** that hath cheated them to serve him, and by the mighty devil Choronzon, their master, whose name is the Second Death, for the blood that they have sprinkled on their Pylon, that is a bar against the Angel of Death, is the key by which he entereth in."

Time (Saturn, Satan, Set, Winter, El, Dagon, Cronus, the Crown, the Ego) cheats the foolish to serve him. By serving Saturn, the Black Mage severs his connection to source, God, and must feed off of others to prolong the inevitable, until finally he meets the Second Death, which is the dissolution of the soul.

The Black Magi are the orchestrators of a spiritual Ponzi scheme that will collapse the moment the majority of their victims grow up and realize what's going on. Once the masses shield themselves, their souls, their soles, from the Black Magi, which cannot hurt you in the body that God gave you, the sorcerers will starve and have no choice but the twofold death, like a rope worm having no choice but to release itself from the walls of the intestines and be expelled from the human body. This information was given to me directly from the mother of monsters. Do what you will with it.

This path of the Inversive Brethren is the left-handed path of nine-eleven. It is why the temple of Set (Saturn) is divided into Pylons, which are groups similar to a coven. In the Greek language, a Pylon is a monumental entrance. In Ancient Egypt, a Pylon was a façade on a cult building, and it symbolized Akhet, a hieroglyph for the horizon. The hieroglyph depicts two hills which the Sun **rose** and **set** between. Rituals to Amun, who later became identified with the sun-god Ra, were performed on the top of temple Pylons. You will see this cleverly disguised in satanic logos that depict the Sun rising between mountains, often referencing "a new day."

This horrible scheme is what they lure the majority of humanity into and why the world has gone to hell. This is the reason for why everything you are taught though their institutions is false, because the only way people make these horrible decisions is through a lack of knowledge. It is also why this work will reach so few initially. There are not many left who haven't unintentionally cut themselves off from God, because that was the main purpose of the high priests of Scientism: to trick the ignorant masses into believing that God does not exist, and that since everything is relative, there is no Truth, so they get to decide what's right or wrong based on their whims. It's the usurpation of God by the ignorant creations foolish enough to think they could become the Creator and dictate the law.

The money and obscene wealth these dark occultists accrued through fraud was merely an ancillary benefit. Their primary function is to lead people astray so that the victims can be harvested as sustenance. Should you do nothing with this information, you will not be absolved henceforth. All who serve Saturn, via the Cross, the Kaaba, or the Hexagram, all symbols of his cube, will be doomed to remain trapped in his construct, beneath the vault of the heavens. For some, it is not too late to reverse course. As long as you are the living flesh and blood, you still have time to do what Crowley and von Braun did by leaving knowledge of the Truth to be discovered by those with eyes to see. It may not absolve you, but it will save others. Perhaps, for once in your life, you will not be among the cell fish.

It is too late for those who have read this to willfully ignore the information and do nothing with it. Those reading this are now watchmen, and thus responsible for what happens, and even though I am not religious, there is a spiritual axiom that is expressed in Ezekiel 33:6 that one should know, "But if the watchman sees the sword come, and blow not the trumpet, and the people be not warned; if the sword come, and take any person from among them, he is taken away in his iniquity; but his blood will I require at the watchman's hand."

It is not coincidence that the seven planets correspond to the seven days per week, which correspond to the seven notes in music, the seven chakras, the seven colors of light in the visible spectrum to the majority of human eyes, etc. The concave pentacle formation that Venus' orbit makes over the duration of eight years is identical to the concave pentacle that is present in the middle of an apple when one cuts it in half. There are observable instances in nature of everything's correspondence to each other across all scales, and in order to elucidate how that pertains to the hue-man, we must break down the seven-fold constitution of man as taught by the Hermeticists.

We must first dispel the black magick of the Orient in regards to re-incarnation and the idea that one's circumstances are due to karma from past lives during their previous incarnations in the material world. The idea of earthly karma being able to penetrate higher spiritual realms and reattach itself to the soul after the soul has evolved to higher spheres is not only impossible logically, it is utterly demonic in concept by suggesting that matter could ever overtake spirit, which is the erroneous epitome and terrible snare of the dark occult. Spirit exists independently of matter. Matter does not exist independently of Spirit.

When a plant or tree releases its seeds, the seeds have the potential to become that species of plant or tree. But the plant or tree never turns back into a seed. You are never coming this way again. You have never been here before. After the body becomes an unfit house for the soul, the soul moves on and the door is closed, and then locked behind it. All life progresses eternally. The human never turns back into a sperm or an egg, as such vessels are not fit to house the evolved soul. This is not to discount past experiences or lives in other worlds or realms, but in regards to this realm, the idea of re-incarnation is black magick that's used to put its victims in a perpetual state of self-loathing and punishment for something they cannot remember doing. It would be like punishing an old dog for chewing up a shoe when it was a puppy. To teach that God would allow that spiritual sodomy to be the mechanism for all creation is utterly depraved and spiritually wicked, and not one word has been minced in saying that.

In comprehending that the soul's progression is eternal, we begin with the first of the seven constitutions of man: the **physical form**. The physical form consists of bones, blood, flesh, and hair, of which are composed from a nearly infinite amount of regenerating cells that each have their own system that is a microcosm of man, who is a microcosm of the universe. This corresponds to the note 'A' in a major scale, or 'Ionian' (Eye-On-ian) scale, or 'Do' in the solfeggio.

The second constitution is the electro-magnetic form that is inseparable from the living flesh and blood, known as the **electro-vital body**. This form mirrors the skeleton and nervous system of the physical form, but is described by those who can penetrate it as pale phosphorescent light and electric fire. The electro-vital body corresponds to the note 'B,' or 'Re' in the solfeggio.

The third constitution of man is the **astral form** that is composed by the magnetic light evolved by the planet. Though it is generated from the universal ether, it corresponds directly to the nature and quality of the planet from whence it came, similar to how the nutrients and minerals in soil and in water correspond to the regions from whence they came. This is also why humans are not suited to travel to any other place in the universe. We are suited for Earth only, and any idea that we're going to thrive somewhere else in the cosmos without drastic alteration to our astral form is pure science fiction. The astral form takes the appearance chosen by the soul of the mental being who pilots it, and can temporarily be made to appear in any image of the dominating mind's scope. It can also be projected, which leaves the human body susceptible to black magick. This is why the overwhelming majority of black magicians operate on the astral plane. The solfeggio frequency that corresponds to this is 'Mi,' or in an Ionian scale, it would correspond to the 'C' note.

The fourth fold in the constitution of man is the **animal soul**. It is the center for carnal, base desires concerned with self-preservation and selfishness. It is formless save for the obvious expressions that it manifests in man's lower nature, which connects him to the animal realms and is confined to the astral and material planes for the duration of its evolution. If we look at the entire seven-fold constitution of man as a microcosm to God, this fold is the lowest arc in the microcosm. The solfeggio frequency of this fold is '**Fa**,' or the '**D**' note in the Ionian scale.

The fifth fold is the divine human form in the soul world where the hue-man becomes an angel. This is known as the **spiritual body**, and it corresponds to the solfeggio frequency '**Sol**,' or '**E**' in the Ionian scale. As Thomas Dalton wrote, "It is the white robe and golden crown given the elect in the Apocalypse of St. John. In other words, it is the soul's expression of the heavenly raiment of the purified man."

We'll explain how these frequencies correspond to Saint John soon, but for now let us continue with the sixth fold, which is the **divine soul**. It is the highest arc in the microcosm of God that is the seven-fold constitution of man. It is the throne of unselfish, moral, good behavior, and just like the animal soul, but in the opposite polarity, it has no form other than its obvious appearance in man's aspirations of spiritual and physical evolution. It is '**La**' in the solfeggio frequencies and '**F**' in the Ionian scale. The satanic Deaf Phoenician will say that '**good**' is a relative concept, to which we respond, "Grow up, naïve little boy or girl. You are wholly clueless and utterly useless in the healthy function of Natural Law, save to be an example to others of what they must strive to not be like should they expect to live in freedom. Relativity is one of your dogmatic tenets, not an axiom of Natural Law. It is a teaching of dark occultists, and those who espouse that ideology are lost."

Six of the folds in the constitution of man correspond to the occult meaning of the hymn to John the Baptist called "Ut Queant Laxis," which are 'Ut-Re-Mi-Fa-Sol-La' as found in the first stanza.

Ut queant laxis Resonare fibris
Mira gestorum Famuli tuorum
Solve polluti Labii reatum

The Latin translation of this stanza is literally, "In order that the slaves might resonate the miracles of your creations with loosened vocal chords, wash the guilt from polluted lip." It highlights the power of the harmonious voice to produce miracles, a gift granted to the hue-man by his or her creator, to channel the Divine.

There are only six ascending notes because the seventh fold of the constitution of man is only embodied in flesh when perfect manhood is attained. Then it is displayed as the **divine Ego**, the spiritual Sun/Son of the microcosm, the pure spirit entity, the '**G**' in the Ionian scale, or seventh state of man, or 'Ti' in the solfeggio frequencies. '**Ti**' originated from '**Si**,' which are the initials of '**Sancte Iohannes**' (Saint John in Latin).

"In the beginning was the Word,
And the Word was with God,
And the Word was God." –Saint John

As we've already shown, or silently sown, the phonetic version of '**G**' is '**gee**,' to "move ahead" or "turn to the right." A 'sin' is "a serious shortcoming" or "a ruined or spoiled state of human nature in which the self is estranged from God."

Thus, to 'sing' is to 'sin-g,' or 'sin-gee,' or in other words, "to make a sin right and to spiritually evolve from it." Hopefully this will inspire you to consider the ramifications of this when the word 'sin' is de-occulted at a later point. When people 'sing,' they 'perform.'

The prefix 'per-' means "throughout," and also, "containing an element in its highest state."

Thus, when one 'performs,' he or she is containing the highest state of the seven-fold constitution of man, 'G,' the pure spirit entity of the divine Ego. This is man made perfect, or 'at-one-ment.' This is why being an artist, in whichever craft you choose, will bring you closest to God. So go ahead, 'sin-g' to your heart's content.

However, it would be wise to guard yourself against those who'd seek to tame and harness that power for their own gains. You won't know when you encounter them right away. They'll come to you disguised as your greatest opportunity, a new influential friend. They'll invite you to parties and extravagant dinners and all the most popular places. They're worldly, eloquent, jovial, and generous. Just remember, there is no such thing as a free meal.

Of all the branches of influence that the dark occult has on industry, nowhere is it more apparent and openly implemented than in the music business and the entertainment industry in general. They give artists the means to perform, which when done properly is extremely resonant with all hue-mans. The Black Magi then harness that energy and attraction to create products that issue subliminal programming and warfare by subterfuge spiritually, mentally, and physically.

The secret of High Magick is found in the triune nature of man, in his thoughts, emotions, and actions. When all in unison, this forms the unity consciousness, illumination, or as the Bible suggests, "when thine eye is single/perfect thy body will be full of light." This is because the universe respects unison, and it is the symbolic meaning of the all-seeing eye that is displayed on the world's reserve currency, the United States dollar, as well as everywhere in the entertainment industry, especially in hand gestures that make triangles between the index fingers and the thumbs of both hands. This is why willpower and the ability to clear one's mind, and focus on only one thing, are so important to the execution of High Magick. The dark occultists know this. The universe does not care about you and whether or not you are willing to learn its laws. It is a cold, impersonal construct that benefits all life forms. Those who can focus on one thought, one emotion, and one action can become the ultimate medium for manifesting their whims because as they think, so they feel, and so they act. That's how the nature of this construct can be programmed, not defied, but commanded. The only thing to protect everyone from an incredibly powerful sorcerer is Natural Law, but specifically the laws of consciousness. The hue-mans are all co-creating this experience, so in order to truly gain control over paradigm we live in, a Black Mage has to dupe the hue-mans to create it, otherwise it will be impossible. This is incredibly difficult to do, because even if the hue-man is retarded to his lowest common denominator, he still has within him the spirit of God. His intuition knows what his other senses do not. And like the Truth, this trait cannot be destroyed unless the hue-man is genetically altered and engineered with machinery, which is what you see happening in the Transhumanism movement. Make no mistake about it. Transhumanism is human extinction, a way for the Inversive Brethren to prolong their existence indefinitely. This is also why it is done generationally, subtly, without too much of the population acquiring knowledge of these deeds. Every time there is a renaissance, an inkling of humanity piercing the veil, the Inversive Brethren take the world to war. If a required amount of humanity acquires this knowledge, the hexes will be undone and the spiritual wickedness in the astral worlds that correspond to the physical Black Magi will be banished from this realm, and hue-mans will again have the opportunity to create a better paradigm.

Getting back to man's constitution, there are only three principles in an active state (**animal, human, deific**), which correspond to the three primary colors of the soul's spectrum (**body, soul, spirit**), as well as the three primary colors of the visible light spectrum of the color wheel (**blue, red, yellow**). This also corresponds to the three genders (**female** (Isis), **male** (Osiris), **androgyne** (divine Ego); "They twain shall be one flesh") and the three types of atomic (Adamic) charges (**negative, positive, neutral**). The process of which an atom (Adam) acquires a positive or negative charge by gaining or losing electrons, resulting in a chemical change is known as Ionization. This is why the Great Work of balancing the sacred feminine and sacred masculine aspects of consciousness (the symbolic left and right hemispheres of the brain; crossing the Red Sea) is called the Alchemical Romance, and in Freemasonry, the Ionic pillar is in between the pillars of Jachin and Boaz. This Great Work is the Royal Marriage of these polarities.

The most easily comprehended example of an ionic compound is **salt**, hence the term '**Salts** of **Sal**vation.' The **Salt** of **Aries**, the Kali phos (phosphate of potassium), is the substance through which God manifests the hue-man, and thus is the occult meaning of the word '**salaries**,' for '**sal**' is "salt" in Latin.

The most common solvent of Nature is water. Neutrality dissolves positive and negative charges. Thus, the solution to the spiritual wickedness of the Black Magi is for the hue-man to get back to God by being a solvent like water, and dissolve the solutes (slavery systems) through conscious moral behavior. This is why if a bank is not liquid, it is considered insolvent. '**Solvent**' comes from the Latin verb '**solvō**,' which means "I solve" or "I loosen, untie."

'**Vent**' is a verb that means "to discharge." '**Sol**' means "Sun," but also "soul" through symbolism, phonetics, and Green Language. Thus '**solvent**' also means "to discharge the soul, to give the soul a means to escape." That's what we're doing here. That's the purpose of the Great Work: to escape duality and unify the polarities of one's consciousness. This is what it means to be '**illuminat-e**': Thoughts, emotions, and actions over duality and ego.

'**Id**' is Latin for "it." The '**id**' is the theoretical source of the human's instinctual drives. It is incapable of judging value, good or evil, morality, etc. The human form is '**sol-id**' because its soul is attached to the material body whose lowest arc is the animal soul/**sol**, which governs the '**id**.' Thus, for our soul to vent, to escape, to be discharged, it must leave its '**solid**' material-world body behind and evolve to higher realms of consciousness. '**Solomon**' can therefore be split into '**Sol-o-mon**,' which would be "Soul of One (mono)," in which '**One**' could be interpreted as '**God**' (macrocosm) or '**man**' (microcosm), or phonetically, '**won**,' as in "victory." This is because the Soul of One is '**G**,' at-one-ment, which is the triumph of the soul, the "Soul of Victory." '**Solomon**' could also be interpreted as the "Soul of the Moon ('**mon**,' but also phonetically Min)." And since '**sol**' is also the '**Sun**,' which is the '**Son**,' then '**Solomon**' could also mean "Son of the Moon," also known as Horus, the Son of Isis, or Jesus, the Son of Mary. We'll get into that in a later chapter, but to tie this into the word '**solid**' and the ramifications that word has on you, the 'id' of the 'soul,' because that's what your body is, you may then comprehend why the Black Magi require you to carry ID (identification). They are trying to keep you attached to the 'id,' your instinctual, scarcity-based, fear-based nature so that you cannot become 'solvent' and 'vent' your soul free from materialist, carnal desires.

The remaining four folds of man's constitution are merely secondary reactions, or forms, that compliment the principles in an active state. The Hermetic constitution of man corresponds to the trinity of the ancient Gnostics like so: The **Body** (physical body (A) and electro-vital body (B)), the **Soul** (the astral form (C) and the animal soul (D)), and **Spirit** (the spiritual body (E), the divine soul (F), the divine Ego (G)), and it also corresponds to the four-fold constitution of the Kabbalists like this: **Body** (A and B), **Astral Body** (C), **Animal Soul** (D), and **Divine Soul** (E, F, and G).

Now we must show how the seven angelic worlds direct the seven creative principles and how they correspond to the content we've just de-occulted. The materialist will never find the missing link, because he willfully ignores the simple fact that though Spirit can be independent of matter, matter cannot be independent of Spirit. Thus, the ignorant materialist, who deludes himself with the belief that he is learned, will never know that the beginning of material evolution is occulted in the spiritual realms because he refuses to see it.

Anyone who takes one day to sit and observe Nature will see that there is a spiritual energy in everything that exists. The name isn't as important as the comprehension of its existence. The duality of this universe is this: it consists of both that which has already manifested and that which has not manifested but will. Things come into existence here, that don't exist in one moment but exist in the next moment, only to return to the unmanifest in a subsequent moment. Everything emanates from the divine Source of the unity consciousness, the spiritual center of all. The paradox is that matter is merely the involution of spirit, an unreal temporary illusion that will eventually return to its domain of at-one-ment through the process of evolution.

Hermeticists teach that everything descends from a Spiritual Sun, Divinity that is a non-atomic, uncreated, self-existent, and formless triune Godhead that is the realm of sephirot, which are described as living potentialities whose existence is infinitely beyond the archangels. Some refer to it as *the realm of unmanifested being.* The Godhead refracts from the first trinity, Love, Live, and Light, which corresponds to the Kabbalistic trinity Love, Wisdom, and Crown, into oceans of force that correspond to the seven active sephirot in the Tree of Life and are the seven principles of nature. However, please note that the Hermetic Brotherhood warns that the Kabbalah's explanations and teachings of the ten sephirot are misleading and nearly useless. Those who remain intellectually sincere will find numerous discrepancies in the correspondences that the sephirot have to the planets, etc., and it is incredibly confusing because the various inconsistencies make their teachings relative. Relativity, especially in regards to morals, is the second major tenet in the ideology of Satanism. So while the Kabbalistic allegories can be beautiful, they are easily misinterpreted, relative, and vague, and as such, the Kabbalah, much like any Bible or man-made text, including the book you are reading right now, is not a practical instrument to spiritually evolve back to Godhead. However, it is still worth researching because there are profound messages and lessons to be gleaned by those who do teach art forms that correspond to the sephirot, such as Tarot.

It helps to incorporate the Christian principle, "From their fruit ye shall know them." Hermeticists teach Natural Law, and do not subscribe to social Darwinism (the third major tenet of Satanism), as all beings have descended from Divinity, thus they encourage veganism because what we do to other beings, we do to ourselves. The kosher way to slaughter an animal is one of the most merciless, immoral acts one can commit, and real Judaism teaches "it is forbidden, according to the law of the Torah, to inflict pain upon any living creature."

Most of us have violated these laws at least once in our lifetime. While this is not a condemnation of anyone, we must bring awareness to how our behavior reprograms our reality, and it is important to know a **tree** (an anagram for 'eter,' which phonetically is '**eater**') by the fruit it produces, especially when it comes to so-called religious people that pretend to serve God. Religions have become as divorced from the ancient Hermetic teachings they base themselves on as mankind has become divorced of its spiritual origins. Their correspondence is the same, meaning they are both approaching the point of no return on their selfish path away from their Divine Source. That is why the human condition is slavery. We'll get into this much later.

For now, let us continue with the seven oceans of force issued from the Spiritual Sun. These seven sub-centers are the true meaning of the heptagram (seven-pointed star) symbolism, and are the seven states of angelic life that issue the spiritual evolution of manifested existence. The heptagram corresponds to the seven days of creation, Babalon (in Crowley's Thelema), Blue Star Wicca, and it is the symbol of perfection that is used and sometimes inverted on many flags and other perversions of Natural Law known as government. These seven blind, unconscious yet harmonious principles manifest the creative design of the universe. For the sake of conceptualization, think of them as neural pathways, circuits that allow the electric current from the master's thoughts to be received by that which will manifest to receive them. This is why the harmony of Nature in the physical world corresponds with the harmony of the intelligence that directs these divine laws from the Realm of Spirit. Ultimately, they are all one and the same, but they exist in layers, like the body, which allows for order and the illusion of separation. It is why there is not one bone in the fossil record nor one observable instance that displays speciation, and this is why mankind will never find the missing link of their origins in the material world. Evolution, though real, is taught in the religious indoctrination factories known as schools to be related to survival of the fittest and those willing to adapt to their conditions, also known as the third major tenet in the ideology of Satanism, Social Darwinism. This is a subtle programming that teaches the hue-man to love his slavery and adapt to it, or go extinct. It is an erroneous, dogmatic belief held together by violence and coercion. In Nature, all things are dependent on each other through symbiotic relationships. Evolution and involution, both spiritual and material, cannot exist without each other. The objective world has evolved out of the subjective world, and this is what is meant by the occult axiom: "Man is a microcosm—a universe within himself."

The seven principles of nature correspond to the seven rays of the solar spectrum, which correspond to the seven states of manifestation. They are called "The Life Waves." They are responsible for the grand scale of material evolution across all scales of the cosmos.

The first Life Wave is the angelic realm of **creation**. It prepares the entirety of the great expanse to receive the manifestation of lesser ethereal forces. This is known as the **Spiritual** world, and is symbolized by *The Word.*

The second Life Wave is the realm of **design**. This is the **Astral** world, the subjective world of causality wherein all the germs, forms, ideals, and other possible potentialities of that system are contained in the astral light. This wave is symbolical of *The Idea.*

The third Life Wave is the realm of **force**, which could be summed up as vibratory energy, that which is ever-moving and creates all forms of light, heat, magnetism, ether, electricity, and everything else that mankind may or may not discover. This wave is symbolical of *The Power*, the **Aerial** world.

The fourth Life Wave is the realm of **phenomena**, the world of matter, the **Mineral** world, and is symbolical of *The Justice.*

The fifth Life Wave is the realm of **life**, the **Vegetable** world. This is the place where the first organic forms are spawned from the water (the chalice; the womb; the matrix). This wave is symbolical of *The Beauty.*

The sixth Life Wave is the realm of **consciousness**, the **Animal** world, where the first expression of consciousness is manifested from the intelligent mind into the lower forms of matter. The easiest way to conceptualize would be to think in terms of how instinct works. It is symbolical to *The Love.*

The seventh Life Wave, the final culmination of all material evolution, is the realm of **mind**. This is the **Human** world that is symbolic to the Kabbalistic state termed *The Glory.*

These seven Life Waves of the Realm of Matter correspond to the seven-fold constitution of man and the Realm of Spirit, which is one polarity of the symbolism behind the heptagram.

At the apex of the heptagram is the angelic world of **Michael**, which corresponds to the Sun, Power, and Kingdom. It is between the colors of red and orange. Moving counterclockwise, between red and violet, there is the angelic world of **Samuel**, which corresponds to Mars, Strength, and Victory. Between violet and indigo is the angelic world of **Raphael**, which corresponds to Mercury, Intelligence, and Splendor. Between indigo and blue is the world of **Zacharial**, which corresponds to Jove (Jupiter), Greatness, and Mercy. Between blue and green is the world of **Cassiel**, which corresponds to Saturn, Patience, and Justice. Between green and yellow is the world of **Gabriel**, which corresponds to the Moon, Fecundation, and Foundation. Finally, the seventh force, or ray, issued from the Spiritual Sun, between yellow and orange, is the world of **Anael**, which corresponds to Venus, Love, and Beauty. Jewish Kabbalists and those that follow Thelema may disagree with this information. But which came first? Is the seal of Solomon from Egypt, which can be traced back to Hindoostan, or is it a Jewish symbol called the Star of David? Perhaps you should ask an art collector. Is the mundane Bible of the Jews an allegory for the science of the stars, or did the science of the stars borrow their story from the mundane Bible of the Jews?

Obviously, all modern religions have been borrowed from Ancient Egypt and their previous origins in Hindoostan. They've aligned themselves in some ways with the Truth, albeit through occult allegories and personifications, but in other ways they have obfuscated Truth so only the initiated could comprehend it. This is the work of the Black Magi.

The Semitic race is predicated on the Semites being descendants of Noah's son Shem. However, since the story of Noah was borrowed from the Epic of Gilgamesh, there was no Noah, thus there was no Shem, and so there is no such thing as a Semite. This means that there can be no such thing as an anti-Semite. The same thing goes for Christians and Muslims. We'll certainly get into Christianity much deeper than anything else, but if one remains steadfast on the path of Truth, he will discover that there is no evidence of Jesus Christ existing or that story being anything other than a personified allegory. That doesn't mean one should throw out the baby with the bathwater. Christianity, Judaism, Islam, Buddhism, Taoism, Hinduism, etc., are all pure sciences when not being perverted by Black Magi, as all of them are based on much older knowledge. People have been murdered for exposing the rise of Islam through the funding of the Roman Catholic Church, and though I'm not afraid to write about it, I'll let you research that on your own so that we don't go off on too much of a tangent. I feel most comfortable exposing the Satanic religion pretending to be Christianity because that's what I came from. I think it's important for the spiritually honest Jews and Muslims to expose their religions respectively so that we can get back to Natural Law, and instead of trying to make our religious beliefs the Truth, we will make the Truth our religion, one which requires no belief. The point of this paragraph is to bring awareness to the fact that something spiritually wicked has taken over this world in the past few thousand years, or longer, and completely wiped out records and people in an effort to obfuscate history and construct an illusory structure to keep humans from knowing who or what they truly are, which creates self-loathing, which creates a race of beings who seek to control others, thus enslaving themselves. This is my attempt to unite all people, through our diversity, and wake up to the hexes that have been placed on us to keep us ignorant, dualistic, and dependent on a system that does not benefit us.

In light of the information presented, there are questions that should be pondered. Are the planets, Sun, and Moon some sort of cosmic DVD player, each color in the spectrum of light being read at different intervals of time? Is Earth the DVD? Is the galaxy the DVD?

The seven planets, musical notes, days per week, are all separated by Time (Saturn). Does this mean that Saturn is that which reads or encodes the information?

'Separated' comes from the Latin word 'septem,' which means "seven." A 'rate' is "a certain quantity or amount of one thing considered in relation to the unit of another thing and used as a standard or measure." It is also the "degree of speed or progress" of something. However, the verb 'rate' is "to estimate the value or worth of" or "to place in a certain rank, class, caste, etc."

Is our 'rate' of spiritual evolution, or involution, being 'rated' by something in terms of seven, or by seven judges?

The noun 'separation' combines 'septem' with 'ration.' The noun 'ration' means "an allotted amount" or "fixed allowance of provisions," but the verb 'ration' is "to restrict the consumption of a person, animal, or thing."

Is our ability to generate, or create, being rationed in this seven-fold rate of existence, hence the need to group people born in different intervals of time into 'generations,' thus manipulating our DNA into **gene rations** (rationing our genes, the genes of Isis: genesis)?

The word '**ratio**' describes the relationship between two things in which the number of times the first thing contains the second. But using word splitting, it can be broken into '**Ra**' (Egyptian sun-god) and '**tio**,' which means "ten" in Swedish. Through phonetics and Green Language, this word could be construed to mean "Son of Ten" or "Tenth Sun." However, it is important to know that Saturn corresponds to the metal lead, which is known to swallow light, or shun it. That's why lead is used to block '**ra-di-at-ion**' (radiation; Sun-god-at-eye-on, a Sun-god in a state of enlightenment due to his activated third eye being on). '**Ration**' is phonetically '**ray-shun**.' Therefore, to '**ration**,' especially a hue-man, is "to shun its rays of light." This is what Saturn allegorically does to the Sun (Set kills Osiris and brings about darkness) and what Satan does to God (Winter kills Summer). This cycle of death and rebirth, of involution and evolution, of entropy and syntropy, is the cycle of Earth, which Saturn's metal (lead) is an element of. The highest constitution of man is '**G**,' or seven, because to transcend to a higher octave, the spiritual entity must first come here and say ten (Satan) to begin the process of involution and evolution.

There are still questions of whether or not this process has been perverted. Are we being rationed by the Sun, or was it created so we could exist in hue-man form? Did our spiritual energy create the Sun or did something that enslaved us create it? Was it merely happenstance, a byproduct of a big bang that commenced the construct? Did we agree to participate in this seven-fold allotment (ration) of frequency? What kind of beings are we? Are we sun-gods being rationed in this reality? Are we caught in, or are we creating a cycle of seven rationed provisions that correspond to the planets, musical notes, chakras (known by the ancients as "wheels of light"), etc.?

We see the world in color. '**Hue**' is "the quality or shade of a color determined by each color's wavelength." It is also an "outcry, war or hunting cry, or a cry of alarm," but in Latin, 'hue' is an adverb that means "hither" or "to the person speaking, this point, place, or degree."

When one let's out a cry, he or she is using his vocal chords. This is the power of *the word.* Is being hue-man a state of existence to measure the degree in the soul's spiritual evolution where it can finally harness the power of *the word,* bringing it hither (nearer, towards this place) to the spiritual enlightenment of unity consciousness (radiation)?

Some say that we are in a 'matrix.' In Latin, a 'matrix' is "a womb." Hue-mans are birthed out of wombs after nine months of gestation. Phonetically, 'birth' is also 'berth,' which is a noun referencing "the space allotted (rationed) to a vessel at anchor or at a wharf," but also "a place, listing, or role; a job or position." As a verb, 'berth' means "to come to dock, anchorage, or moorage." We will explore this more when we delve into Commerce, and it will cause us to contemplate if Earth is a womb, or maybe even a wharf. Is it a playground or perhaps a prison or farm? Were we birthed on Earth or did our citizen ships merely berth here?

The symbol for the Earth in astrology is a circle with a cross. This is also the mark of the beast. The arms of the cross indicate the equinoxes and solstices. A circle is also a circuit as well as a cycle. A circle has 360 degrees, and a prophetic year has 360 days. Is our circuit/cycle crossed, quartered, and/or quarantined? I am not the arbiter of Truth. My intention is merely to spark your creativity so you see the world through yourself, anew, for the ideas and innovations that come from you casting away the rationed worldview that your masters imposed upon you will undoubtedly spark another evolution for those who encounter your work.

6 A PLAY OR A PLEA?

The old Akkadian moon-god, approximately 2100 BCE, was **Sin**. But approximately two millennia before that, an estimation of around 4400 – 5000 BCE, the lunar god of fertility was **Min**, and this came from predynastic Egyptians. Between you and me, I think everything we've been told about history is bullshit and I don't trust any of these timelines. However, these are the lies that people agreed upon to use as our "history." 'Min' is the spirit of the words 'mind' and 'minutes,' as they both are symbolic to the Moon, just like the word 'hours' is an anagram for **Horus**, the Egyptian sun-god. In the name '**Solomon**,' both essences of the "Sun and the Moon" are contained. As you'll notice, these shifts occur approximately every two thousand years. There is a scientific explanation for this, although most will never teach it to you because it disturbs the current religion of Scientism, and that explanation is found in the cycle of the ages of the Zodiac, in which each age retrogrades and lasts for 2160 years. For example, if we started at Capricorn, the signs of the Zodiac would normally progress in the order of Aquarius, Pisces, Aries, and so forth. But since the ages retrograde, the Age of Aries would last 2160 years, then retrograde into the Age of Pisces, and then after another 2160 years into the Age of Aquarius, and so on.

This brief digression was necessary to highlight how each religious age corresponds to the age of the Zodiac. For the past two thousand years or so, it has been the Age of Pisces, a Water sign, which is why there is so much fish symbolism involved with Christianity and the laws that govern Commerce, specifically Maritime Admiralty Law, the Law of the Sea. The ruler of Pisces is Jupiter, or St. Peter, and he is known as a benevolent energy, which is why Jesus forgives everyone and the church preaches the Golden Rule, etc. But prior to that was the Age of Aries, a fire sign, the ruler of which is Mars, and this is the reason for God having such a hostile, warlike, fiery nature. Currently, we're transitioning into the Age of Aquarius, which is an Air sign ruled by Uranus and Saturn. This is the age of Man, the water-bearer, the Age of Freedom. Though we may go through dark ages for three to five centuries during the transition, the end result will have been the collapse of all these man-made religious institutions and black magick, and an age of mankind realigning itself with Natural Law and standing in Truth.

The past two ages, or aeons, were ruled by masculine planetary dominants in Jupiter and Mars, but before that was the Age of Taurus, ruled by Venus, a female energy of love and beauty. Venus is Lucifer, an aspect of Isis, which is why the Catholic Church made it the enemy of God. The current order that controls the world is a solar cult of male dominators. Prior to that, lunar cults that embraced the sacred feminine aspect of consciousness were in power. This is why they tell you not to sin, because they're secretly programming you not to worship the Moon: Sin, or Isis, or Diana, or Taaraa (where Terra comes from). This is why the main "enemy" of the War on Terror/Terra (Earth, Taurus, ruled by Venus and exalting the Moon) was named ISIS. They are waging a war on the Truth, the sacred feminine aspect of humanity's consciousness that cares, feels empathy and compassion, nurtures, loves, and creates. This is why the Black Magi perform a ritual called the Cremation of Care, because care is the Generative Principle, the root word of which is the Latin verb 'generare,' meaning "to create, beget, produce," because what we care about generates and creates the quality of our experience in this world. The majority of humans have become sociopaths that only serve themselves. They have been divided by egregores, collective thought forms, and thus have become divided ones: demons. They have been converted into practicing Satanists, but they aren't aware of it because they've never actually studied the ideology of Satanism. One cannot know that which he refuses to know.

Does all of this seem like lunacy to you? That's because it is a lunar sea. A 'demon' is a deity of the Moon. The word 'demon' comes from the Latin word 'dæmon' that stems from the Greek word 'daimon,' which is a protective spirit. This is where the word 'diamond' comes from. Now do you understand the occult meaning of "shine bright like a diamond?" This is why 'diamonds' are a girl's best friends.

The prefix 'de-' has multiple meanings, like most words, and it could be "to remove or remove from, a departure from, or to reduce, degrade, reverse," or it could be "derived from," as in "derived from the Moon," or "deity of the Moon." Thus, 'de-mon' could mean "removed, reduced, departed, or reversed from one," the Creator (the One) or the Moon depending how you use 'mon,' what some may term 'singularity.' In simpler terms, 'demon' is "a dual one, divided one," or "duality."

This is corroborated in the word 'diamond,' as the word 'dia' means "twofold." Thus, 'dia' + 'mon' means "the twofold one," or "the twofold Moon," and phonetically the '-d' sound is the same as '-ed,' indicating it occurred in the past, thus changing the meaning to "one who has made himself, herself, or itself dual," or "one that has been made dual, or been divided," the same as a 'demon.' But also, it could mean "Moon that has been divided or made twofold." Does this indicate that the Moon was part of another body at one point in the past, perhaps Saturn, also known as Time? That would support the idea of the occult spirit of the word 'maritime,' which I've suggested means "Mary-Time, Moon-Time, or Moon-Saturn."

Notice how the solar cult made Eve, a female, responsible for eating the **Apple of Sin.** Look at the word 'apple.' Phonetically, it can be split into 'a-ple,' which one could choose to pronounce as "a play" or "a plea." **Si**nce Sin is the Moon, is the **Apple of Sin** a "play for Isis, the Moon" or a "plea from Isis, the Moon."

The word 'play' has over fifty meanings. The reader is encouraged to explore it further, but suffice to say, it could mean "theater, a game, or an elusive change" as a noun, but as a verb it could mean "to perform, act the part of, to engage or contend against."

'Apple' can also be split phonetically to be 'a pull.' Thus, the

Apple of Sin could also mean "a pull of the Moon." People noticed that there is a correlation between the phases of the Moon and the affects that they had on people's minds. This is where the terms 'lunacy' and 'mania' derived their meaning. 'Luna' and 'mani' are both words for the Moon. This is why the mind corresponds to the Moon, and why in astrology the zodiacal sign in which the Moon was when a person was born reflects his or her mind and reactive nature.

The organ that corresponds to the mind is the brain, and the cerebrum is the seat of reason, or center of understanding, symbolized by the all-seeing eye, the 'mind's eye,' 'one-eye,' 'mono-eye,' 'moon-eye,' or 'money,' hence the reason the all-seeing eye is placed on the sigil that is printed on the reverse side of the one-dollar bill, the world's re-serve current-sea and the most used 'money' on the planet. The irony of it is that it is not money. It is an IOU debt note that isn't worth the paper it's printed on. The United States dollar is a proxy for money, a black magick snare to trick people into believing that if they have more money, they'll be closer to attaining that singularity, that unity consciousness, that seat of reason, the objective of human evolution. They colored it green because green is the frequency of Nature, of the Earth, which is the heart, so this further penetrates our subconscious mind into using their black magick money and binding us to their slavery system of Maritime Admiralty Law, the Law of the Sea, the Moon-Saturn Sea, or lunar sea (lunacy; mania; madness of the monkey mind). To transcend the monkey mind is the key, the moon key. But we can't attain the center of understanding if we are in a state of duality by using dishonest money. Thus, we must demonetize all fiat, debt-based, non-competitive currencies or we will continue to be demonized by Black Magi who control the institutions of Government, Money, Religion, Science, and Politics.

The mind, the brain, is housed and protected by the 'skull,' which is phonetically the same as a 'scull,' a "light, narrow racing boat propelled by oars," or an "oar mounted on a fulcrum at the stern of a small boat." As a verb, 'scull' means "to propel a boat with sculls."

Why was our money made to be debt? Debt is not real. It is dead energetically, in reality, which is why people charge and discharge debt to buy and sell things. Only our thought-forms make it real. So it begs the question, is the Moon a ship powered by the dead? Are we the dead that are powering the Moon, which is towing, or pulling, our citizen ship? Is that 'a pull of the Moon?'

A 'scull' is an 'oar,' but 'oar' is phonetically 'ore,' a "metal-bearing mineral or rock, or native metal, that can be mined at profit."

The word 'mineral' can be played with both by word-splitting and phonetics to be either 'min-ur-al' or 'min-ra-l.'

The irony of this is that Min became Sin, so when the solar-cult of Christianity discourages one to sin, they are discouraging them (in an occult way) not to worship the Moon.

'Als' are demons of childbirth that interfere with human reproduction, fertility. They steal the lungs, livers, and hearts of women. 'Women' can be split into 'wo-men,' and phonetically that would also be 'wo-min.' 'Wo' is the same as 'woe,' and 'min' represents the Moon, so 'women' also has the spirit of 'woe moon' or 'Moon of Woe' in it, but since the Moon and 'min' also represent the mind, it could mean 'woe-mind,' and another word that relates to 'woe of the mind' or 'mental woe' is 'lunacy,' because those who suffer from mental illness experience tremendous mental woe (sorrow, grief, misfortune).

As discussed, Min is the god of Fertility (Egypt), but is also Pan (Greek), and thus Ammon-Zeus and Cernunnos. He is the Protector of the Moon, a lunar god of lunacy. Ur was the Capital of Akkad, the last king of which was Naran-Sin, succeeded by Shar-Kali-Sharri. Note that Kali is associated with the Indian goddess of Time, Creation, Power, and Destruction, and she is worshipped as the ultimate reality, Brahman, and Rama, the seventh avatar of Vishnu, which is where Abraham comes from, originally Abram, because it is symbolic of Aries, the house of God, the Spirit in man, the Ram ('ram' is the Sanskrit word for "high"), the optic thalamus (light of the chamber), the Eye of Providence, the guardian of all things, the substance of all things, the seat of reason, center of understanding, the Eye Single (all-seeing eye), the cerebrum, the material of light ('mater' meaning "mother" in Latin), the Lamb of God, the spiritual electricity known as Kali phos.

'Kali' means "she who is black or death" in Sanskrit, the root word of which is 'kal,' meaning "time." This corresponds to Saturn, Father Time, as seen in the word 'alkaline,' with the word 'al' being Hebrew for "upon, over, or above." In Vedic astrology, Kali is the dark aspect of the Moon, so 'al-kal-ine' literally means "the substance of or pertaining to the nature of that which is above or beyond the darkness, Death, Time, Saturn," or "over the Moon." The idiom *over the Moon* refers to "a state of elation or great happiness." Therefore, the spirit of the word 'alkaline' is also "a state of elation or great happiness," which is why diseases cannot exist in alkaline bodies. What must one's PH level be above in order for his or her body to be alkaline? Seven: G, the pure spirit entity of the divine Ego, at-one-ment, at one mind, unity consciousness. Can you see how maintaining one's body in an alkaline state corresponds to, and is necessary to achieving, the highest state in the seven-fold constitution of man? What happens when meat is introduced to the body? It puts it in an acidic state. What happens when raw fruits and vegetables are consumed? The body maintains an alkaline state above the PH level of seven, or in other words it is performing the way it was meant to. This is the primary reason for why humanity was deceived into practicing Carnism, the consumption of dead flesh. It lowers the body's PH level and prevents it from attaining at-one-ment.

What is necessary for a body to remain healthy? **Minerals.** The word could be split to mean '**mine Sun-God**,' as though it were ore (**mine-Ra-El**, El being a phonetic sound of 'L'), which corresponds to orange, a color associated with the Sun and the most valuable ore, **gold**, hence another occulted meaning of the word: **Min-Ra-El** (Min (phonetically) + Ra + L (El, phonetically). If you translate the correspondences to the names of these gods to the names of their planetary bodies as well as their alchemical elements, the word 'mineral' becomes **Moon** (Min/Silver) + **Sun** (Ra/**Gold**) + **Saturn** (El/**Lead**). What other word has Silver-Gold-Lead occulted inside it?

Israel. '**Israel**' comes from the combination of '**Isis + Ra + El**' (**Moon-Sun-Saturn; Silver-Gold-Lead**). What is the symbol for 'money,' or 'moon-honey,' or 'mono-eye,' the almighty dollar? It is **Isis**, also known as $. They put the Eye of Providence on the seal of the dollar because it is the Eye of **Ra**, the pineal gland, which is also the Third Eye, the Eye of Horus, the Sun, the Phoenix, which is what the eagle is an occulted symbol of, hence the reason a hexagram (made up of pentacles) is above the eagle's head on the back of the dollar. The hexagram is a symbol of the cube, which is a symbol of Saturn, or God, who is the father of Ba'al, the Sun. The third part of this equation is **El** (Saturn), Time, which is why we get paid by the **hours** (Horus) we work. This is because Horus' movement, the Sun's path through the sky, dictates the hours which divvy up our day until Saturn (El) comes out to rule the night, who is often accompanied by the Moon (Isis).

The Obelisk in the District of Columbia is Osiris' penis. Congress, which is "sex," is in D.C. as well. The Oval Office is symbolic of the ovaries. There are also obelisks in Vatican City (from Heliopolis) as well as the City of London. This is the trinity of immoral Roman Civil Law, known as Commerce, the Law of the Sea, because Commerce also means "sex." Columbia is Virgo, the Virgin Mary, which is Isis, so it is really the District of Isis.

Who also has an erect penis, and is the brother of Horus and son of Osiris? Min, the Egyptian lunar god of fertility. We've already discussed that the Moon and Min correspond to the mind, which is why **'minister'** and **'monster'** are the exact same. They are moon-stars. If you are under the hexes of your ministers, or monsters, your mind is in a state of **'dis-aster,'** because you are being deprived of the story of the stars, or in other words, you are apart from the stars due to priestcraft sorcery, which cuts you off from God.

'Min' is also an Egyptian boat built by Hatshepsut called **'The Good Ship Min. 'Mente'** is Latin for **'mind,'** which comes from **Min** (Moon), and thus The Good Ship Min is also **'The Good Shipment.'** Our thoughts seem to be the real money here, as our lunacy is the currency that we ship to the Moon, the good shipment, by the Good Shepherd. Perhaps our mania is what feeds or generates the construct.

We live in a mental universe. Though the word **'mental'** describes the nature of the mind (mind + all), the opposite polarity of the word describes that which its fertility is susceptible to: mind (ment) demons (al). This is why the internal struggles that people face are often referred to as *battling demons*, deities of the Moon or divided/degraded ones ('de-' + 'mons').

The 'universe' is the 'one verse' because 'uni-' is a Latin prefix that means "one." 'Se-' is a Latin prefix that means "apart," however, using word-splitting, 'universe' can be decoded as 'uni-ver-se.' 'Ver' means "to see" in Spanish. But in Latin, 'ver' means "true, real, proper, suitable, right, just." In Old English, 'ver' is connected to 'wær,' which means "true, correct." This is all related to the nature of this construct because it is here where every person is a microcosm of the universe, or 'one to see apart' (uni-ver-se), otherwise known as an individual. Though we are all connected to the one verse, the universe, we are also individually experiencing, or seeing, the universe separately in space, motion, and time.

Since Time seems to be the fabric that separates everything in this construct, we'll look at how it connects to Truth, or 'ver.' The Roman goddess of truth is Veritas. She is the Daughter of Saturn. This is why Jesus is also the Truth, because he is Ba'al, the son of Dagon, who represents Saturn. Truth is the progeny of Time. Time becomes Truth, and Truth is masked by Time. Life becomes death, and then life is again born from death. This is Saturn's construct. This is also why Veritas, Truth, is the mother of 'Virtus,' the Roma version of Arete, a Greek deity of bravery and military valor, but 'virtus' is also a Roman virtue meaning "manly marshal courage." In order to serve Truth, one must have the courage to seek it and then speak it, and it is related to the marshal energy of war, which is similar to 'wær,' because the Truth is always at war with lies, yet it soundly defeats them at every encounter, which is why one only needs to stand in Truth and let those who oppose him be destroyed by Truth. This is what the saying, 'Omnia Vincit Veritas,' or "Truth Conquers All Things" means. That is also why 'Virtus' is depicted on the continental currency of Virginia in 1776. Virginia is the Virgin, or Virgo. Did you think it was coincidence that Virginia and Maryland are right next to each other? They represent the Virgin Mary, the mother of Jesus Christ, the Truth.

Before we continue, there must be a brief digression to explain Saturn. Even though it is symbolic of Death, Father Time, Satan, Winter, Kronos, the Crown, Lead, the destroyer of light, etc., the occulted symbolism is rarely brought into light, correspondingly so. This will finally put to rest the confusion as to why Ba'al is the son of El, Apollo is the son of Zeus (Jupiter) who is the son of Cronus (Saturn) who is the son of Uranus (the other ruler of Capricorn), Jesus is the son of God, or the Sun is the progeny of Saturn, light the progeny of darkness, life the progeny of death, manifest the progeny of unmanifest. It's important to remember that we are dealing with symbolism and allegories of historical observations, not actual historical accounts. The Saturn/Sun symbolism corresponds to the transmutations of life, the caterpillar's journey to becoming a butterfly, and the soul's journey from God to man and back to God. This is the jewel of the lotus. The occulted symbolism of Saturn is that he is actually the Angel of Life. The experiences that the old man acquired transform the skeleton with a scythe into a divine youth with a crown of light and a rod of power, the jewel of eternal life, the conqueror of evil. This is Christ born in the manger of Capricorn, the Goat. Who rules Capricorn but Saturn? That's why it corresponds to Winter, or John the Baptist, who is also Aquarius, the Water-bearer, Horus, and Man. John the Baptist is Baphomet, the Baptism of Mentis, the goddess of Wisdom, thus the Baptism of Wisdom. Jesus was not a physical Jew, but a symbolic Jewel, the Jew-el, the Jew-God, of eternal life. Get it? He is symbolic to both the Angel of Death and the Angel of Life. He is the Lamb of God (Aries) and the Fisher of Men (Pisces), the alpha and omega, the beginning and end of the cosmic cycle that is self-similar across all scales of life. The reason people choose Barabbas over Jesus is symbolic of how most people choose the comfortable lie over the uncomfortable Truth. Misery loves company and people like being the cream of the crop, but they also like to do this in the least inconvenient way, which is why they despise competition. They want to live in a world of no responsibility where they can fool themselves into believing that someone is coming to save them from their self-imposed condition rather than understanding that within them is the seed of their own destruction and resurrection, the Divine Spark from the Will of Creation. It will carry them through life, death, and then life again.

Continuing with the de-occultation of the word 'universe,' we established that 'ver' is connected to Veritas, and that Veritas comes from Aletheia in Greek mythology, the daughter of Zeus. Zeus is Jupiter who is also Saint Peter. In English, 'verse' is also "a succession of metrical **feet** composed as **one** line." The word 'feet' indicates more than one, so we see that 'verse' indicates many composing one, which we've covered as an occult meaning of '**monopoly**,' ('one' + 'many,' or "from many, one"). The universe is a monopoly of mental energy, or an ocean of mental frequencies that compose one verse, one Truth. Thoughts create currents and thus are current-sea. That is the real 'ore' that can be mined (mind) for profit (prophet). This is why prophets are seers, ones who see Truth in separate places, times, and motions.

Those who originally hid the Truth from their subjects would send their own kind to university to learn this sacred science. A '**university**' is also a universe city, a city for seers, where one goes to learn or see the Truth.

'**City**' can be split into 'ci' (101 in Roman Numerals) + '-ty' (a suffix that denotes 10), which would make it III, or 111. This corresponds to the three pillars of man's temple, Jachin, Boaz, and the Ionic pillar, but also the triune nature of God and of man, as well as thoughts, emotions, and actions in unison, also known as the unity consciousness.

The Eye of Providence, the optic thalamus, the mono-eye (money), is the real "ore." But if you are in debt, you are a debtor. The spiritual implications of this are in the hidden phonetics. To be a debtor is to be '**dead ore**,' but also a '**dead oar**,' because a dead oar cannot row the '**citizenship**,' the '**city-zen-ship**' (Trinity-Enlightenment-Ship).

Without the unity consciousness of an activated cerebrum, you are lost at sea, shipping your mind, your money, your minerals, to the inverse, unholy trinity of the Moon, the Sun, and Saturn that are responsible for the creation and sustaining of this construct in which you are trapped. You make payments to them. Pay-ment is to pay mind, thus you pay mind to them. We must eliminate debt so we can harness the fruit of our labor, our '**lab-ore**.' A '**lab**' is a "place to experiment." To '**experiment**' is to "experience mind," (experience + mente), which is to experience the **ore**. Does this seem too far-fetched? Research the lunar wave and study it for yourself. When you behold the matrix through direct experience, it becomes much more challenging to ignore.

We must transcend both the earthly monetary system as well as the cosmic monetary system. 'Monetary' can be split into 'mon' + 'et' + '-ary.' The suffix '-et' indicates a "small, lesser, or diminutive force." The suffix '-ary' means "belonging to." Thus the word 'monetary' indicates a system belonging to the diminutive force of a small moon, or a small mind, which is symbolic to the monkey mind, the animal nature that is represented by Taurus, a symbol for Isis and the cerebellum, "Adam's contending against God."

This is the moon-key. The soul must transcend the monkey mind. That's how it gets out of the dualistic zoo known as the zodiac. It must transcend the flesh on the macrocosmic scale, but it must transcend consuming carrion on the microcosmic scale. Trust me. I know how difficult it is. Perhaps no one struggles with this more than I do. But it must be done. I didn't access this knowledge till I went mostly vegan for a couple of years. The beings in the Realms of Spirit won't trust you till you demonstrate your commitment to stop harming others. The Black Magi duped us into transforming ourselves into the walking dead. Now it's time for us to reverse our status.

7 THE PRICE OF PASSAGE

What are you willing to sacrifice in your service to Truth? What are you unwilling to sacrifice? The answer to that question is the measure of your character, as well as the quality of your service and how far you will go on the path to Truth.

The Truth is the great equalizer, the panacea for all conditions. It will take down the mightiest foes and dissolve the most spiritually wicked of lies. Relationships are one of the most illusory delusions in this construct, but the paradox is that the ones formed in Truth will transcend Saturn's zodiacal Ouroboros. Speaking the Truth will dissolve most of a man's relationships. It may end his career and make him infamous in the minds of the dead. But in the minds of the living, the conscious, he will be revered as a hero returning home. The material world is not about acquiring things, but purifying the soul and dissolving untruth so that he may return in perfect form: 'G.' But who are the authentic men and women among you? Who will serve Truth? You? I doubt it, but I'd love to be wrong.

Remember, you are in this world but not of it. You are a passenger. But what is a passenger? The word 'passenger,' which is "a wayfarer, traveller," comes from the Middle English word 'passager,' which is "a passing, temporary messenger, harbinger, scavenger, or popinjay."

The word 'pass' is "to move past or go by something."

'Eng' comes from an Old English adjective 'enge,' which means "narrow." It was later used in Scotland as 'eng' to have the same meaning, but is now obsolete. In German and Dutch, 'eng' means "narrow, tight," but in Danish and Old Norse, 'eng' is "a meadow." In Proto-Albanian, 'anga' was related to the Lithuanian word 'angùs,' which means "sluggish, lazy, idle." How ironic that the Aberdeen Angus breed of cattle, something that is both lazy, idle, and sluggish while it grazes in a meadow, originated in Scotland. The Albanian word 'eng' means "deaf and dumb," and it comes from the Lithuanian word 'angùs.'

The suffix '-er' denotes occupation or origin of someone, but also some characteristic of someone or something. It also denotes action or process of a noun, such as 'teach-er.' Let's not forget that it also has a phonetic value of 'err,' which is "to be led astray."

Since 'passenger' comes from the Middle English word 'passager,' let's take a look at the meanings of 'passage.' It could mean "a verse, a musical work, the freedom to pass," or it could mean "a route, a voyage," or "to cross."

If we contemplate all the meanings and infuse the Language of the Birds related to 'passenger,' we could define it as "one who is free to pass through Truth (verse), the one Truth, the uni-verse, but in this Truth is the possibility to be led astray by the aster-rays (star rays (Ra/Re = Sun); star suns)."

What are passengers allowed to take aboard airplane flights? Carry-on bags, or carry-on luggage. Phonetically, carry-on is 'carrion.' What is carrion? It is "dead, rotting flesh." Therefore a carry-on bag is a "bag of, or made of, dead flesh."

If we split the word 'luggage' phonetically, we get the words 'lug' + 'age.' To 'lug' is "to pull with force, vigor, or effort." An 'age' is the length of time during which something has existed, or as I would offer, the duration which you are ruled by Saturn, Kronos, the Crown, which are all symbolic of Father Time, hence your life unfolds in chronological order; chronological having its origins from Chronos/Cronus.

Before we continue, let us comprehend the word 'airplane,' which can be split to 'air' + 'plane.' The 'air' is "the invisible gases that make up the atmosphere," also known as the 'aether/ether.' When given the option to choose between 'either or,' choose the phonetic equivalent of 'ether ore,' the "spiritual energy that your body harvests to cleanse and replenish itself and function properly; inspiration and expiration."

A 'plane' is a "flat expanse." Notice how the vehicle people use to fly to their destinations is called an 'airplane,' not an 'airplanet.' But phonetically, it gets deeper. 'Air' is also the same as 'err,' which is to go astray in thought or belief." 'Plane' also means "a level of dignity, character, existence, development, or the like."

'Carry-on luggage' is 'carrion lug-age,' and using the Language of the Birds, we see that it can mean "dead flesh being towed through time, or towing its time through the air in or on a plane," or "a pledge ('gage') to lug dead flesh ('carrion')." However, if we take the newly established Green Language, the word 'airplane' becomes 'err-plane,' which facilitates your 'ether ore' (spirit) to tow its dead flesh (body), ruled by Time (Saturn), on a flight path (pass) that will lead you astray from your level (well-balanced) thoughts, emotions, and actions, to a mind (moon) of lunacy (lunar/moon-sea of madness, irrationality, imbalance, and duality).

Still want to trip (Fall) on an err-plane? Or would you rather trip (dance) through Truth (verse) on a level (balanced) playing field? Do you see how you get to decide 'either or,' or ether or ore?

What happens to your 'ether ore' once it docks at its destination? It sits in its 'berth' and becomes 'docked ore.' This is why 'doct-ors' help deliver bay-bees in a process known as childbirth. At the same time, the idiom 'give a wide berth to' means "to shun," which is essentially what the mother's womb is doing to the baby as it births the child. Docked ore is ore in its berth, or ore that has been "deducted, cut short," or "placed where a prisoner is kept during trial" (dock).

What does it really mean for doctors to 'de-liver' babies? They dock (cut short, deduct) their umbilical cords too early to deprive them of biological nutrients, and for the males, they dock their foreskins. Then the doctors take the babies and stamp their soles (souls) on birth (berth) certificates (documents evidencing ownership or debt), thus selling them into legal fiction slavery (corporate law). Why? Because they are producing a manifest to document which goods are being brought into, or onto, the citizen-ship.

The word 'corporate' cannot exist without its root word 'corpse,' a "dead body." By making you corporate, they turned you into a 'corpse Or (the Sun) ate.' The Cult of Or is the Cult of the Sun, the Cult of Death. They have also turned your ore into debt, which is dead ore, which is why corporations are dead entities, and thus the Black Magi can absolve themselves from what they do to you, because in their mind the dead cannot be killed. They cremate their care as they cremate a corpse.

Since corporations are corpses, they are not **live** men and women, thus they are not 'livers,' which are "dwellers, inhabitants." By registering a baby with a birth certificate, doctors truly **deliver** (de-liver) people, the same way religions **de-liver** people by removing, negating, reversing each baby's status as a live sovereign, a liver, and put them into the realm of the dead, also known as the undead or the walking dead.

We are **de-livered** through the cervix, the lower end of the uterus. 'Cervix' can be split into 'cerv-ix.' Phonetically, 'cerv' is 'serve,' and 'ix' is 'nine' in Roman numerals, so 'cervix' means "serve nine."

One could write a novel on the significance of the number nine. There are nine months of gestation, nine openings in the body of man, etc. Nine is a number of completion, of deity, but it also represents the ego in Gematria, and acts like a zero in equations regarding addition. For example, $3 + 9 = 12$, but $12 = 1+2$, which is 3. So adding nine, ego, to anything does nothing for it spiritually. It's equivalent to a zero ($3 + 0 = 3$ just as $3 + 9 = 12$, which equals 3 ($1+2$)).

The symbol for a zero is 0, which is the shape of a cycle and a circle: the perfect form. This is completion, the beginning and end, the equation of the universe. How many degrees in a circle? 360. $3 + 6 = 9$. Therefore, if one seeks to get out of this cycle, or loop, he or she must transcend nine.

Anton LaVey, the founder and high priest of the Church of Satan, wrote in his book *The Satanic Rituals*, "Despite others' attempts to identify a certain number with Satan, it will be known that Nine is His number. Nine is the number of the Ego, for it always returns to itself. No matter what is done through the most complex multiplication of Nine by any other number, in the final equation Nine alone will stand forth."

To give an example of this, let's take the numbers of my birthday and convert them into a value: 7/23/1983 = 7,231,983. 7,231,983 x 9 = 65,087,847. Using Gematria, 65,087,847 = 6 + 5 + 0 + 8 + 7 + 8 + 4 + 7 = 45. 45 = 4 + 5 = 9. Nine alone will stand forth.

Through the cervix, we are de-livered by serving Nine, the Ego, and thus cut off from the living, separated from source, de-sired, and thus, the way back to the Divine Ego is to transcend the monkey mind of lunacy that's imprisoned by its ego, the old religion of "me, me, me," also known as the modern day ideology of Satanism.

8 JESUS, THE ROCK STAR

Of all the unique attributes that differentiate men from women, perhaps none are greater than that of the womb. Each womb-man is a portal to another world, a vesica piscis that the spiritual fire of man can open for another soul to enter this realm.

Some women sync their menstrual cycle up with that of the Moon, which is symbolically feminine. The word 'menstrual' can phonetically be 'men's true al,' as in men's true fertility demon, and as we've already explained, a demon is a divided or degraded one, a deity of the Moon. Under these circumstances, a menstrual cycle is a 'moon-strual' cycle, but is also correlated to the mind through phonetics because 'mens' is Latin for "mind." Does this indicate that the Moon is the mind's true demon? The waning Moon is symbolic of sorcery. Is Mary sending her son to fish the souls of men, or is he her lamb to be sacrificed to save their souls?

Aries, the Lamb of God, was known as Gad in ancient Tsabaism (who some believe is Shaivism, part of the Vedic tradition), which is where God comes from, because Aries is Green Language for **Rama**, which means "most high, great, elevated" in Sanskrit. 'Aries' is the Latin word for "ram," which comes from the much older word in Egypt, '**Arez**,' meaning "Sun," and thus is connected to Zor, "the Lord; God; the Rock." This is seen in words like '**Caph-Arez**' ('caph' being the **rock**, the Zor, that temples were built upon), just like '**Chan-Arez**' relates to '**Chan-Or**' ('**Or**' being another word for Sun, hence '**or-ange**') and '**Chan-Amon**,' from which we get the word 'cinnamon,' because they are all related to the Sun, or Apollo, Zeus Ammon, Baal Hammon, Pan, Cernunnos, etc. Look up any artifact with a depiction of Jupiter Ammon, and you will see he has ram horns, because he was the most high, which corresponds to Aries, the great "I am." On is the City of the Sun, Heliopolis, so AM—ON is the "fire being." Contemplate the hidden power contained in the phrase "I am on." It is Green Language for the nature of the symbol of Aries, the Hill of Mars, the cerebrum, the Eye Single: "Eye Fire Being." Regardless of what any Deaf Phoenician may tell you, when a Christian finishes a prayer with "through Jesus Christ our Lord. Amen," they have been duped into saying, "through **Jesus Christ our Lord Ammon**," as in Jupiter-**Ammon**, Zeus Ammon, because Jesus Christ is **Ammon**, the Sun, as admitted in the Revelation of St. John 3:14, "And to the messenger of the assembly in Laodicea write: These things saith the **Amen**, the witness, the faithful and true, the chief of the creation of God."

Why? Because Jesus is Jupiter-Zeus, the Amen, or Ammon, the chief of the creation of God, the most high: Rama, the ram, Aries, the Lamb of God: the Sun. Arez of the East is connected to Bel, Baaltis, Ba'al, and also to **Dysares**, the Arabian God, and one will note that the Greek version of Mars is Ares, because Mars rules Aries. They are all symbolical of the Sun and *fire*, which is why the Sun is exalted in Aries, the sign of cardinal fire. Another layer of the symbolism regarding the Sun being worshipped as Jupiter Ammon, Jesus, is the 'J' that looks like a fishhook, because he is the fisher of men, Pisces, which is ruled by Jupiter. Note that after we penetrate a deeper layer of Jesus, we will expose why Galileo named Jupiter's fifth moon IO.

The 'J' was not used till approximately the fifteenth or sixteenth centuries. The Romans used 'I' as the 'J,' which is seen in Iesus, but it comes from something much older. This work is not intended to offend anyone, or attack anyone for his or her beliefs. However, to undo the hexes that have been cast upon humanity, it will undoubtedly make some readers incredibly uncomfortable. The early Christians named their "savior" Christ after an ancient name of Bacchus, spelled in Greek as Iota, Eta, Sigma, which is Ies, Jes, or Yes. This is the occult meaning of the English language affirmation

96

of consent, 'yes,' and the common translation that Deaf Phoenicians will use to justify their ignorance and maintain their self-imposed slavery is that 'amen' means "a declaration of affirmation, so be it, or it is so," which ironically is synonymous with 'yes.' This is because Bacchus is Yes, and Yes is Yesus, or Jesus, the Amen, the witness, the faithful and true, because 'yes' is a "pledge of fidelity and truth," hence Jesus Christ our Lord Ammon (Amen) is the Truth. Who are the father and son? They are Dagon and Baal, Zeus and Apollo, Saturn and Jupiter, the Angel of Life and the Angel of Death, etc. There is no need to deny that Jupiter-Zeus, Jesus, is the Christ, the father and son, and the Christ, *the Cristos*, is the oil in the flesh that can only be raised by abstaining from the consumption of flesh. So before you mistake the Truth for the deception of the antichrist, another one of your mythical non-existent entities, you had better do the Great Work and discover how entrenched in the psyche of man this black magick actually is.

"To whom God did will to make known what is the riches of the glory of this secret among the nations – **which is Christ in you**, the hope of the glory, whom we proclaim, warning every man, and teaching every man, in all wisdom, that we may present every man perfect in Christ Jesus, for which I also labor, striving according to his working that is working in me in power." – *Colossians 1:27-29*

Christ rises, and Jesus dies. Unfortunately, Bacchus' ancient name (IHΣ) is used in an even more deceptive way on Christian alter and pulpit pieces, under the occultation of IHS. The phony Phoenicians and their hexed minions will tell you that IHS means "*Iesus Hominum Salvator*, Jesus the Savior of Men."

The awful reality is that it is an occult symbol of Bacchus, the god of Wine, hence the consumption of the sacramental wine, the blood of Bacchus, the one of great fire, the Sun, as confirmed in Hebrews 12:29, "For our God is a consuming fire."

Even still, the Deaf Phoenicians will deny Truth till their dying day, for there is no Truth left in them. Keep this in mind, because Moloch, one of the deities that these phony Phoenicians murder babies in ritual sacrifice to, is the Sun, Herod the King, the Hero of the Skin (Lion of July), Hercules, the universal light, the Ruler, the

Regulator, the Monarch of the solar system (Israel) who rules the day. He doesn't kill Rachel's two sons (Joseph and Benjamin); he "passes through" them, or "puts them away," because they are Gemini, and the Sun's effulgence blots them out during May. The perverted sun-worshippers who sacrifice children are yoked by priestcraft sorcery that turns them into religiously insane degenerates. It doesn't help that they are sexually inverse retarded psychopaths due to thousands of years of inbreeding to preserve "well-born" bloodlines. You have eyes to see. Look at how incredibly ugly they are. They look like demons because they are. As long as you are their concubines, you allow them to hijack your good DNA and conceal their seed in your offspring. Were it not for you doing this, the generational inbreeding wouldn't be able to conceal itself. Make no mistake. There is a stark contrast between a spouse and a wife, just as there is a stark contrast between marriage and joining in holy matrimony. You idiots keep marrying them and producing offspring for them so you can live a life of luxury at the expense of all their victims. You will pay. Make no mistake about it.

Gemini plays an incredibly significant role in our western way of life, and the Sun's transition through it occurs from May 21 – June 21. But who rules Gemini? Mercury, who is Woden, hence Woden's Day is Wednesday, the day of the week attributed to Mercury, and it is right in the middle of the week, or the weak, because Gemini is the June month, which comes from the Latin word 'jungo,' meaning "a joining, or joint," and since Woden is Mercury, Woden's Day joins the beginning and the end of the week, or the weak, because the 'weekend' is phonetically the same as the 'weakened.' In the world of elements, Mercury is a solvent of metals that can separate gold and silver from the impurities of other ores. 'Quick' means "living," so 'quicksilver,' the chemical name for Mercury, is also called 'argentum vivum' in Latin, which is "living silver." Mercury is the carrier of the spiritual electricity, the messenger of the gods, the mind-fluid, that enables the Sun and the Moon (Solomon, the Soul of Man) to accomplish the Great Work. The Sun is exalted in Aries, the Moon is exalted in Taurus, and the twin souls split in Gemini. Mercury utilizes the spiritual fire from Jove, the Father of all gods, the giver of all good things, and as you'll find in Latin etymology as well as that of legalese, 'merx,' the root word of Mercury, means "goods, or merchandise, articles of trade that can be bought and sold" and is evidenced in the Latin phrase *Merx est quicquid vendi potest*, meaning *merchandise is whatever can be sold*. This comes from an even older Greek story in which Hermes, son of Jupiter and Maia (the daughter of Atlas, who supported the heavens, which is also the name of the C1 vertebra that supports the skull), was also the messenger of the gods and the father of merchants and thieves. He was the god of oratory, symbolizing the necessity of becoming a good orator so that one can perform the Great Work of seeking and speaking the Truth, and in order to do this, our minds must be filled with 'merx,' good merchandise through which it can deliver *the goods* in its fulfillment of expressing itself.

How does the week begin? On Sunday, the Sun's day. How does it end? On Saturday, Saturn's day. What sign is the Sun exalted in? Aries. What sign is Saturn exalted in? Libra, the balancing of the scales corresponds to dusk, when day gives way to night, but on the grander scales, when Summer gives way to, or begins its descent (Fall) into Winter, but moving to the greater macrocosm, when the Spirit succumbs to the illusion of matter and descends into the material world, the Fall of Man.

Looking at the angles of the Zodiac, we see that Aries and Libra are beholding each other, which, according to Ptolemy, means that they are of equal power because their days and nights are equal to each other when the Sun moves through each sign at different times of the year, and each sign rises and sets from the same locations of the horizon during those periods. They are opposite reflections of each other, just like the Sun and Saturn. Why? Because the father is the son. Dagon is Baal. Saturn is the Sun. God is Jesus, etc. Where is Jesus crucified? On a hill called Golgotha. But what does 'golgotha' mean? "The place of the skull" in Greek, which is related to the Aramaic word 'gulgalta' and Phoenician (Hebrew) word 'gulgoleth,' which both mean "skull." What is that synonymous with? 'Calvaria,' the Latin word for "skull," the cap of the skull which is symbolized by the skull cap that the Jews and the Popes, cardinals, and bishops wear, and also where the Latin word 'calvarium' comes from, the "dome of the skull," and thus where the name 'Calvary Cross' comes from, which Jesus was "crucified on," which is why 'Calvary' is also a term that means "an experience of extreme suffering." And the anagram of 'Calvary' is 'cavalry,' a group of warriors on horseback, because Castor and Pollux, the twin stars of Gemini are horsemen. Which is why the Angel, or Angle, directly across from Gemini is Sagittarius, the satyr, ruled by Jove, Jupiter, the Great Teacher, the Guru, which is why Chiron is a centaur and a great teacher. Gemini and Sagittarius are reflections of each other. Gemini relates to the Vedic mythology of **Yama** and **Yami,** the twin siblings who later become husband and wife, which is what the archetype of Adam and Eve evolved from. The Sanskrit word **'yamati'** literally means "hold, subdue," like what is done to a horse by one who holds the reigns, the bridal, and tames animal nature, Tau-rus, the unconscious mind, the cerebellum, the seed of war. Why? Because this is the anatomical location where Spirit unites with Matter, Father with Mother, Fire with Water, Sun with Moon, the Temple of Solomon, Positive with Negative, the Royal Marriage, the Great Work, the alchemical process of turning lead (Saturn, Death) into gold (Sun, Life). This is because the beginning is the end and the end is the beginning of the next octave of evolution or involution, depending on which path the soul chooses through free will. This is the crossroads, the 11:11 catch 22 nature of our reality, and Tau is the 22nd and last letter in the Hebrew (Phoenician) alphabet, hence its association with Saturn and the Tau Cross, because the cross bends and folds itself up into a cube, a symbol for Saturn, which is why Taurus is the earthy dew cross where the Manna descends to form Man, the red cross: **Taurus.**

The Divine Man is suspended, or crucified, on the cross of matter, a tree that is made of nerves where the organism of man is projected from, which corresponds to the word **'gemmation,'** because is it allegorical of Gemini, who is ruled by Mercury, because Woden hanged himself on the Tree of Yggdrasil (the tree of nerves) for nine days so he could bring the wisdom of runes to his people. In Tarot, the Hanged Man represents this. The trunk of the tree represents the union of the earth, the heavens, and the underworld, or as Tolkien called it, Middle Earth.

In Kabbalah, Wisdom (Chokmah, Male) is gained through Understanding (Binah, Female), and beyond them is Keter (Crown,

Will) on the Tree of Life. What does the crown rest on? The head, the skull, the Calvary or Golgotha, because man is the microcosm of God. The process of spiritual involution and evolution begins in the Mind, the most high, the Rama, the Ram, the optic thalamus, the Eye of Providence, the Lamb of God, and as it is above, so it is below; as on the earth, so in the sky. Truly, the outward doth from the inward roll, and the inward dwells in the inmost soul.

The Calvary Cross that Jesus was crucified on, the Kabbalistic Tree of Life, the Sacred Fig tree named Ashvattha from the Bhagavata Gita, the Bodhi Tree that Buddha meditated under to gain enlightenment, the World Tree named Yggdrasil, the esoteric meaning of the Druids (which according to Pliny the Elder's etymology can mean "Oak-tree Magi, Seers, Prophets;" the oak is the tree of sacrifice and the oak leaves on military uniforms mark the soldiers for death/sacrifice), the Epic of Gilgamesh and his quest for the plant of life which was stolen from him by a serpent (3,000 years B.C.E.), the mystical Tree of Great Merit, the Golden Tree at Kumbum in Tibet, etc., are all different allegorical stories conveying the same knowledge. They are macrocosms to the different languages people speak. People from various regions who speak different languages can all convey the same message, but each language will sound different and appear to be different. It isn't until someone who speaks multiple languages comes along that we can have our comprehension of this knowledge expedited by their gracious efforts to teach us. For us to remain ignorant in the presence of such gifts is what invokes the hexes of our slavery. That does not mean that the merchandise, the goods, the message, is different. They convey the same Water of Life, the argentum vivum that the individual bodies convey, just on a larger scale. The fact that people cannot see this and still fight with each other over allegorical stories is evidence that the human race has been severely degraded over thousands of years. Some people may find this fascinating, but it's boring to those who have eyes to see. It's an awful experience to see war and ignorance plague this world, and then be ridiculed by Bolshevik-indoctrinated bluestockings every time we make this knowledge public. This is why the secret orders hide it from you. You and your ancestors have proven, time and time again, that you are not worthy of it, that you actually love slavery and no matter how much you insist you seek freedom, your behavior and the merchandise with which you trade suggests otherwise.

The Calvary, Golgotha, is where the nerves from the head branch off to form the body, for the base of the brain is where 75% of the nerves meet and cross, or get crucified. This is seen in just about every culture known to man, for the cross inside man is a microcosm of the solar cross in the Zodiac. For those who would like to verify this, search for the Latin Cross, the Papal Cross, the Cross of Lorraine, the Greek Cross, the Celtic Cross, the Maltese Cross, Saint Andrew's Cross, the Tau Cross, the Pommée Cross, the Botonée Cross, the Fleury Cross, the Avellan Cross, the Moline Cross, the Formée Cross, the Fourchée Cross, the Crosslet, Quadrate, and Potent Crosses, etc. Surely you can see that these are not coincidences. These nerves fork and branch off to the ends of the body's extremities, which we call the left and right, or the masculine and feminine aspects of our consciousness, and the cosmology of the heavens also corresponds to the two souls commencing their evolutionary process of becoming one flesh again.

Popular instruments and tools that were modeled after this process were the thermometer, barometer, and syringe. Mercury expands and rises based on the vibratory frequencies of heat that it is exposed to, and the tubes represent the spinal canal. The word 'syringe' comes from the Latin word 'syrinx,' meaning "a reed, tube, pipe, reed pipe, panpipe," which is why it corresponds to the lungs. A syrinx is also a voice organ in birds, which makes it not only correspond to music, sound, and science, but also the Language of the Birds: Green Language. This is why the Green Man, **Cernunnos**, is also Pan, who has panpipes, corresponding to the Latin 'syrinx.' Reeds correspond to lungs, which there are two twin versions of in each healthy body, and Gemini is the sign of the Twins of May. But to tie in the rest of this to all of the Sun-gods, Gemini was called **Al Tau'aman**, which if you break down means "the hidden cross," or "the Occult Cross of God." To quote Bulwer Lytton, "All that we propose to do is this: To find out the secrets of the human frame, to know why the parts ossify and the blood stagnates, and to apply continual preventatives to the effects of time. This is not magic; it is the art of medicine, rightly understood."

102

That's what Alchemy comes from: 'Al' + 'Kimia,' meaning "the Hidden, the Occult." Everything about your essence, your being, is occulted by your own Creator. Why? Because it is the honor of God is to hide (occult) a thing, and the honor of kings to search out a matter, and by learning the occult one can know thyself, and understanding the law of affinities, *Similia similibus curantur*, "like cures like," one can know how to raise the Christ, the Cristos, the oil, the Water of Life, the living silver, up the spinal canal to the **king dome** of God, the most high, the cerebrum. That's how we inherit the kingdom of God, and why Jesus says in John 14:6, "I am the way, and the truth, and the life. No one doth come unto the Father, if not through me."

Remembering all the different characters we've linked through Sun-god symbolism, now we see how they also physiologically and chemically correspond to Christ, the Cristos, the oil, the Water of Life that enables the cerebro-spinal system to generate and carry the physio-chemical electricity through the body, the oily or fatty nerve fluids from the sacral ganglia to the cerebrum that, once raised, enable reason to conquer, tame, and subdue (yamati) passion so that the body may exist in a state of purity, harmony, perfection, and equipoise. This is the natural state that humans evolve to if not hampered, obstructed, or thwarted by wrong-living, as evidenced in Exodus 23:20, "Lo, I am sending a messenger (Mercury, the living silver, the Water of Life) before thee to keep thee in the way, and to bring thee in unto the place which I have prepared."

The appearance of the glory of god, the honor of Jehovah, Jove, IO, the Sun, is later described as "a consuming fire on top of the mount" in Exodus 24:17. Where else have you seen that "fire on top of the mount" symbolism? Contemplate it. Call it what you will: Mount Olympus, Mount Meru, etc. If you know the sacred science, you can apply it anywhere you go, and if you don't serve God, you can manipulate people with it. This is the causality of our world's slavery. They believe your stories because you didn't explain the allegories to them, and now we have adult children, who hate themselves, trying to control others, also known as chaos.

This brings us to the twin stars of Gemini, Pollux and Castor. Castor comes from the Latin word 'castus,' meaning "morally pure, guiltless, chaste, pious," which High Magi must be in order to be successful. The caster must be castor, castus. He or she must 'cast ore,' or become light, as in illuminated, or Illuminatus. Francis Bacon admits this, "Nature, to be commanded, must first be obeyed." And if you really want to know how the Black Magi are summoning demons, daemons, jinn, and shayateen, then you should read the Goetia so you can learn how they invoke them in the name of God. What gives them that authority? They know Natural Law better than you know yourself. The truly powerful are pious, and if they choose to wield that power for selfish purposes, they must be experts at sidestepping the karmic laws of cause and effect by wholly comprehending the way nature works. Castor corresponds to the conscious God-mind of Aries, the cerebrum.

What is the opposite of the conscious mind? The unconscious animal-mind of Taurus, the cerebellum. This corresponds to Pollux, the other polarity of Castor. If we look at the Latin words that compose this name, we see 'pol' + 'lux.' 'Pol' means "forth," and 'lux' means "light," so quite literally, Pollux means "to shine forth light," or "bring forth light." Who rules Taurus? Venus, Lucifer, the bringer of light, because Taurus brings forth Gemini, the Twins: Castor and Pollux. What brings forth light? The darkness of rest. It is always darkest, and coldest, just before dawn. What lures the soul towards mortality? The illusory pleasure and impurity of the material world, the night, which corresponds to Scorpio, Judas' Kiss of Death that is symbolical of sex. Interesting to note that Judas' name in Greek corresponds to 'Iou-Das' in English. 'IOU' is a Green Language acronym for 'I owe you.' IO is the Sun from which we get Jove and love, but phonetically, Iou is pronounced as 'Jew,' where we get Zeus and Jew' Peter (Jupiter) from. Do you see where it leads? If not, keep pulling that thread and you'll expose the Inversive Brethren.

In this sense, we see how the Latin word 'polluo,' which translates to "I defile," ties into the real meaning of Pollux, despite what the unconscious Deaf Phoenicians of my era say. 'Luo' is "to dissolve, rot, spoil," and when combined with 'pol,' we see that it means "To bring forth or cause rot, defilement, spoilage, or dissolution," hence the English word 'pollute.' To defile something is to pollute it. To cater to the unconscious animal nature defiles and pollutes the body, mind, and soul and thwarts spiritual evolution. The process in the yearly cycle of the Sun that corresponds to this is known as the Fall, which brings us to one of the most used and recognized symbols of all time, yet the meaning of which is hardly known.

The 'caduceus' is derived from both the Latin words 'cado,' meaning "I fall, I die, I cease, I decay," as well as 'cadus,' which is a "vessel or jar." The body is a vessel for the Spirit, and once it's been defiled beyond its capacity to heal, it becomes unsuitable, and so Spirit departs. This event is known as death, which is why a dead body, known as a 'cadaver,' shares the same etymology, because it is a "dead vessel." Just like a thermometer is a vessel that contains quicksilver, Mercury, a correspondence to the living silver, the Water of Life, so too does the human back bone, the human vessel.

The caduceus is a symbol that conveys not only the Sun's rise and fall between Winter and Summer, but also the Cristos, the oil, the living silver in the spine that facilitates the rise and fall of man's physical and mental involution and evolution, which corresponds to the spiritual involution and evolution of the soul from its departure from the Creator to its ascension back to at-one-ment. Raising the Cristos up the spinal canal and into the cerebrum, where it is crucified on the Cross of Matter, is what enables this, thus allowing the individual to experience the Christ Mind, the conscious mind, the God-mind.

Mercury originates in Mount Olympus, the cerebrum, Aries, where the Sun is exalted. He is gold, and descends into the cerebellum, Taurus, where the Moon is exalted and he becomes silver, and then transitions into quicksilver, the living silver, argentum vivum, the Water of Life that moves down the spinal canal as the Divine Messenger. His winged hat represents the hemispheres of the brain, his winged pole is the Tree of Life, and the two serpents are the left and right sympathetic nervous systems on each side of the spine that fuse together at the base, corresponding to the Tree of Knowledge of Good and Evil. It's the same stick of Brahm in Hindu literature, Rod of Hermes, Rod of Moses in Phoenician (Hebrew) mythology, and Crucifix of Christ in the Christian allegories. It's all beautiful symbolism, or different languages, for communicating the same knowledge. So when you revisit the Bible story and realize that Joseph and his bright multicolored coat represent Mercury, the mind, overcoming death by dividing his merchandise, his goods, his thoughts, and feeding the other parts of the body their daily bread from heaven, and that the River Jordan and the Euphrates are metaphors for the spinal canal, then you can use this allegorical Truth and apply it to your own life.

However, it helps when you study all the traditions that you can access because the more you know, the more you can purify it and syncretize it. Most people will die in their coffin of consciousness, buried in the soils of their own ignorance, hating their fellow human being merely because his macrocosmic religion of choice didn't use the same microcosmic language to express the same esoteric Truth. This is the epitome of being yoked by priestcraft sorcery, and hopefully, by the end of this, you will be prepared to walk a path less travelled, and not accept one word of this work as Truth, but use it as an inspiration to seek what the Creator has hidden for you.

The Water of Life makes the creation of the bay-bee possible. The wand, like the caduceus, is the spine, where the focus of our minds directs our spiritual electricity. The Door of Brahm is the suture of the skull, the chimney opening where Santa Claus, Spirit, leaves and enters the body. This is why the dwelling place of Spirit is also Brahmarandhra, which is symbolical of "the Bee" and why the cave of Brahman is also the cave of the bumblebee: the Sun. Jupiter, the Guru, the Master, the magister, the god-star, Mithras, etc., comes to the worm in the form of a bee and lays the worm on a lotus blossom that was brought back to God by the angel at sunrise to unite with its creator. It is all symbolism of the Sun.

Since a bay is a body of water, the bay-bee is a water spirit, a näkki. Jesus, the Lord Fish, also symbolizes the Water of Life that is the living silver, the *argentum vivum*: Mercury. It originates in Aries, the Lamb of God, Brahma, Rama, the most high, Mount Olympus, Mount Meru, and enables the Great Work as the messenger of the gods, the mind, the rise and fall of man, Summer and Winter, the quick (living) and the dead, the Sun and Saturn, the Cycle of Necessity.

My apologies for the repetitive nature of this work, but it is necessary to remind those who seek to retain this information about how it syncretizes. Let us continue. The shiny bright one is Phanæus, hatched from the Orphic World Egg by Chronos (Time) and Ananke (Inevitability/Necessity). The Orpheus states, "First-born Phaëton, Son of the far-shining morning," and the Romans mistook this for being the Son of the Sun, rather than the Sun itself. Phaëton is Phanæus, Phanes, the Ram of March, Eros, Cupid, which is why God is love, as the Babylonian Phoenician writer Sanchuniathon wrote over a thousand years before Christ, through the works of Philo Biblius (Byblius) who translated it from Phoenician into Greek, "When the Spirit became enamored of his own perfections, he begat Cupid—for Cupid was the beginning of the creation of all things." Notice how both Cupid and Jesus are both the holy child, conceived by the Holy Ghost, and then contemplate the writing of Ian Fleming, "Once is happenstance. Twice is coincidence. Three times is enemy action." How many times will you let the enemy get away with pawning this black magick creation story as historical fact to dictate their whims to you?

The foundation, the rock, of their stories is that God is light, love, etc., which is all esoteric, beautiful Truth, but they encode that knowledge in stories that only those whose eye is perfect, single, initiated, can comprehend. In Ephesians 5:13, it states, "And all the things reproved (criticized; critiqued) by the light are manifested, for everything that is manifested is light." Then in John 1:5 it is stated that "God is light, and in Him is no darkness at all." What is the only thing in this world that you've never seen darkness (the absence of light) in? If you say anything other than the Sun, you're a fucking liar.

The Sun is the God-star. This is the cornerstone to priestcraft sorcery, the rock, if you will. Why? Because the God in Hebrew, **Sur, Zor, Sir,** also has a name which means "rock," and it comes from one of the oldest religions of Sun worship that there is: the cult of Zoroaster, hence the meaning of Deuteronomy 32:31, "For not as our Rock is their rock, and our enemies are judges." This is because 'rock' is God, 'Zor,' so what they're really saying is that their god is not as our God, because it is not Zoroaster, which is derived from the words 'Zor' and 'aster.'

As demystified, 'Zor' means "rock," which is why the sacred rock of Mithraism is called 'Petra,' which also means rock, hence the names Peter, Jew'Peter, Jupiter, Pator, Pater, which means "father," and is the reason that Jupiter is literally the God-father, or god of the light and sky. *Yes, sir.* He is the Sun. 'Yes,' Yesus, Jesus, is the Sun, and 'sir' is God. Thus the occult meaning of 'yes, sir,' in the context of the deceit, is 'Sun, God,' or 'Bacchus, God.'

The Black Magi give you this hidden knowledge in the form of the 'gospel,' which is the 'God spell,' because it is a hex, certainly not from God, because it is so powerful that you can connect nearly every one of the thousands of dots that compose the grand picture while those under the hex will cling to every last unconnected dot as their excuse to reinforce and remain under the hex of the gospel. The masses love their slavery as much as they love their black magick.

Who is responsible for bringing this hex to the western world? What was the original name of Tyre, the capital of Phoenicia? Sur, pronounced Zor, or Zur. It's all phonetically the same because it's from the phony phonics of the Phoenician Canaanites. Zoroaster is the god-star, because 'aster' means "star," and if a star is not in a favorable position, it is said to be a 'disaster,' hence all the disasters occur when the stars are in unfavorable positions. This spirit is also contained in the name Dis, the Roman god of the underworld.

Zoroaster literally translates as "rock star." Let that marinate in your mind for a moment. This is why you have rock stars in the entertainment world, and companies with the name Rockstar, because they are continuing to hex you with the gospel, the God-spell, not to be confused with anything from God. This is the magic of mankind, for it is illusory.

Magia was originally a name for the science of astronomy. This is what words like 'magistrate,' a "judge of a police court," and 'magister,' the Latin word for "master," are derived from. It all comes from the old Akkadian word 'imga,' which meant "wise, holy, learned," and it was used to title men of knowledge who formed a caste of priest-kings, or priest-masters. Imga gradually morphed into 'mag,' which is where 'magi' in Latin comes from, which corresponds to the Greek word 'magos,' hence the integration of this into the Bible as the *wise men*, the *masters*.

They are masters because they create their own paradigms and dictate their whims to others. This invariably makes them slaves to the paradigm, because the master is the slave, which is why you cannot appeal to them to change it. They can't. They bound themselves to their iniquity. This is where the word 'mason' came from. A mason is builder. He may either work with matter or energy, but both require mental imagery: imagination.

The "freemason" imitates the Egyptian Mason, and knows nothing of freedom because he swears oaths to individuals other than God. He, just like most religious people, knows nothing of the allegories involving Hiram, his master, or Solomon and his starry temple. Most masons know nothing of Hiram just as most Christians known nothing of Christ. Who else was "the Master" besides Jesus and Hiram? Mithra.

Petra, the sacred rock of Mithraism, is where Peter, the apostle whose original name was Simeon in Hebrew, received the name Cephas because he was the foundation of the Christian Church, a corner stone, and a fisherman, a fisher of men. Petra, Peter, and Cephas, all mean the same thing: "rock." This corresponds to the symbolical advice to build one's house or temple on rock. The following will reveal the "rock" that the wise men, the magi, laid the imagery of their priestcraft sorcery upon.

On March 25, the Feast of Annunciation (Lady Day) occurs, commemorating Gabriel's visit to Mary in which he informs her that she is pregnant, "Hail, full of Grace, the Lord is with thee."

It occurs exactly nine months prior to December, 25, the first day that the Sun rises out of the lower meridian, the nadir, which is Capricorn, the Manger of the Goat, the Stable of Bethlehem, because in the physical world, this is where the Sun's position is at the lower meridian, where it stays from December 21, the Winter Solstice, through December 25, rising on the date of the latter by one degree. This is the south, Winter, sur, rock, foundation, the love, light, and beginning of the cyclical life of the Sun, which corresponds to our souls, as well as to God.

At this time of year, the Virgin, that is to say, the constellation Virgo, is on the eastern point of the horizon, and in her elbow is the bright yellow star Vindemiatrix (the Grape Harvester), the star that the magi see in the east, the East Star, which also is contained in the occult spirit of the word 'Easter,' in Matthew 2:2, "Where is the newly born king of the Jews? For we saw his star in the east, and we came to bow to him."

During this time, the magi, the wise men, the imga of Orion's belt rise from the east in the evening to the southern sky, hence they come to bow to him, because by the time the Sun is being "born," they will be setting, or "bowing" to him, in the southwest. Orion's belt is symbolical of the Three Kings, the Magian Kings who set just after the Lamb of God (Aries) in the western horizon, and they behold the star in the east directly across from them in the eastern horizon. They present gold, myrrh, and frankincense, which have been used throughout the ages as religious offerings to sun-gods. They are certainly not unique to Christianity, but further illustrate that Christianity is nothing more than Sun worship in its exoteric application. Where does myrrh and frankincense come from? Arabia.

There is symbolism that must not be overlooked in regards to this day. It is called Christ-mass, because December 25 is the symbolic birth of the god star, the rock star named Jesus. The most high, the Rama, the Ram, the High Ram, as in Hiram, or Chi Ram, because Chi is X, the Sun, hence the abbreviation of Christmas as X-mas.

The XX symbolism that is visible in cult institutions and their logos comes from the days when people were buried with their name and XX inscribed on their grave, meaning "Good man—good-by!" This is a play on the names of the Chrests and Chrestians, the good men or good fellows, hence the Chrest, or Christ, is the Good Shepherd. They are nothing more than Jupiter worshippers, as the XX represents the death and resurrection of the Sun.

These are also known as St. Andrew's Crosses, and they are symbolical of the two crosses of the equator that the Sun makes, by the ecliptic, at the equinoctial points in Autumn, when the Sun dips below, and then in Spring, when the Sun crosses again from below, or "rises again from the dead."

The Cross of St. Andrew is also known as the Cross Saltier, or Crux Decussata, and not only was it the flag of Scotland, but it was also used as the symbol for the 29° of Scottish Rite Masonry, known in title as Knight of Freemasonry. Keep in mind 'mason' was derived from 'mag,' which comes from the same etymology as the 'magi,' the wise men: 'imga.' The Cross of St. Andrew is the sign of the Good Shepherd, and all variations of the solar cross contain the X, representing change and transition, and the O, representing permanence and stability, which mirrors the two of disks in Tarot, change being the support of stability. This is also the meaning behind the mark of the beast as well as the game Tic Tac Toe, and the prophetic casting of lots, also known as Cleromancy, which is an act of sortition that Ancient Athens utilized to pick the 'magistrates' for their governing committees by choosing random candidates from a larger pool of candidates, an act that is comparable to rolling dice or flipping coins with the intent that it will reveal the Will of God in a decision making process.

You will see this XX symbolism everywhere, especially on the logos of organizations controlled and owned by the Black Magi, and it goes beyond all religions, but you had better believe Christianity is under that umbrella. Still think the Christians are Good-fellows? With the tax-exempt 501 (c)(3) status they receive, it's obvious that they are *goodfellas*, just like all the other members of religious institutions such as government, politics, science, academia, healthcare, banking, etc. They are gangsters, members of Mafia families. Only a Deaf Phoenician natural born idiot would attempt to deny this.

So when you partake in the dark occult ritual of drinking the sacramental blood of Bacchus today, contemplate the meaning of the word 'rite' and 'ritual,' which come from the Latin word 'ritus,' tracing back to the Sanskrit word 'riti,' and is the Greek equivalent of 'reo,' meaning "the method or order of service to the gods."

Do you serve God? Or do you serve only yourself?

9 SARA'S MONEY

Under Maritime Admiralty Law, the Law of the Sea, you are a water product and considered lost at sea, a lost soul, discharged from the cerv-ix, the service to Nine (deity; completion; wholeness; the divine Ego), and until you declare that you are no longer lost seamen/semen and that you stand on land as a sovereign inhabitant, you are granted liberty (short leave), not freedom.

Our current-sea, our electrical currency, is used to charge their system through the moon-key mind in our skulls, the sculls (oars, ore) that we use to row and make roe (eggs) as well as to fertilize them. Remaining trapped at the monkey-mind state of duality is the cycle of our mind's true demon (mens-tru-al), and should we not transcend it, we call out to be rescued, re-skewed (harpooned), by the false light of Je-sus, the fisher of men, who says, "Come ye after me, and I will make you to become the fishers of men."

You were born in Sin, the Moon, and so you must be lured to die in her by the Son of the Moon: Solomon. The Eye-Fish, as we've referred to him, is a spiritual concave lens that distorts reality, which corresponds to the fish-eye lens in most cameras.

Why does everything in our laws and way of life revolve around water? The Latin word for "water fluid" is 'serum,' which comes from the root word 'ser,' "to run, flow." The word that indicates plurality for 'serum' is 'sera.' This is why a 'ceremony' (phonetically 'sera' + 'mony') involves the plurality of water products.

Perhaps the most popular of all ceremonies, as far as the Whore of Babalon Roman Maritime Admiralty Law system is concerned, is the marriage ceremony, for it binds two water products into one business, which is why the spouses are partners. The moment you do this, you are taking yourself off the land and into the sea, because a marriage is a "lunar sea-oath," the root word of which has the spirit of the Latin word for the sea: 'mare,' and the Dutch word for an oath: 'eed.' When you said "I do," you bound yourself in a sea-oath because you were 'mare-eed.' 'Cera' is the Sanskrit word for Sarah, which means "flowing," as the phonetically similar word 'sarit' is a "brook" or "river." This is why the occult meaning of the relationship between Sara and Abram is 'cerebrum,' the optic thalamus, the conscious God-mind.

There is no temporary solution to having your relationship recognized by the government while not being bound by the laws of Commerce, for the whole system is black magick and needs to be abrogated so that it matters not how we refer to things. However, the physical and spiritual solution is to avoid turning your relationship into a 'marriage' so that it is not bound by Commerce, and instead of getting married, you will 'join in holy matrimony.' Under no circumstances should you refer to your husband or wife as your 'spouse,' for this is a commercial term. The husband and wife are each other's property for as long as they agree to be in that relationship. They are not to allow any government to interfere with it, no matter how well intentioned. Does that mean you won't receive benefits from the government? Damn straight, it does. Benefits are privileges, and once you accept privileges from the Black Magi, you enter yourself into a contract and agree to be their slave as far as they are concerned. Some of you may find this terrifying. They're waging commercial warfare against you. Did you really believe that the government was there to benefit you? It's time for you to grow up. They are secret orders of pirates, ones with fire, and they are pretending to be government so they can assault you with contracts, rape you, and then sell you into slavery. Ignoring Truth will not save you, so you might as well pretend you've already lost everything and confront it while you still have resources, because the direction that the Roman Cult is steering the world in will strip you of all real property before this century is over. You've been warned...

As we've stated, 'mon-' is a prefix to represent the Moon, hence the name Monday, because it's all about the money, the mooney, which is why married people are usually moany about trivial things like money instead of being concerned with the real issues facing humanity. To avoid becoming moany, avoid participating in the sea-oath ceremony. Of course, your black magick hex is already causing you to have an emotional reaction, so perhaps it will be easier for you to stop reading and continue down your path of dying as a Roman Slave also known as a US Citizen.

As previously covered, though phonetically different, the spelling of the Latin word for the sea and the English word for a female horse is identical: 'mare.' During a sea-oath ceremony, the male partner is called the 'groom,' which is "one who grooms horses and stables," because the house of marriage is nothing more than a stable, where a mare-groomer, who bridles the 'bride' with a bridle, headstall, bit, and reins of a harness that restrains the mare (female) as she draws the carriage, the flesh-I-age, the flesh that Iesus (I, Ies, Bacchus) preserves, which is a female-drawn carriage, and is also known as a mare-iage (marriage).

The groom dis-charges his semen into the bride's egg to create another fetus for Sin (the Moon), thus more fish for Iesus, because from their perspective, when you create a 'fetus,' you oblige their phonetic command, "feed us," by engaging in an act, or a deed of ingenuity, a feat of creation for them. This corresponds to the three principles of this construct: 1) Charge and Discharge, 2) Centripetal and Centrifugal, and 3) Spatial and Counter-spatial (magnetism is polarized, which is spatial, and dielectricity is counter-spatial). Delve into the work of Ken L. Wheeler for further study on this matter.

Through word-splitting, 'ceremony' is 'cerem' + 'ony.' Phonetically, 'cerem' is 'serum,' which is "blood." In Scottish, the antiquated word 'ony' means "any." Thus, 'ceremony' is also "any blood," because anyone can partake in it. However, phonetically, the first half of the word corresponds to 'sera,' a Latin word meaning "lock," because when one participates in a marriage ceremony, they are locking each other's money, from that point on, into a business institution. 'Sera' is also a name for the "evening, night." The word 'even' means "fair, level," so not only is 'evening' a word for the night, but the process of "making something square, fair, or level."

What always seeks its level? Water. Thus the nature of money and the Moon is water because it can always be balanced, or made even, full, whole, new, used to facilitate society, or used as black magick to enslave it. It has a certain magnetic quality about it, and can be gained or lost in a manner that corresponds to the nature of those who use it. Money contains the energy, the frequency, of everyone that's ever handled it. It is the lifeblood of every civilization, regardless if that's a good thing for humanity or not. So when we look at the plurality of 'serum,' which is "blood," we have 'sera.' Money related to any ceremony (sera-money) is blood money because a dowry is essentially the restitution for the loss of sovereignty that one incurs through marriage.

In Celtic, 'al' means "harmony, stone, or noble." Marriage is a custom that is accepted as 'normal.' 'Norma' is a "carpenter's square" in Latin, and when experimenting with word-splitting, one could discover that the combination of these words could mean a "noble carpenter's square," or a "stone carpenter's square," and if something is 'normal,' it has the nature or form of a carpenter's square in the sense that it makes things level, balanced, or harmonious in terms of the status quo. What is a carpenter who builds with stone? A mason. What was Iesus? A carpenter. What were homes in the ancient Middle East built with? Stone.

Another tool that a woodworking carpenter uses to make wood smooth and level is a 'plane.' When a builder, carpenter, mason makes something even, he levels it, and by some degree destroys what it was, or brings it down through reduction, and thus the saying of making something "fair and square" arises.

'Square' is another one of those words that has over fifty meanings, but to layfolk it is slang for someone who is ignorant of current fads. To masons, being 'on the square' is also a derogatory statement that mocks someone for being in base consciousness.

The word 'fair' as an adjective alludes to any of the following: "free from bias, ample, moderately good, promising, bright, sunny, or fine." As an archaic noun, it is "a beloved woman," hence a fair maiden. Its phonetically identical counterpart is 'fare,' which could be any of the following: "price of passage, food or diet (feed us), and something offered to the public for entertainment, enjoyment, or consumption (feed us)." But as a verb, the word 'fare' means "to experience" or "to eat and drink" (feed us).

To 'square,' as a verb, is "to pay off debt, which is to get out of debt, or not be dead ore (a debtor), to even the score, set right, or bring into agreement." As an adjective, being 'square' is "not owning anything." Do you see how the Black Magi are squaring you by depriving you of property?

Perhaps it is worthy to consider that the purpose of this construct is to teach individuals to respect all life, including their own, and that no living being may ever be owned. Tending one's own 'garden' is not only "to mind one's business," but also "to guard within, to guard oneself internally (guard in)." But if we look at the word 'gar,' it is "to cause, compel, or force something, or someone, to do something." When you tend to your own garden, it will bear fruits that compel, or cause, others to tend to their own gardens, because if your garden is fruitful, it will inspire others, and language is breath, inspiration and expiration, deep or shallow, hence by guarding within, you are garring your *den*, your lair, your temple, your body to be perfect. As you tend to your own 'gar-den,' you will transform your own language, hopefully under the intent remitted with love as its foundation.

'Remit' is "to transmit or send, usually a payment (pay mind), to give back." In law, "to send back (usually to an inferior court)." However, if you take a closer look, the word 'remit' is also the word 'timer' in reverse. A 'timer' is "a person or thing that times, measures, or records times."

Since we have the gift of memory, does that make each of us a timer that is capable of remitting our time to the court of an inferior game? But what if each of us is a 'time-err,' "one who is led astray, in thought or belief, by time?" What if our *existence* is a remittance, a timed sentence, and we sent tension because our *egg is tense?* What if we remit our mind, the payment of our spiritual currencies of time and attention, to an inferior place where justice (just ice) is administered, a place where they try to court (win) our favor? After all, Winter is Satan, and it's cold as hell right now.

What if they put us on ice to pre-serve (age) us, thus when we hold office, we are off ice? What if we are dice? 'Di' equals two, hence '**divide**' is "to see double" because '**vide**' is Latin for "see." What if we are double ice, di-ce, and they put us on the rocks and then cast us (castus) into a garden of eating (Eden)? After all, '**castus**' means "guiltless, pure, chaste, pious" in Latin, and we do start off in this construct as virgin (pure, original) beings.

Are you awake? A '**wake**' is "a watching, or a watch kept, for some solemn or ceremonial purpose; a watch or vigil by the corpse before burial." When you go to a marriage ceremony, are you keeping watch over Sara's money, the blood money, the lifeblood, before a mare and her groom turn their relationship into a corpse, a dead legal fiction known as a corporation? That would be a night**mare**.

A '**vigil**' is "wakefulness at night," and to be '**vigilant**' is to be "ever a-wake." Are you vigilant? Are you forever a wake? Is our existence a solemn or ceremonial purpose to be watched? A '**wake**' is also "a path or course of anything that has passed or preceded; a track of waves left by a ship." Are you a wake left by the citizen-ship?

Who is Sara? She is '**cere**,' the "seed." But the seed of what? Both '**brum**,' the most high, Rama, **Abram**, **Brahm**a, and also of '**bellum**,' war, contention, antagonism, rebellion. Is she the Whore of Babalon? '**Baba**' is the Father, and the Father is the Sun, the most high. What happens after you take the sea-oath for Sara's money, the marriage ceremony, the blood of the Moon?

10 THE SEA OF DIVIDED SOULS

What do married couples go on after their wedding sera-moon-ey? A honeymoon. After any blood (serum-ony) becomes locked money (sera-money) through ceremony, it is now the water fluid (serum) of the Moon: mooney, money, the Moon's honey, money of the Night (Sera), the honeymoon.

When couples conceive on their honeymoon, they create a fetus, known as a bay-bee, for the Queen Bee, the Whore of Babalon (Baby-lon), the whore of the Father god of the Sun: Jupiter Ammon. They make money, honey. But the moon-honey that is created on the honeymoon feeds something.

Who is the "us" that the fetus feeds? When one is married, he or she takes the female horse oath (mare-eed), which is also the sea-oath (mare-eed), and thus the couple is said to get 'hitched.' As a verb, 'hitch' is "to harness an animal to a vehicle."

But what is an 'animal?' The word comes from 'anima' + 'mal,' which literally means "bad soul." The word 'hitch' also means "to catch, snag," like fish being caught by the fisher of men, the King-Fish, I-Fish, Je-Sus, Dagon: El. The de-sire to get hitched will quite literally turn you into a de-mon, one who is divided and cut off from source. It's a business. Marriage was never designed for souls to find their mates and continue the process of becoming one flesh, as we've been deluded into believing. That process will happen without the satanic laws of men interfering and turning that process into a business.

After the couple is hitched through a female horse-drawn carriage (mare-iage), and a bay-bee is produced, they cycle has restarted. A 'bay' has four different meanings worthy of your consideration. It is "a body of water that forms an indentation in a shoreline." A 'bay' is also "a compartment, as in a barn for storing hay." Relating to the sense of sound, a 'bay' is "a deep, prolonged howl," but "a situation of powerlessness due to being actively opposed by an animal or person, or... something else?" This is where the term 'at bay' comes from.

Why do wolves 'bay' at the moon? What keeps them at 'bay?' I love you, bay-bee. I love you too, honey. What do horses eat? Hay that is stored in a 'bay.'

The sera-mooney (watery fluid of the Moon) is a body of water, a bay, and since hue-mans are mostly water, it is only fitting that they are called bay-bees, bees made of water that produce honey (Cristos, plasma) for the Moon, the Queen, to feed "us" (fetus). *But who is us?*

Is the Moon a giant female horse drawing the carriage of her marriage to the Sun? Is the Moon the illusory carriage of Cinderella, which is phonetically **Sin**-derella, Sin being both the name for a wicked deed and also the Moon? '**Cinder**' is "burnt ash or ember," while '**ella**' is the Spanish word for "female." Is this merely symbolism that indicates some sort of electromagnetic relationship between the two heavenly bodies of the Sun and Moon, Solomon?

What does Cinderella's carriage turn into at midnight, mid-sera? A pumpkin. What color is a pumpkin generally associated with? **Or**ange, **or**-ange, **ore**-ange, hence the Sun symbolism that corresponds to that color, as well as to the jack o' lantern, which you light a candle in, because as they've told you, "our God is an all-consuming fire."

'**Horse**' is almost phonetically identical to '**whores**.' So perhaps the giant female horse is really a giant female whore, as in the Whore of Babalon. Where is the Queen of this system? London. Interesting that Babylon, one variant of the spelling, looks like Baby-lon, as in Baby London, or Bay-bee London. Perhaps the City of London is the bay-bee of Vatican City, or was a bay-bee loan.

Marriage is also phonetically Mar-Age, and if using the Spanish word for the sea, '**mar**,' it would make it the Sea Age, or Aeon of the Sea, governed by water, where couples produce bay-bees, which in turn grow up to make more money, moon-honey, honeymoons, and sustain the fetus cycle that feeds us. If you tamper with the phonetics and pronounce 'us' as 'you-ce,' while keeping the same spelling of 'u-s,' you get another identical Latin phonetic in the word 'jus,' which means "right." This is seen in the masonic claim 'Deus Meumque Jus,' which means "God and My Right." Why? Because the satanic ideology that runs all the orders, that control the corporations and the governments, adheres to Social Darwinism, the idea that they are in the positions of birth and power due to their genetic code. They believe they have descended from gods and thus have a divine right to rule people of lesser fortune and beings of lesser consciousness. This is known as the Divine Right of Kings. The color of honey is amber, or golden, just like the money of kings has historically been gold. So while the world wastes away in fraudulent paper and electronic currency, those who run the system use it to buy up the real assets so that when the music stops playing, they'll have all the chairs.

If a divine right to rule came from anywhere, where would that be? Most people would point to the heavens, the stars, and one of the most important concepts we'll ever decode is the Zodiac. The word 'zodiac' can be arranged in several ways, one of which is 'zo-di-ac.'

The word 'zo' is a variant of 'zoo,' indicating a limited artificial construct or habitat for animals, bad souls (anima + mal), for the viewing pleasure of beings with higher consciousness. 'Di' means "twofold, twice," and it corresponds to words like 'dia,' 'dea,' 'dios,' 'deuce,' 'dice,' and 'divide.' It indicates duality, or polarity, not singularity. The suffix '-ac' means "pertaining to." So quite literally, the word 'Zodiac' (zo-di-ac) is "pertaining to a dualistic zoo."

But you and I have never drunk shallow draughts from the Pierian spring, so let us drink deep and look at the Green Language of 'c,' as in 'Zo-dia-c,' which is phonetically 'see,' or 'sea.' I have provided sufficient evidence that we are water products, and that every system known to man is based on water in some way or another, so it's no stretch of the imagination to behold that another meaning for 'Zodiac' is a "Sea of Divided Souls," which we have already established as demons because the very word 'de-mon' means "degraded one, divided one," because they have been cut off from their sovereign creative power by desires. But demons are also "deities of the Moon." And to go one step deeper, the dualistic deities of the moon are crucified on their own crosses of matter, their 'cadus,' their vessel, which enables those watching us to "See Divided Souls," the other meaning of 'Zodiac.' They say that we are born in Moon (Sin) and that we die in Moon (Sin), so does that mean we are all demons? Perhaps that is why the Holy Sea considers us 'lost at sea.'

When looking at previous words that correspond to 'di,' we find that 'dea-' is a prefix that means "good" in Irish, which comes from 'deg-' or 'dag' in Old Irish, meaning "good, well," but also "goddess" in Latin and Italian. Interestingly enough, the word 'God,' is just 'good' without an 'o.' If we look at 'Dagon,' who is El, Saturn, father of Ba'al, we see the combination of 'dag' + 'on.' Building off of our foundation, we see that 'Dagon' can mean "Good Sun," or "Good Son," which ties him right into the XX seal of Saturn, and its Chrestian roots of meaning "Good-fellow." Is Dagon, Saturn, Father Time, the Angel of Death that becomes the Angel of Life, the Sun, the original "Good-fellow," or should I say, "Goodfella?" What does Dagon wear on his crown? The head of a fish. Why? Because the fish rots from the head down and he comes from the deep, the abyss, just like his son, the Sun: Ba'al. Just like Abaddon, who is called Apollyon in the Greek tongue, who is also the Sun. Just like Jesus, the Lord Fish, who comes from the Pure Sea: Virgin Mary (Mare), because the Sun rises and sets out of the sea, and those with an ocean view of this occurrence witness the Son of God walk on water.

'Dios' means "God" in Spanish, which is phonetically similar to 'deus,' the Latin word for "God." Further connected to 'di' is another word for "two" known as 'deuce,' which is especially used in card games that involve gambling. Another gambling device is the 'die,' which usually are cast in pairs of at least "two," so we call them 'dice.'

Do we die because we failed to get out of duality during the time we gambled with the 'dice' in this Wheel of Fortune known as the Zodiac? Jupiter, Jove, is the giver of all good things, and so he corresponds to Fortune. However, Jupiter Ammon is also the Sun. Perhaps we reach singularity when we die, because 'die' is the singular version of 'dice.' There is a saying that we come into this world alone and we die alone. A 'die' is also "an engraved stamp for impressing a design upon some softer material, as in coining money."

Is our soul the die that the Moon uses to impress Dagon's design upon our flesh vessel, to coin her moon-honey, her money? Or is the Zodiac the die that impresses our soul with its design, as astrology indicates? 'To see' the Truth, our eye must be perfect, single, initiated, so our body may be full of light. However, 'to see' is phonetically 'two see,' which is also 'divide,' 'di' meaning "two" and 'vide' meaning "see." It indicates double vision, because to divide is also "to split," or "to part the seas," hence the other phonetic arrangement of 'two sea.'

The Zodiac is divided into two seas, life and death. Life is from Aries to Virgo, and then Judgment Day occurs at the beginning of Libra where Father Time (Death, Saturn) is exalted, on September 23, and lures the Spirit into the illusory world of Matter, which is Winter, where the soul reaches its state of crystallization, also known as death. From December 25, the soul takes its accumulated energy and begins its journey toward life again till it reaches the final state of completion, Pisces, and then it is born again into the next cycle of evolution or involution. This is the real meaning of the swastika, what the Nazis stole it from. You will also note that it indicates the four positions of Ursa Major, the Big Dipper, the Car of Osiris, as it circles Polaris, the North Star. Each position indicates a season, and so no matter where you are, you can always tell what time of year it is. When the handle of the ladle points to the south, it is Winter. When it points to the east, it is Spring. When the handle points to the north, it is Summer, and when it points westward, it is Autumn. The seven milkmaids of the sky circle Polaris just like the shape of the swastika. This is a microcosm of the Cycle of Necessity. The beginning is the end, and the end is the beginning. This is Dagon's construct, and in order to escape the rule of Time, Chronos, Saturn, we must transcend it through our behavior, for even though this is a mental universe of vibration and energy, it is ultimately our actions that program this reality.

11 DICTION OF ARIES

The primary sources of definitions for Deaf Phoenicians are the dictions of Aries that can be found on the Internet, otherwise known as **'online dictionaries.'** When Truth threatens the childish worldview of coincidence theorists, they need to cherry pick as many cross-reference dictations from the airy diction of dictators as possible. These dictators are known as "authority" figures.

The Deaf Phoenicians are totally incapable of comprehending the whimsical and magickal nature of language. Very few of them understand that all languages are religions that require people's belief as established compilations of symbols and sounds, otherwise they have no effect on those who do not subscribe to them. It's easily provable by trying to communicate with someone who speaks a different language. If you cannot comprehend what he's saying, then his words have no power over you when they are used to make fun of you and insult you openly. You will likely feel no emotion as the words are whirled at you, unless you get frustrated with the situation, the same way that you feel nothing at the sound of birds chirping, unless you find those sounds to be delightful or annoying. The speaker/caster only has to conceal his tone of voice and body language, and then you won't suspect that he is insulting you if you cannot comprehend his words. But the moment someone uses words that have specific egregores attached to them, that you can identify with, and insults you in a way that is inappropriate, you may be evoked to respond with vitriol or even violence. This is the primary reason for why magi prefer symbols. These occult languages do not reveal themselves to the uninitiated. Even if the profane can identify patterns in the usage of the symbols, the language still protects itself from them. Understanding how the minds of magi work will benefit one's journey towards learning the Language of the Birds and being able to syncretize all of the mystery traditions.

There is nothing wrong with using the Internet for research and cross-referencing one's findings, however, to think that a digital world of instant access cannot be tampered with is utter naiveté. Dictionaries, whether modern or ancient, are merely the opinions of their authors.

There is no such thing as '**authority**' in nature outside of the esoteric meaning of the word, which is '**Au**' (the abbreviation of gold from the Latin word '**aurum**') + '**Thor**' (Jupiter, the Sun). So in the real world, in terms of the Language of the Birds, the only '**au-thor**' is the Sun, hence the occult meaning of King Arthur, Golden Thor, Jupiter Ammon, Zeus Ammon, Jupiter-Zeus, the Amen, Jesus: the Sun. It is a myth that conveys a deep allegorical Truth.

For anyone who thinks that authority is real, a natural phenomena that Nature creates for different beings based on the level of consciousness that they manifest as, the onus probandi is on him or her to show the rest of us where in Nature we can find someone who is born with more or less rights than others, as displayed by Nature, not circumstance, and as such, has an observable right to dictate his or her whims to others.

I created this work to help you tap into and cultivate your other senses so that you can activate and operate from your cerebrum, your optic thalamus, also known as the conscious God-mind, or Aries. As you get familiar with this process, you will learn to see the world through yourself, and tap into the spirit of the energy that exists all around you so that, in addition to accumulating the discoveries of others, you can discover the Truth through experience, thus making the transition from being a believer into a knower.

That's my objective. There is nothing I want. This work is here to facilitate you, through your own free will, to penetrate the deeper mysteries of the world you live in, whether it be this octave or the next. It is merely a cornerstone, and nothing in this book that should be accepted, but rather considered.

It's great that you're reading this, but at some point, you must get out of the matrices of men, get off the page, get out of the digital ether, and apply your knowledge into the way you behave. That's what makes it wisdom, and that's how you transcend the zodiacal Wheel of Fortune.

Till then, the Black Magi will keep mocking you, stripping you of your reality, and replacing what previous races valued in Nature with illusory digital substitutes. A good example of this is found in entertainment. As James Bomar notes, the original matrix is Nature. Who created it? The Creator. What you choose to call it is irrelevant, for it is ineffable.

What did the original matrix give us, in terms of fixed things that we could use to find our way through the days, the months, the years, and even our location on the earth? The stars. The races of the past looked to the stars to know who they were, where they were, where they were going, and where they had been.

The Inversive Brethren created metropolitan areas with light pollution, and made a paradigm that provides the most benefits to those who live in the human farms known as cities. They replaced your stars with Hollywood stars, so instead of looking up to empyreal splendor of what God created for you in the firmament, you look to what service-to-self demons created for you in an artificial, digital simulation.

But what does 'digital' mean? Don't ask a Deaf Phoenician. They're clueless. Split the word for yourself and you'll find that 'di' means "two, dual," a 'git' is "a foolish or worthless person," and 'al,' amongst other things, is "a fertility demon" that can cause sterility. Simply put, 'di-git-al' is an adjective that "pertains to a dualistic, worthless, sterile thing."

This is further evidenced in its etymological origin from the Latin word 'digitus,' which means "finger" but comes from Greek words that translate as "to point out, the finger with which we point out, the forefinger, and each finger being one of ten." What's the lowest number between one and ten? One.

Which finger do we point with the most, and is also used to represent 'one' the most? The index finger: forefinger. So even in this context, 'digital,' from 'digitus,' indicates the least value. One cannot accumulate generational wealth that is stored in digital ether, or digital currency, for we have so clearly demonstrated that the nature of 'digital' is nothing more than a sterile, dead sea of dualistic, worthless denominations conjured by divided ones, demons, and sustained only by collective egregores.

So how do we reprogram a word like 'digital?' We have to reconstruct a word in the opposite consciousness and then create an egregore powerful enough for it to be understood by many without defining it. What's the opposite of dual, or something that is 'in piece,' or phonetically 'peace,' because to rest in peace is to be dead, hence the Todesrune, the Schutzstaffel rune of death that is seen in the peace symbol? Whole. So the whole solution could be encoded in a word like 'wholution.'

Or, if you'd like to keep it based on the polarities of their words, you could use the words 'whole,' 'light,' and 'balance,' and form them into 'wholitance.' The possibilities are endless. This is an example of how language can be constructed any way we want it to be, but in order for it to last, an egregore must be created by the spirit of the words, otherwise, no one will know what the idea conveyed by the word is.

Only when one's solutions are coming from a place of wholeness, light, and balance will they be able to raise consciousness. Using digital currency is, by its very spirit, the equivalent of using a sterile, dead sea of worthless demons as a measure of one's worth. If that's what one's worth is to be valued in, then it's obvious why the majority of humanity is worth nothing in these whimsical Deaf Phoenician terms.

When the illusion of the sea-oath, the female horse-drawn carriage of Jesus' grandmother, Saint Anne, who phonetically is Satan, is exposed, it will turn back into its earthy, orange form, a pumpkin, because orange is the new black (death) and it isn't worth jack. It's a Jack O' Lantern worth zero. That's why they named Orange County after Saint Anne, Satan, but the Deaf Phoenicians will never admit that.

What color is Judas' hair? Orange. Because after Judgment Day, September 23 in the yearly cycle, which corresponds to 6pm – 8pm each day, the soul, the sol, the Sun, is weighed on the scales of Libra before it is given the kiss of death by Judas, Scorpio, and then it burns in orange hues as it dies, or sets.

This is known as Fall during the yearly cycle, but it corresponds to 8pm – 10pm on the daily cycle. There are many symbols for it, from Scorpio to Judas, the White Eagle, the Serpent, the Fish, NVN (mother of Jehoshua in the Hebrew Bible, Jesus), etc. Why NVN? Because Scorpio is the water from which the spiritual fire of God, IO, Jove, JHVH, Jehovah in Sagittarius, sends his Sun to be born in the very next sign, the manger of the Goat, Capricorn.

This eleventh hour of the day in Sagittarius (10pm – 12 pm), is when God (**El**) is **even**, hence the middle of this sign corresponds to **el-even** o' clock in the **even**-ing, which culminates at **mid**-night, the Eve, the watery feminine half of the ecliptic that corresponds to night.

This part of the cycle is announced by a hallo, a shout of exultation, on Halloween, All Hallows Eve, October 31, the eve of the **el-even**th **mon**th. Some call it Samhain. '**Sam**' is the Hebrew name meaning "bright Sun," and the Sun is brightest in Leo, the House of Judah, in Summer.

The verb 'hain' means "to save, to cease, restrain, resist, be tolerant or to be patient in the face of provocation." God save Richard, the brave and strong king(dom) ('**ric/richi/rikja/rike**' + '**hard**') of the Sun, the heart of the Lion, Lionheart, the Sun in Leo.

To save is to prevent from dying, harm, or loss, but in a monetary sense, it is to avoid spending currency for the purpose of accumulation, whether that is physical money or the spiritual currencies of Time and Attention. What ore is associated with the Sun, the money of kings? Gold. To save the Sun, the gold, is to make a profit, a prophet.

Samhain thus means "to save the Sun, the gold ore, the profits of one's labor (laboratory ore) for the cold winter, and be patient in the face of provocation."

'**Hallow**,' as a verb, means "to worship, to honor as holy or consider sacred." But phonetically it is '**hollow**,' which is an adjective describing something as "insincere, false, empty, not solid, meaningless," as well as a verb that is "to make hollow." '**Ween**,' a verb, is "to think, suppose, expect, hope, intend, or **imag**ine."

This brings us to the polarities of '**Halloween**.' Phonetically, it is "to withdraw, or make hollow, one's ability to think or **imag**ine." But etymologically and literally, it means "to consecrate or honor one's ability to think or imagine, or his ability to use willpower to wean himself from certain tendencies."

Of course, we see the keystone of both arches being 'imagine,' which is composed of that ever-important word 'magi' that comes from 'imga,' indicating that each hue-man has the potential to be a wise, holy, and learned creator within the bounds of the construct that his macrocosm, God, created for him or her.

Tiamat, another goddess that corresponds to the sea, gave birth to eleven guardian monsters that surround her. If she were a sign in the Zodiac, then there would be eleven other signs or guardians left. Who else's mother is the Pure Sea? Jesus. What numerical value does the name Jesus have in basic numerology? J (1) + e (5) + s (1) + u (3) + s (1) = 11. It corresponds to simple Gematria value, which would be 74. 74 also reduces to 11 (7 +4).

This is not the be-all and end-all of Truth, but merely to show you how if someone was creating a story with these systems, you could see the value in creating names that correspond to the systems across as many scales as possible. In the cycle of the soul and Sun, December 21 is the apex of crystallized rest, just as June 21 is the apex of spiritual rest. These dates are the duality of the Zodiac, just as we've seen how the microcosm of the languages also reflects this duality.

Audio is literally a golden god, a sun-god, just like the god of the solar system and the daytime half of the daily cycle is the Sun, and the god of the seasons is Summer, and the physical god of the human anatomy is the heart. How would a dark occultist invert this knowledge? By making night the god of the daily cycle, Saturn the god of the solar system, Winter the god of the seasons, bones the god of the body, and they would make silence golden.

If the carriage of Sin-derella turning into a pumpkin symbolizes a dying Sun, then perhaps that's why they named it a pumpkin. A 'pump' is something that propels fluid (serum) or transports energy." Is that the function of God in the machine, *Deus ex machina?* As a verb, 'pump' means "to free from water or other liquid by means of a pump, to supply or inject, and to seek to elicit information from a person."

'Kin' is "of the same family, kind, or nature." Are we pumping more kin for Sin, the Moon? Are we supplying the Moon with more sera-mony, blood money, or moon-honey, by pumping kin on our honeymoons or in our sea-oath businesses known as marriages?

Is the hollowing out of the pumpkin a ritual for what is being done to us and to the minds of our kin? Are the Inversive Brethren replacing or pumping out the seeds of our imagination, our spiritual light, our existence, and then replacing them with a hallowed false candlelight that feigns illumination but is nothing more an illusion?

We sure do hallow a lot of hollow stars and idols that were created by the Hollywood of Druidic wands, and we've covered that the Druids are the Priests of Apollo, the Cult of the Sun, which is the same as the Magi of Persia and Phoenicia, as well as the Priests of Egypt and Hindoostan.

It just dawned on me as I finished writing this that it happens to coincide with the eleventh chapter of this book. This is exactly how syncromysticism works, and how you know that you are on the right path, standing in Truth, and your will is aligned with the Will of God, the Wheel of God, the TAROT, TORA, the Law, ROTA, where 'rotate' comes from, hence the Rotary Club, because it is honoring the Wheel composed of Yod, Heh, Vau, Heh, JHVH: Jehovah.

Yod is Scorpio, Heh is Aquarius, Vau is Taurus, and Heh is Leo. Scorpio is the White Eagle, Silence, Wisdom, the Serpent, the Fall, Autumn, and the procreative organs. Aquarius is Horus, John the Baptist, Baphomet, the New Age, Winter, Satan, Death, Man, and the ankles (Ankh Les, the Life). Taurus is Isis, the Moon, Spring, fertility, and the unconscious animal-mind, the cerebellum. Leo is Osiris, the Sun, Summer, Life, God, Jupiter Ammon, and the Heart. This is the Riddle of the Sphinx, known thousands of years prior to any of your modern day religions, yet so dubiously encoded in all of them.

Could it be any more obvious? When reading Ezekiel 1:4-10, he describes a vision of God as the heavens opened, and it states, "And I look, and lo, a tempestuous wind is coming from the north, the great cloud, and fire catching itself, and brightness to it round about, and out of its midst as the color of copper, out of the midst of the fire (Sun). And out of its midst is a likeness of four living creatures, and this is their appearance; a likeness of man is to them, and four faces are to each, and four wings are to each of them, and their feet are straight feet, and the sole of their feet is as a sole of a calf's foot, and they are sparkling as the color of bright brass; and hands of man under their wings—on their four sides, and their faces and their wings—are to them four; joining one unto another are their wings, they turn not round their going, each straight forward they go. As to the likeness of their faces, the face of a man (Aquarius, Horus, H) and the face of a lion (Leo, Osiris, Sun, H), toward the right are to them four, and the face of an ox (Taurus, V, Isis) on the left are to them four, and the face of an eagle (Scorpio, J) are to them four."

It's one thing to not know this information because it's never been presented to you or you've never cared enough to look into it. But after all I've given you, if you still can't see that the Zodiac is what's being described, then stop reading and give this book to someone who isn't blind, deaf, and dumb. Though Jupiter is in his house of rulership, Sagittarius, as well as the Eighth House in my natal chart, all the gifts from the giver of all good things are not enough for me to break the hex that has been placed upon you by the indoctrination factories and the television programming of the Black Magi. I can raise the dead, but I cannot raise those who willfully cut themselves off from the One.

God gave you Nature. Man rightly understood it. Corrupt men perverted it. Now they've enslaved the world for perpetual remembrance thereof by obfuscating that knowledge. So remember that the next time you spew your ignorance all over someone's work with your drive-by character assassinations. Just because you don't like someone's work or can't access it, that doesn't mean it's bad. You're a slave because you have no knowledge. If you cannot see the obvious, stop eating dead flesh as much as possible, stop drinking fluoridated water, stop putting any man-made pseudo-scientific products in your body, and for God's sake, stop getting your information from the mainstream media, your religious and institutional figures who are nothing more than Priests of Ba'al, and your know-nothing cultural Marxist "professors" who take paychecks to hollow you out like a Jack O' Lantern, so by the time you leave their Universe Cities, you don't know jack and the only thing you're prepared to be is an order-following knave.

12 THE GREAT ENUCLEATION

If one were to ride a horse bareback and without a bridle, what would there be to hold onto? The mane. One reigns over another by physically or metaphorically pulling on the mane. Removing this option is the logic behind military men shaving heads.

A 'mane' is defined as "a head of distinctively long and thick or rough hair." This is connected to the German noun 'pony,' which can mean "pony, fringe, or bangs." In English, a 'pony' refers to "something small of its kind," usually a horse. But in Indonesian, the phonetically similar 'poni' means "bangs." In Dutch, 'pony' is a noun that refers to "a pony or bangs" but also "a hobby." This can be done, with this very word, in about twenty other major languages so I'll spare you, but they are all similar. This is how connected everything is.

What position, in the world of Commerce, is the most common indicator that it is a slavery system? A 'manager.' If you answer to a manager, you are not free. A 'manager' is "a person who has control or direction of an institution, business, or of a part, division, or phase of it." Therefore, if one who has a manager is not free, then one who is a manager is also a slave because of the master-slave relationship in which both are dependent on each other.

But what is a person? In a status quo dictionary, most definitions of a 'person' will convey "a human being, adult or child, as being distinguished from an animal or thing." However, we will see, when we cover the blackest of all magick, that a 'person' is also "a corporation that has the same rights as a human being," and a 'corporation' is "an artificial person, a legal fiction or dead entity," hence its phonetic root word: 'corpse.'

The word 'person' comes from the Latin word 'persona,' which is "a mask, figure," and since actors wore masks, they showcased a different 'persona,' which is "a character, part, or person represented."

In English, the word 'persona' is "a person's perceived personality or character, their public image." Actors 'impersonate' people because they "assume or act the character of" them, which is why slaves are not really slaves. They are "human beings assuming or acting the character of a slave," hence the reason people in the legal system use the term 'bad actor.' They really mean "bad slave," or a "human being not acting like a good slave."

More often than not, you will find that a person's public 'persona' is nothing like his or her natural character beneath the mask, and this is the critical element of illusory magic: perception. In the world of Commerce, the true nature of a person, whether natural or artificial, is nearly irrelevant so long as a public 'persona' can mask it.

What is another word for 'slave' as far as the language that is concerned when your freedom is on the line, the Roman laws that you are governed by? An actor. In legalese, an 'actor' is essentially a "slave who tends to his or her master's business affairs." You will see this conveniently covered up in most legal dictionaries, but it's there as an egregore, if not as an actual definition.

When the nature of a person and a slave is enucleated, the rest of the system will be much easier to comprehend. In the 1924 7th Edition of *Jurisprudence*, which is composed of Civil Law decisions by courts, not based in Common Law, it is stated that, "In the law there may be men who are not persons; slaves, for example, are destitute of legal personality in any system, which regards them as incapable of either rights or liabilities. Like cattle, they are things and the object of rights; not persons and the subjects of them."

This entire philosophy or "science" is satanic on its face, based in moral relativism, because nowhere in Nature, the only real and authoritative system in this world, will you find a natural born slave. Therefore, in reality, there is no such thing as a slave, and thus no such thing as men who are destitute of legal personality, rights, or liabilities. This is where black magick is implemented to affect perception by creating personas, masks, where there are none.

However, in the heat of the moment, it does not necessarily matter what is real or illusory, because if someone can be made to believe in the erroneous Social Darwinism dogma, that there is such thing as a slave, and he is willing to act on his beliefs to steal freedom for a paycheck, then all the knowledge in the world will be of no use during the actual confrontation where the thief manifests the harm into the plane of effects by violating one's inherent rights through the use of coercion, whether it be physical violence or violence through Mentalism.

The status quo definition of 'actor' is "a person who acts in performance art," or simply put, "one who participates." Formally, a 'manager' was "a theatrical producer" in British lingo, therefore, if not a master, a manager could certainly be seen as a handler or a taskmaster.

Where did theater originate? Greece. The first performers were tragedians called Hypocrites. The Greek Tragedies were gospels performed during religious festivals, hence they were God-spells. This is why theater is the perfect term for them. 'Theós' means "God" in Greek, the feminine name that encompasses this spirit being Thea, but 'thea' is also "a seat in a theater," or "a viewing, seeing." 'Theater' comes from the Greek word 'theatron,' which is "a place for viewing." However, '-tron' is a Greek suffix that denotes an instrument, therefore 'thea-tron,' the origins of 'theater,' denotes "an instrument of beholding, of God, of God's Spell, the gospel, or the hex of God."

Who were these Hypocrites, these Greek tragedians? The priests, of course. What did they wear while performing tragedy and being Hypocrites? Masks, different 'personas,' the Latin word for "masks."

What is a 'hypocrite' in English? It is "a person who puts on a false appearance of virtue or religion!" In other words, a 'hypocrite' is "a person who puts on a mask, a persona, and pretends to be something that he is not," i.e., an 'actor.'

What are the priests of religions if not hypocrites? They're a bunch of silver-tongued deceivers pretending to be pious while, in the meantime, they're raping, murdering, and cannibalizing children, orchestrating mass ritual blood sacrifices known as wars, destroying and plundering nations, burning books, and eradicating whole peoples under the pretext of prophecies and service to God. They have enslaved the world with their black magick for perpetual remembrance thereof, and instead of uniting against them, the masses attack everyone who tries to point out the obvious, that the priests, the hypocrites, are waging war against humanity.

If you're not crying or laughing out loud right now, you don't appreciate the Divine Comedy of this Greek Tragedy we're stuck in. We're all a bunch of tragedian hypocrites playing the part of slaves in a theatron, a theater, a place for viewing, hence the Shakespearean expression from *As You Like It*, "All the world's a stage, and all the men and women merely players; they have their exits and their entrances; and one man in his time plays many parts."

Wipe your tears. I'm not going to leave you with the phony Phoenician Hypocrites. Let us continue to dispel the hex of the gospel, but in order to do that, we must repent in every sense of the word. The literal translation of 'μετάνοια' is not just 'repentance,' but 'metanoia,' which means "comprehending things in such a wholly different way that not only changes one's mind entirely, but also his or her inner constitution." The Great Work will not just change the way you think. It will change the way you feel and the way you behave. The Great Work will change who you are.

The chief principle, or 'main' importance, of the word 'mane' is found in the Italian word 'maneggiare,' which means "to handle, to work, to deal with," and is etymologically connected to the English word 'manage.'

This brings us back to managing the persona, the mask, of a theatrical performer, an actor, a slave, by pulling the mane of the artificial person, the legal fiction dead entity known as a corporation, that the human being has agreed to play, through willful consent or nescience, in the direction that he or she is willed to go by the manager.

This is how the horses, the whores, the prostitutes who sell themselves to the highest bidder, are corralled. That's what we do when we work for a manager. We prostitute ourselves: our minds, bodies, and souls, to engage in labor that benefits the business, the commercial activity of the artificial person, the corporation, in exchange for a paycheck.

They've herded us by pulling on our manes, to make sure we comply with their system of laws, or statutes, and if we don't, they sick their dogs, their police, their **pole-ice**, after us.

Behold, the language of the beast system is constructed by Black Magi that hijack the principles of Nature, but specifically electricity, magnetism, and water. As Mark Passio explains, the pole-ice are frozen on the pole of consciousness, thwarting all who try to ascend it including themselves.

What degree does water unfreeze at and become liquid? 33° Fahrenheit, which corresponds to the degree of enlightenment in Freemasonry, as well as Golgotha, which is the skull, the 33rd level of the spine where the Cristos, the Christ, is raised into the cerebrum. To live at a level of consciousness that is anything less than this is to be frozen, or on ice.

The **pole-ice** pets follow orders from those who are off ice: **off-icers**. The **pole-ice** order-followers spiritually and physically charge others with crimes so that they can arrest them. An 'arrest' is a "seizure or forcible restraint to deprive a person of his or her sovereignty." An 'arrester' is "a person or thing who arrests."

However, an 'arrester' is also "a device to protect electrical power systems from over-voltage." What kind of volts does the **pole-ice** state protect the Black Magi against? **Re-volts**, surges of powerful wavelike rises or sudden swells of the seas, the current-seas, which correspond to the way consciousness, time, and attention work.

People say that the Truth hurts. This is because the Truth 'hertz.' A 'hertz' is "a unit used for measuring the frequency of sound waves, electromagnetic waves." Nothing activates an unconscious mind as effectively as the Truth. This corresponds to the alternating current of the sine wave, the sin of Eve as Santos Bonacci so eloquently correlates it, which is how electrical energy is distributed in accordance to the Cycles of Necessity. The reason that the Truth is the most powerful force in this world is because it cannot be destroyed. It is an absolute frequency that distributes all energy in this universe. There is only Truth. Everything else is an illusion.

The primary pitfall that those who **re-volt** fall into is the use of violence. The **pole-ice** know how to bring **just-ice** to violent **re-volters**, therefore, do not use violence and you will avoid their circuit courts, which are nothing more than a path between two or more points along which electrical current of the soul can be carried in order to deliver the **re-volters** to **just-ice**. Did you think that the Roman Cult named the agency responsible for enforcing over 400 of its federal statutes regarding Homeland Security with the acronym ICE by coincidence (Immigration and Customs Enforcement)? If so, then this book was named after you.

In the circuit courts, plaintiffs bring charges. As an adjective, 'plain' means "clear to the mind, evident, manifest, or obvious," but as a verb, it means "to complain," which comes from the Latin words 'planctus' and 'plangere,' meaning "to beat or strike in mourning or grief." As a verb or noun, the word 'tiff' is associated with "a petty quarrel," which is "an angry dispute or altercation."

A 'plaint' is "a lamentation, wail, protest, or complaint," which is why in legalese a 'plaint' is "an action, real or personal, in writing, made by the plaintiff to a court, asking for redress of a grievance."

As seen, a 'plaintiff' is "someone who brings obvious and clear charges to courts that manifest petty altercations," thus enabling the court system to generate electrical currents, or currency. But how does one avoid being shocked by the charges of the plaintiff? How does he ground the charges, if you will, to avoid electrocution by the judge of the circuit courts? After all, if the charges are serious enough, one could find himself in an electric chair.

If you are a component that helps close, or complete, the circuit, then you will get charged and electrocuted. So in order to avoid being charged, you must avoid the behavior that people can claim as pretext to make you participate in closing the circuit.

The primary function of pole-ice, liars (lawyers), judges, circuit courts, and anything else involved with man's laws, is to dupe people into thinking they must become part of the circuit and close it. Those who are grounded stand their ground, but also stand on the ground, the land, and not the sea, which is the law of Commerce that all modern courts operate in: Maritime Admiralty Law; Roman Civil Law. The courts mirror Nature. It is unwise to be in courts ruled by the laws of water while being charged, just as it is unwise to be in water when electric charges are present. Water conducts electricity. Since 'city' means 111 (ci (101) + ty (10)), a trine of this would be 333: 'tri-city.' 333 is the number of Choronzon, so to elect 333 (elect-tricity) is to elect Choronzon. Perhaps you should keep your affairs on land, where it isn't as easy for the Black Magi to elect that mighty devil from the abyss.

They who stand in the absolute Truth do not understand (stand under) any of the charges, and thus ground the charges to nullify the effects of electric shock, hence parents using the term **'grounded'** to convey a long-term punishment to children that usually involves stripping the child of privileges.

When a citizen-ship is grounded, it has run ashore, either through ignorant navigation that left it in shallow water, or intentional mismanagement for the sake of pillaging its cargo. Someone who has already been grounded is no longer a threat in terms of the ability to shock, which is why **'grounded'** also means "to be sensible, down-to-earth, on land," and is also why a child can claim to be grounded as a reason for not being able to play.

In terms of electricity, the ground can be used as a return path to complete a circuit. By facilitating this process through technology, it makes the return path unnecessary, and thus protects the environment from hazards like fire or other electrical damage that can cause fatalities.

However, this language existed long before man discovered the nature of electricity, so where did **'circuit court'** derive its name? In terms of the law, who traveled the land, completing a circuit from the kingdom to the countryside, hearing cases and making decisions that would protect the system of human slavery from hazards? The judges. They used to ride on pre-set paths known as circuits, thus the terms circuit judges and circuit courts were born.

What did the judges ride on in the 13th Century? Horses and carriages, because they are **el-ected** whores and the preserved flesh, the aged car, of the archons. They settle disputes, plain tiffs, so that the **el-ectric** system of rule is upheld, in exchange for a more comfortable existence in that system, a preservation of flesh, of material world self. This self-preservation is the first major tenet in the ideology of Satanism.

If the charges are serious enough, and one is found guilty in a circuit court, he or she may end up a prisoner in a prison. But where in a prison is the prisoner stored? A cell. And a group of prisoners are stored on a cellblock that furnishes electric current for whoever owns the prison. Why? Because they were charged with a crime and found guilty of it. Now they are grounded cells, which is why a cell that furnishes electric current is also called a battery, because prisons are batteries, large groups of people that are used together to generate electrical currency profits for corporations that own them, who are in turn owned by the Crown, which is owned by the Vatican, which is owned by the Black Magi.

The slavery of the prison system is an act of battery in itself, because 'battery' is "a harmful or offensive touching of another, usually through assault." This is why warships are worshipped, because they have batteries, artillery guns, and they put the fear of God in us because they are used to assault (batter) other militaries and nations. A citizen-ship without batteries has no ability to defend itself, and thus no respect from those would engage in battery (assault) of that unarmed citizen-ship. This is why the second amendment shall not be infringed, and anyone who attempts to infringe upon it should be dealt with in any way one sees fit.

This type of person, who would infringe upon one's rights to own and travel with his or her property, may be disposed of with zero karmic consequences of Natural Law, God's law, for if they are not dealt with, we will become their prisoners. But what is a prisoner? Through word-splitting, 'prisoner' can be separated as 'pri' + 'son' + 'er.'

Phonetically, 'pri' is also 'pry,' which is "an inquisitive person." Those who destroyed and enslaved the world on behalf of the Catholic Church and the Vatican called their crusade 'The Inquisition,' because they were also connected to the 'Pry-Sun,' the prison, the 'Priory of Sion.'

A 'son' is "a male descendent," but phonetically it is a 'sun,' which is both "a self-luminous heavenly body" and "heat and light from a sun (electricity)." We've noted that 'er' is 'err' through Green Language, which is "to lead astray in thought or belief."

The spirit whirled in the word 'prisoner' is "an inquisitive person whose energy, light, and electricity have been led astray, or trapped, and imprisoned in a cell, a battery, and as such, has become the ore of the prison: prison-ore."

This is done, among many other ways, through Trapezoidal hexes and sigils, hence the Order of the Trapezoid, which later became a governing body of the Church of Satan. Satanism, and all other collectives that embody the dark occult, invert everything that pertains to the Divine Will of Creation.

The symbol of a circuit historically corresponds to that of a cycle and completion. It looks like a circle, because electricity, like animals and humans, 'races' around circuits, which is "to run, move, or go swiftly" along a pre-constructed path of necessity amidst, or against, other conscious beings. We are the electricity of God, racing away from and back to our Creator on spiral tracks of involution and evolution.

To conceptualize how this symbolism is perverted, I bow to the greatness of Mark Passio, who I heard speak while I was writing this section of the book, and the syncromysticism only lines up with the Truth we're conveying to you. It only confirms that we are in fact serving God, the Angels, the daemons, and all the other sentient beings that exist in the upper Realms of Spirit who are fed up with the degraded Black Magi who invoke them for selfish gains in this world.

Whether this is his writing or someone else's, I heard it from the voice of Mark as he spoke, "In Satanism, the Trapezoid represents imbalanced, ego-driven consciousness and identification purely with the physical self. It is considered a perversion of the divine shape, the Circle, since its angles total 360 degrees (just like the Zodiac). In its Satanic connotation, the Trapezoid is considered a soul trap, symbolizing going around in circles of base consciousness. LaVeyan Satanists use Trapezoidal altars in many of their rituals."

Does this seem like a stretch to your imagination? Re-search images of one of the most Satanic governing bodies known to man, the United Nations, and describe the shape of its meditation room: a Trapezoid. This is because the UN is a body of the satanic Roman Cult.

Next, look at the shape of the coffin of that Dagon-imitating demon known as John Paul II. What shape is it? A Trapezoid.

Purge the incredulous snarky remarks you make of me in your mind and under your breath, because your 'prison' comes from the Old French word 'prisun,' which is derived from the Latin word 'pensio,' meaning "a capturing."

They captured your soul with a 'pension.' What do people say when their photo is captured? "Cheese," because that shot was money, the money shot, and you're gonna make that cheddar, because business is commerce and commerce is sex, so they're fucking you good and hard out of your sovereignty from the House of 'Congress,' which is also another word meaning "sex," located on a hill named after Capitoline Hill in Rome.

God's not coming to save you from yourself. Jesus isn't coming to save you. Buddha's not coming to save you. Muhammad's not coming to save you. Krishna isn't coming to save you. No one is coming to save you. You're here to realize the real lies with your real eyes so that you can take re-sponsibilty for yourself and re-spond by taking up the service to Truth. You save yourself by serving the Creator and aligning with the laws of morality.

Where did they put the most demonic soul trap hex that's ever graced the earth? On the back of the world's reserve currency. And they put the Eye of Providence above it, indicating that they are going to cap that pyramid and sever the entire race from God in a mass ritual of global self-deification. I guarantee at some point in your life, you've had some of those black magick IOU debt notes known as the United States One Dollar Bill and been foolish enough to think they were money. You thought you were in possession of them, but it's them who possessed you.

That's because all of you religious folks worship Ba'al, Bel, Bull, the Sun, but you were never curious enough to know what you were doing. You just kicked back on your circuit of spiritual involution, believed the stories of the Priestcraft Sorcerers despite the obvious impossibilities, and assumed those guiding your experience loved you, were well-meaning, knowledgeable, and Truthful. Then you woke up one day and found yourself to be a Roman slave. Little did you know they were having sex with children and murdering them in ritual sacrifices. Don't ever confuse love with knowledge or morality. They have nothing to do with each other. Yes, Ies, you can love someone who is a bad person that sacrifices his or her conscience to steal freedom for a paycheck. That suffering is the price to pay for your ignorance. This place is not hell. The suffering you experience is from the divine mechanism of the Creator, teaching you that you suffer because you violate the Natural Law of this world.

That's why slavery is being manifested, and you can't vote it away, you can't ask for someone else to re-present you and absorb your karma, and you can't pass your bullshit, billshit, bailshit, belshit, bolshit, bylshit, ballshit, baalshit, onto someone else. There is consequence for the violation of Natural Law, which is why you see scales in the Trapezoid. God has a sense of humor. Know it. Imagine if you had the power to filter your own cancerous cells at will.

Don't follow us. Don't believe us. Don't serve us. Take up your cross, your conscious mind, and serve Truth so you can eradicate this demonic infestation that has ravaged our paradisiacal world. This construct is perfect. It is not a prison like the Inversive Brethren view it as. Do not subscribe to that belief. This place was created for you to learn how to live in harmony with the Will of Creation. Anyone who doesn't know that hasn't trodden upon the Path of Truth and lacks the most common of all sense.

13 THE VAULT OF HEAVEN

In addition to Chaos Sorcery, there are many other ways a being can be de-lighted, de-sired, and have his or her soul trapped. Ironically, another technique that is rampant in the entertainment industry also corresponds with or-ange, a color associated with the Sun and the House of Nassau.

There are far better works than this book to delve into this particular subject, but this type of sorcery was declassified as Project MKUltra (Manufacturing Killers Utilizing Lethal Tradecraft Requiring Assassination) in the 1970's. Its name may have also been a play on 'mind,' the German word for 'control,' which is 'kontrolle,' the designation of 'ultra' (by the British) as the most secret classified of material during WWII, and the project's association with Nazi scientists from Operation Paperclip, which would make it the most secret mind-control technique. As we've covered, 'mind' comes from 'Min,' which is symbolical of the Moon.

Without digressing too much, Project MKUltra evolved into Monarch programming, the primary function of which is trauma-based mind-control through the implementation of paraphernalia, psychiatric and psychological abuse, hypnotism, sensory deprivation, electroshock, ritual sex abuse, and other forms of trauma, for the sake of creating dissociative identities, alter-egos, within the same subject, that can be activated by triggers, from phrases to other programmed cues, that will evoke the desired alter within the subject without any of the other alters knowing about it, creating Manchurian candidates that have unknowingly done the bidding of their handler, master, or archon, their one ruler: a monarch.

To be so naïve as to think there isn't a spiritual component to this is as grave a mistake as one could make, and just to satisfy the Deaf Phoenicians, we'll prove it. The Latin word 'psyche' means "animating spirit," and it came from the Greek word 'psykhe,' which is "the soul, mind, spirit; breath; life, one's life, the entity which occupies, animates, and directs the body," but also the "departed soul, spirit or ghost." In Ancient Greek, the symbol for 'psykhe' was a moth or a *butterfly*. Thus the very nature of Monarch programming is not just programming the mind, the psyche, but also the *soul* of the victim.

Splitting the psyche into multiple personalities, especially through black magick rituals, enables the conjurer to not only create a demon, a divided one, but also to invite other demonic entities to possess and feed off of each alter, something that we've previously covered in terms of obsession and willful desire. Some of the alters in the victim may be aware of each other, but some of the more innocent alters may have no idea that the other depraved ones exist.

How else did you think these multi-generational Satanic families were sustaining their power for thousands of years throughout every culture that's ever existed? A good business model? No. They program their own, and they even kill their own, the ones who refuse to go along with the hive-mind agenda. No one is born that depraved. Even those born into these families have the spark of God in them, and were they raised right, they'd grow up to be moral and never participate in this rape of humanity.

Abuse is what creates the psychopath. Empathy, care, must be cremated. Why do you think they are so obsessed with bloodlines and eugenics? Some of these covens are so strict that if you marry outside of the bloodlines, you are cut off from the generational wealth.

At some point one has to grow up and stop using the logic of a child if he or she is to comprehend what is really going on in this world. It is not difficult to determine who is under Monarch programming. The symbols are everywhere. Simply re-search which celebrities are mocked, and marked, by moth and butterfly symbolism.

If we split the word 'monarch,' we see through 'mono-' and 'archon' that it means "one ruler, master or lord." Therefore 'monarchy' is "rulership of one." However, not once have we been satisfied with the mythological authority of the status quo.

On its face, we see that 'monarch' is also 'mon' + 'arch.' Since 'mon-' is also a prefix denoting the "Moon," and an 'arch' is "something bowed or curved," as well as "a gateway having a curved head," we see that 'monarch' is also the "arch of the Moon," the "Moon's arch."

As a verb, 'arch' is "to cover with a vault," and as previously unearthed, Vau is symbolical of Taurus. Which heavenly body is exalted in Taurus? Isis, the Moon. As an adjective, 'arch' describes something as being "mischievous, cunning, and sly," but also "superior, expert," because it comes from Greek origins, and so 'arch' is also a noun for a "chief, leader, or ruler."

As previously covered, Taurus is also symbolic of the 'cerebellum,' the seed of war, the unconscious animal-mind of instinct, as this is the abode of the most cunning intellect of the animal plane, and thus of the Black Magi.

The element associated with Taurus is Earth, where the dead are buried, and since Vau is Taurus, it only makes sense that a 'vault' is also "a burial chamber." It is also "an arched structure and an underground chamber reserved for storage and safekeeping, especially such a place as a bank."

As a verb, 'vault' means "to leap or spring over something." What season is Taurus in the peak of? Spring. It is right in the middle of the 90° angle formed by Aries and Cancer, and it marks the process in the soul's evolution where it longs to regenerate and unite with the Higher Self, and once complete, it passes through the Moon to merge in eternal love on the plane of Atma (according to Buddhists.) How appropriate it is then, that Taurus is the keystone in the arch between Aries and Cancer, the vault of Spring.

'V' is the Moon (Taurus; Vau), 'Au' is gold, 'L' is El (God; Saturn; the Angel of Life and Death, of Light and Darkness), and 't' is the Cross of Matter on which the Son, the Sun, is crucified in the skull, or Golgotha. The Cycle of Necessity, the sojourn of the soul through Israel, the solar system, of erecting the starry Temple of

Solomon, is encapsulated in this word, 'v-au-l-t' (the Cross of the Solar System, of Israel; Isis-Ra-El; Sol-o-Mon; the Moon-Sun-Saturn-Cross; the Cross of Day and Night, of Life and Death, of Summer and Winter, and of Spirit and Matter).

Cancer, June 21, is the keystone in the North, the Arch of Day, of Summer, of Life, which is ruled by the Moon, and this arch spans from the East, Aries (March 21) to the West, Libra (September 23). This is the Gate of Heaven, the house of physical conception, the formation and fertilization of Aries, the Lamb of God, the Word, the seed. This is the Sun's highest degree in the ecliptic, hence the commencement of the Summer, the peak of which is ruled by the Lion of Judea, Leo, Herod the King, the Heart, and it marks the baptism of Mithra, the purification by Fire, the Pyrrhic dance. The longest days and shortest nights of the year occur here.

Capricorn, December 21, is the keystone in the Arch of the Night, of Winter, of Death, which is ruled by Saturn, and this arch spans from the West, Libra (September 23; Judgment Day), through Winter, the South, and back to the Vernal Equinox of Aries, March 21, completing the cycle at the end of Pisces. This is the Sun's lowest degree in the ecliptic, marked by the longest nights and shortest days of the year. These are the Gates of Deluge, the Flood, the purification by Water. This is where John the Baptist appears out of the wilderness, the Baptism of Wisdom (Metis), the Baphomet. This is the House of Spiritual conception, because it is in the arch of Capricorn, the manger of the Goat, that the Sun begins its ascent back to the Gate of Heaven, or is born.

Berosus, the Chaldean priest of Bel at Babylon, wrote that there were ten kings before the flood. Which sign of the Zodiac does the Gate of Deluge occur? The tenth sign, after which Oannes, a half-man and half-fish creature, came out of the Red Sea and preached to the first race of men in Babylon.

They called him John the Dipper. It is important to note that Berosus is a priest of Bel, of Ba'al, Apollo, which is what the Druids are. He was a sun-worshipper, so it should come as no surprise that this half-man and half-fish named Oannes is eerily similar to Dagon, whom the pope imitates: Saturn, the ruler of the Gate of Deluge, of Flood: Capricorn. Also note the similarity of Jesus, with 'sus' also meaning "fish" and "swine" in Latin, which ironically is in Bero-sus.

But who is this Chaldean fish-god Oannes? According to Reverend Robert Taylor, the name comes from the Ammonian radicals—I–ON, ES, which means "the Sun, the Being, the Fire; the name of God, the Sun—that is, of the Son in the sign of Aquarius, who pours his stream of water into the mouth of the great Southern Fish, and hence became Jonas, swallowed by the fish, the Matsya Avatar, or first incarnation of Veeshnu, in the form of a fish, of India, the Jonas of the Phoenicians, the Ιωάννης (I-oannes) of the Greeks, Janus, the first of the Great Gods of the Romans, and January, the first of the Great Months of the whole world."

The Greek name for 'John,' that is similar to Jonah's name in the Greek Old Testament, is Ιωνας. Thus, it is quite obvious, since January coincides with Aquarius, that in the Language of the Birds, 'Jan-uary' is in fact 'John-uary.' He appears from the wilderness because the constellation Aquarius finally appears above the horizon at this time of year.

When is the festival of the nativity of John the Baptist? June 24th. John said, "I am not the Christ, but that I am having been sent before him; Him it behoveth to increase, and me to become less. He who from above is coming is above all; he who is from the earth, from the earth he is, and from the earth he speaketh; he who from the heaven is coming is above all."

Why? Because John the Baptist, Aquarius, appeared from the wilderness above the horizon in John-uary, and after the Summer Solstice, from the days of John (June 24-25), his birthday being so close to the Sun's highest point in the sky (the mountain of the Lord), June 21st, the days grow shorter and shorter as the constellation of Aquarius dips back below the horizon till late August, thus it suits him, or behoveth him, to become less. After December 25, it will suit Jesus, the Sun, to increase.

Is the grand picture beginning to formulate in your mind? They've told you all along. The Father is the Son, but also the Sun. They are one and the same. The allegorical story of the scriptures is encoded with the science of the stars and the soul. This is how the ruling priest-kings preserve the sacred science while keeping it occulted from the profane. What better place to hide something than in plain sight? There is nothing that confuses the masses more, and nothing that causes more chaos and division than priestcraft sorcery. It is by far the best form of magick to conquer people.

What did the Knights Templar confess to worshipping while being tortured during The Inquisition? The head of Baphomet, the Baptism of Metis (Wisdom), because not only is it symbolical of John the Baptist's skull, but also because they did in fact learn how to shrink heads and other various magick from an Arabic book *Ghayat al-Hakim* known as *The Goal of the Sage*, also known in Latin as *Picatrix*.

So go ahead, pick a trick. It makes no difference. It's all sun worship, or dare I say sun **whore**ship, from the pentagrams of Satanism, and Zeus Ammon, to the Cross of Jesus. They are hypocritical sides of the same fraudulent coin minted by bad actors who think they have a divine right to rule you on a carousel of fear that's spinning wildly out of control in a Hegelian dialectic fueled by ignorant carnies.

They're laughing at you as you fight with each other over the same bullshit, like sunfish in a fishbowl thinking the sea is at hand, too cloddish to figure out what's really going on. Remain as indignant as you'd like, it won't alter the Truth that you're still whoring out your souls to these Black Magi whose man-made religions have nothing to do with the Will of God, the Wheel of God, other than being a cheap imitation of our Creator's glorious science.

The Summer Solstice is a 90° square from the Vernal Equinox on the Zodiac. John said, "In the beginning was the Word, and the Word was with God, and the Word was God." The Word is Aries, the great I am, the seed, and John is *the Voice.*

Knowing that John is also Baphomet, who has a Goat-head that corresponds to the Gate of Deluge: Capricorn (the Fish-Goat), hopefully you can now appreciate why he is so important to the music industry and the spoken word of spellcraft, hence the occult meaning of the reality singing show by the same name: *the Voice.* This is also why you see so much Saturnine symbolism in that industry as well.

In John 1:23, he said, "I am a *voice* of one crying in the wilderness." What do singers, the ones who **sin-g/sin-gee** (to make a sin right), take to heal their voices, *the voice?* Wild honey. The ancient Arabs depicted Leo as a Bee, which they called the 'honey-fly.' As we've covered, '**Sam**' means "Sun," so in Judges 14:14, the riddle of Samson, "Out of the eater came forth meat, and out of the strong came forth sweetness" refers to the Sun moving past Leo. Samson is Sam's Son, the Son of God, the Son of Sam, the Sun of On (Heliopolis).

John is beheaded by a younger Herod. When is the festival of the beheading of John the Baptist? August 29th. As John decreases, the Sun in Leo is still the hottest time of year, and on August 29th, at 4:30pm in the blazing hot afternoon, Sadalsuud, the brightest star in Aquarius and the left shoulder of John, rises above the horizon while the rest of his body remains below it.

Which constellation rises and opposes Aquarius at 2:30am on August 30th each year? Look at the Zodiac. Which sign is opposite of Aquarius? It is none other than the constellation of Leo: King Herod. The fixed Air of Aquarius feeds the fixed Fire of Leo.

Cancer, the sign of cardinal water, is the ocean of the Great Mother, the Pure Sea or Virgin Mary, ruled by the fertile Moon. The Moon carries the light from the Sun, the Seed of the High Born (Aries), and the Great Bear of Ursa Major, the Big Dipper, is a constellation in this decan of Cancer. It becomes the Car of Osiris, the Ark of Moses, the Good Ship Min, the Good Shipment, sailing south to God's Land, because south of Cancer is Capricorn, where the Sun is born, but also south is the path through the gates of heaven that consist of the locations of the equinoxes and solstices (Aries, Cancer, Libra, and Capricorn).

Cancer is Tammuz, the Sun that is slain in June after the solstice. This is the Cross of Tammuz that corresponds to the 't' in the word '**vault**,' as '**solstice**' means "sun still" ('**sol**' + '**sistere**'). The far distant temple that Ezekiel was taken to in spirit is Jerusalem: Aries (the gate in the east that none doth go in because Jehovah came in by it). And then he is brought to the front of the house of Jehovah by the way of the north gate: Cancer (Ezekiel 44:4).

This is the Will of God, the Wheel of God, contained in the Zodiac, the Tarot, and the Torah. Cancer was symbolized as the scarab in Egypt, which also represented resurrection and rebirth, just like the cicada did to the Roman and Greek Priests of Apollo (Sun). Which sign is at the keystone of the Royal Arch in Freemasonry? Cancer. The beetle would lay its eggs in dung, push it backwards up a sandy slope, and then let it roll down to compress. Though seemingly silly, the ball of dung was compared to the fiery ball of the Sun.

It doesn't take a genius to figure out the mechanisms of men. But it takes knowledge to dissect where everything comes from. Like an owl, one must train him(her)self to see in the absence of light, and from a superior perspective.

And who could rule the Gate of Deluge, the Earth, in Capricorn but the God of Seeds, of Sowing, the Lord of the Rings, the black fertile soil, the lead of the Earth, the lunar god of fertility also known as Min, the maker of gods and men? Saturn. To the Greeks, he was Pan. Why is this so confusing? Because it is not to be taken literally. Min is also Osiris, Amun, Ptah, Sokari, Harmachus (Horus), because the father is the son, the Sun. This is why Min was also associated with Leo and Taurus, the Bull, because they correspond to the Sun and Moon.

But isn't Min the Moon? No. During those days the Moon was Isis. However, Min was a lunar god, and the Akkadians modeled Sin after him, which was their god of the Moon. It's all a bunch of Black Magi encoding the same sacred science into the stories of their choice. In Latin, they called her Luna, and in Greek, she was Selena. In Hebrew, she was known as Lebanah.

It is vital that we do not get caught up trying to make sense of the stories through literal interpretation, as though they are historical accounts, but instead see them for the Truth of the stars and seasons that they carry as their spirit, their psykhe, their seed.

The arches are the vaults that seal us for safekeeping. As a verb, 'vault' is also "to leap or spring over something, the leap of a *horse*," because we are the whores that ask, when the archons tell us to jump, "How high?"

To be 'over the Moon' is to be "extremely happy." Well, no shit; ever see an animal get out of confinement and see the God-made wilderness for the first time? We quite literally, not figuratively, must get "over the Moon" to be happy and free. This is the occult meaning, within the keystone of Cancer (because the Moon rules Cancer), that holds the moon-arch, the Monarch, together.

Is our ruler the Moon? Is that our Queen Bee? Have we been

buried at the bottom of a watery firmament and sealed in a starry vault for safekeeping at a cosmic bank? Or is all this symbolism the magi's way of teaching us that, to spiritually evolve and be happy, we must get over money? It was 11:11pm as I wrote this sentence, so hopefully it'll activate you to manifest a way out of this sentence and look to a new beginning.

14 CAPUT ALL

Who is the one that sentences the prison-ore? A judge. What does a judge sit on? The bench. What is a bench? It's "a bank of the earth," from the Proto-Germanic word 'bankiz.' The judge sits on the bank of the earth, and to approach the bench is to approach the bank.

As previously stated, commerce is sex, so when you go to a court, to play a game of commerce, someone is bound to get fucked. This is why 'bench' is also a verb that means "to take out of the game," because the judge is the one who takes the prison-ore off the court and out of the game, and then sticks him or her into a cell, a battery, and makes the prison-ore become dead-ore, a debtor, who has to pay his debt to society.

Make no mistakes while observing Truth. One needn't be in a prison to be a prison-ore, just like a wild animal needn't be in a cage to be enslaved on a farm or zoo. Perhaps nowhere is this more apparent than in the world of entertainment.

As established, a 'cell' is a "battery." The word 'ebb' is a noun that refers to "flowing backward or away; decline or decay, the point of decline; the flowing back of the tide as the water returns to *the sea*." A 'writ' is "a written document under seal and in the sovereign's name."

Filing under seal protects something, usually documents, from being viewed by the public, but as covered in the previous chapter, the verb 'arch' is "to cover something with a vault," or in other words, "to close tightly, fasten, bind, or block so as to prevent escape or entry," the very definition of 'seal.' A 'seal' is also "a symbol that evidences authority," as well as "something that keeps a thing a secret," like a vow.

The suffix '-y' means "characterized by or inclined to." Put all of these phonetics together and the word 'celebrity' is formed. Another name for a celebrity is a 'star.' Most service-to-self entities dream of becoming stars. To my fellow servants of Truth, do not accept these terms, for the stars are what they use to seal you off from your Creator. They themselves are sealed by a vow of silence, and sealed by the occult symbols of their masters.

Through Green Language, a 'cell-ebb-writ-y,' in addition to being "a famous or celebrated person," is also "a battery in a sovereign's name that is sealed beneath a starry vault, whose energy current is in decline and being transferred back to the sea." Which sea? The lunar sea, the sea of stars: the Holy See. Come on, kid. We're gonna make you a star. You'll have tons of fun and make a lot of **mooney.**

A person cannot become a star unless he or she is willing to loan his or her celebrity to the Black Magi. A celebrity is just an illusion, a shell of a person, a mask of a hypocrite, a battery in a sovereign's name. Just like the birth certificate.

Do you remember being born? Do you remember agreeing to create a legal fiction Cestui Que Vie trust that is phonetically identical to your name but spelled in block capital letters? The document may surely exist, but do you remember entering into that contract and being sealed under Maritime Admiralty Law by it?

A birth certificate is really a berth certificate. A 'berth' is "a shelf-like sleeping space, as on a ship," because you are a lost soul on a citizen ship, a Roman slave ship, lost at sea, so the Vatican has declared itself to own everything about you, through a trust, till you return on land and declare your sovereignty.

To be 'berthed' is to be "docked, anchored, or moored," but in this case, your vessel (body) is berthed in a depraved system of slavery, and according to the Black Magi, your 'berth,' your "position, rank, place, listing, or role," in that system is a slave.

The symbol for spirit is the trine with its apex upright. The two-dimensional representation looks like a pyramid (middle fire). As explained previously, through the Trapezoidal pyramid on the Great **Seal** of the United States One-Dollar bill, to cap something's middle fire, its pyramid, is to sever it from source and imprison it.

What is the middle fire? The heart, hence the reason the Sun pulses, because it corresponds to Leo and '**courage**,' the etymology of which comes from the Old French word '**corage**,' meaning "heart, innermost feelings; temper," which came from the Latin word '**cor**' that also meant "heart." Courage is the "rage of the heart," but also the "age (aeon) of the heart," which is why it is associated with both bravery and wrath.

If there ever will exist human freedom, it most certainly will be in an Age of Righteous Indignation that attains a level of enlightenment and bestows upon the people the courage to serve Truth and use the word of all power against those who would claim to have authority over them, and that is the lost word '**No.**' When's the last time any of you heard someone shout "no" at their boss, or at another figure of "authority?" My point exactly. You'll know when a true mass enlightenment of the population has occurred when the word of all power is ringing through the halls of power.

Till then, expect the middle fire in all beings to be capped with capital, '**cap-it-all**,' block letters of legal fiction corporate names: corpses; trusts. That's how the debt (the dead) is settled. The bay-bee debtor, dead-ore, is liquidated and made into merchandise through the birth certificate.

Welcome to sin, the Moon. You were born into it, and you will die in it. To '**liquidate**' is also "to get rid of or do away with, to break up with," hence they also liquidate your partnership with the Divine Spark of God through the birth certificate ritual, where they take the imprint of the baby's sole, its soul, and trap it in hell by its heel. They seal it with a seal.

All the mockery you can muster against me will not break the hex. I did not do this to you. I'm merely the argentum vivum that's giving you the required knowledge to defeat the Inversive Brethren. It makes no difference to me if you water these seeds or not.

Should you continue to ignore that which is before you, it will quicken your fate with Choronzon. I have no more of an interest in your destiny than the heart of a body has in the destiny of a hemorrhoid; I view the profane as merely being a pain in the cosmic ass that will be removed one way or another, and it has nothing to do with me. My only point of contention is that the reason you are so ignorant and unlearned is that you were programmed to be that way from the beginning, so if I can help it, I'd like to arouse the Divine Spark of the Will of Creation inside of you, so that you can at least have a chance, a freewill choice in the coming chaos. You will either serve Truth and help end slavery, or you will resist Truth and be destroyed by it. I've already declared victory in the honor of God. I couldn't care less if this race destroys itself or ascends to the next octave. I know where I'm going. My guardians and I are doing what is permissible within the bounds of morality, the rules of Natural Law.

You came out of your mother's berth/birth canal after her water broke, because you are a liquid asset to those who claim to be your masters. You are stock, livestock, and if you come from a wealthy family, you are preferred stock because you are worth a lot of moon-honey.

But what is stock? 'Stock' is "a supply of goods kept on hand for sale (sail) to customers by a merchant," which is a sea chanter. Why? Because 'mer' is a French (and Old French) word that pertains to "the sea." This is found in many languages, from Latin's 'mare,' to Finnish's 'meri.' It's also connected to the Hungarian word 'mer,' which is "to have courage to do something," and also to the Icelandic word 'meri,' which is a "mare, a female horse."

We see how 'mer' not only pertains to 'marriage,' but also the Virgin Mary, the pure sea, because in Italian, 'mero' is "pure, simple." Perhaps this connects it to the word 'merry,' as a common expression around the Winter Solstice is "Merry Christmas," a holiday that has more to do with consumerism and commerce these days than its beautiful shamanic origins.

We see the use of 'mer' in creatures that pertain to the sea, as in mermaids, but we also see it in words like mercy (mer-sea) and merchandise, and even in the sacred mountain in Hindu cosmology, Mount Meru. In French, the word 'dise' means "to say; to tell." A 'mer-chant' is "a chant of the sea sung by a chanter of the sea," and this is reflected in the word 'mer-chant-dise,' which is "to say, tell, sing, or vocalize sea chants."

We have allowed them, through the consent of golden silence, to turn us into merchandise, stock that is alive: livestock. They have made us into capital through the use of capital block seals, sigils of legal fiction black magick.

In Latin, 'caput' means "head" and is also a noun meaning "the greatest authority." In the dark occultist ideology, the greatest authority has the right to control. 'Caput-all' thus means "to control all by right," hence the ideology of the Divine Right of Kings, Deus Meumque Jus: "God and My Right."

What is the All? The All is mind: mente. Thus, 'caput-all' means "to control mind, everything, the All." Where else have we seen this? 'Gubernare' + 'mente' also means "to control mind, the All." This is the commerce of Government.

Capital is the current-sea, the liquid asset medium of exchange for the sea-chanters to mercilessly control everything with. 'Head' has several meanings as a verb: "to lead, outdo, direct the course of," and also "to take the head off; decapitate; behead." The Eye of Providence is the cerebrum, which is in the head. So when they cap that middle fire, the pyramid, they are also beheading you with that black magick Trapezoid sigil.

Through this chaos sorcery, the merchants get you to make transactions with them. Like sirens, they lure you with their sea-chants, their deals, and the best way for them to make a trance-action is to put items on sale so that they can make a sale (sail) by selling you their wares, their mer-chant-dise.

What happens during a sale involving currency that is made of fiat paper notes or digital ether? Someone discharges debt. 'Dis' is "a Roman underworld god," where the dead (debt) go. When one discharges debt, he has elected to charge Dis with his electricity by directing his charges to Dis. In Scandinavian mythology, 'dis' is "a female deity, especially one promoting fertility," the plural of which is 'disir' (dee-seer). How ironic, given its phonetic affinity to 'desire,' which we've already established as "severing a sovereign from his procreative essence."

But if we look at 'seer,' it's "a person who sees, but also who prophesies." Therefore, a seer is a prophet, and to 'de-seer' (disir) is "to remove one's ability to see, to unload a profit (prophet)."

To 'discharge' is "to relieve oneself of an obligation or burden, to remove," but also "to send forth." Thus, when we give payment to a merchant, we lose or give up a charge of our el-ectricity, our current-sea, and send the charge forth to Dis, the god of the underworld. However, the positive polarity of this transaction is that, since we use IOU Federal Reserve Notes, when we send them forth we also relieve our obligations and free ourselves from their burden. At any moment, the IOUs can be gotten rid of, the same way paper and digital currencies can be devalued, changed, or destroyed by those who believe in them. An ounce of gold or silver remains an ounce of metal regardless if anyone sees value in them. Their properties were forged by Nature and will exist independently of mankind till the death of this world.

The conscious solution, the wholution that breaks the hex of dishonest money, is to discharge worthless IOUs to someone who believes they are worth something in exchange for gold and silver, or other tangible assets that preserve wealth and can be held in allodium. Convert imaginary units into gold and silver. It's that simple. The more people that do this, the more they will take back all of the real property in this world and return the worthless slave notes to the bankers and their overlords who created them, thus leaving the Black Magi with no wealth and no power. If the transfer occurs right before the people destroy the egregore of fiat currency, then the people will win and be protected from the system collapsing. If the people make the wrong choice and agree to lock themselves into a cashless digital system, when the egregore of fiat currency is destroyed, the bankers and their Black Magi masters will win. This is the game. People who own nothing cannot win it.

The greatest opponent is Satan, the adversary: the Ego. Defeat your ego and quell the de-sire to get wealthy through gambling, and then make the transition back to producing real value with your labor. The lottery mindset of getting rich quick and getting something for nothing will always produce a party that loses. When the majority of humanity is participating in deals in which both parties win, then we will know harmony and prosperity.

No matter how well intended, usury always runs out of solvent parties to do business with, and thus degenerates to the usurers finding new victims to sustain and preserve the lending institutions. Oftentimes, this can only be done through war, which is why you see the Black Magi using propaganda and the military industrial complex to target countries in the Middle East like Syria and Iran. They are the remaining countries who do not have Rothschild-owned central banks, which means Rome does not control them.

If we discharge more currency than we have, we go into debt and become a debtor, and thus dead ore, to the merchant. When they charge us, they make a profit (prophet). They now have our current-see, the ability to see the currents of influence that cascade from the conscious God-mind down through the Realms of Spirit and into most crystalized recesses of matter. The sapiens use their *nigromantia,* their black divination, to harness these currents for good or ill, but either way it comes from above.

A 'sapiens' is "a sage, a wizard, a mage." The Black Magi further mock you by calling your species 'homo sapiens,' which literally means "man-sage, man-wizard, man-mage." But they programmed you to be a literalist, materialist ignoramus who believes, not knows, that we evolved from an apelike creature despite there being no observable instances of one kind changing into another kind. Perhaps if the hypothesis were that we're devolving into apelike creatures, then there would be plenty of evidence to upgrade it into a theory.

You subscribe to this Social Darwinism, the third major tenet in the ideology of Satanism, because you are in fact a Satanist. But you're so ignorant of what Satanism actually is that you don't even realize the ideology you espouse. Then they infested your psyche, but also psykhe, with Relativity, the second major tenet of Satanism, because if Truth is relative, then there's no such thing as right and wrong, so you get to decide what they are based on your whims. It's black magick deception.

We do not live in a gravitational universe. There is only dielectricity and magnetism (radiation) that results in electrification. There is convergence and divergence, charge and discharge, space and counter space, and centrifugal and centripetal forces. The only thing the Priests of Apollo are sending into outer space is your common sense, because without it, you have ignored the rest of your other senses and even the most basic of provable experiments that don't require you to be a member of the Cult of Science to conduct. What good are eyes to those who cannot see? What good are nerves to those who cannot feel? What good are ears to those who cannot hear?

The speed of sound is slower than the speed that the Priests of Apollo tell you the planet is rotating at by about 250 miles per hour. Since the planet allegedly spins eastward at half the speed of some rifle bullets, one should not be able to hear anything in the west, because the speed of sound can't catch up to something that's moving faster than it by approximately 250 miles per hour. Yet you can hear the sound of thunder or fireworks in the west just fine. The reason for this is found in Airy's Failure.

Enough. I'm already bored of the obvious. It is in your name. You are inherently a sage, an imga, a mage, a mason, a builder, a creator. You don't have a choice. Act like one. Take responsibility and stop allowing people in positions of imaginary authority to dictate their whims to you, including me.

'Dis-' is also a prefix indicating "reversal, negation, lack, deprivation, removal, and release." As a verb, 'charge' is also "to impose or ask a price or fee, to hold liable (lie-able; able to lie) for payment; enter a debt against, or to attack by rushing violently against." As a noun, it means "a liability (lie-ability; ability to lie) to pay." Therefore, a 'discharge' is "a release in liability," which is why we must discharge our debt. Contemplate what a release in one's ability to lie about his debt would mean.

When we discharge capital, we remove or negate our right to control our current-sea, our energy *in our gee* (NRG), our G, the seventh fold in the constitution of man. We remove, or caput (head), our greatest authority of all, our capital, and so we behead our seat of reason, our center of understanding, our cerebrum, the conscious God-mind, the optic thalamus, which is why so few of us are able to break free of the mind-control. But it is possible. There are prerequisites, however, you can restore the Cristos to the Throne of God.

15 THE DEATH PLEDGE

There is no greater service to God than the pursuit and study of the knowledge of Truth. Knowledge is the greatest gift bestowed upon hue-mans, for it always expands and increases. It can never be unknown or destroyed, and the acquisition of knowledge cultivates behavior that is aligned with morality.

Whosoever claims to possess knowledge but lives in a manner that harms others does not in fact possess knowledge. However, though knowledge never diminishes, it is not augmented unless he or she who wields it is passionate enough to keep seeking it through free will. The Language of the Birds will not give up its secrets until knowledge is acquired.

The most important knowledge is that of the Creator and that this realm and everything in it was made by the most high. The Black Magi know this, and if you are unwilling to discover it for yourself, you have no probability of defeating them.

In order to understand the material world in which you exist, the celestial world must be observed, and above that, the spiritual world. They are all one and the same, however. Like a master chef, the Creator has baked layers into the cake of existence.

The spiritual realm is the layer where perfect Wisdom and the Truth of all things are generated. This is the layer of the causality of generation and corruption, as well as the correspondences, of all things beneath the Creator. It is self-sufficient and self-generating, for nothing else gives it its qualities. The ancients called it *the One,* hence Neo being referred to as *the One* in the Matrix Trilogy. The ancients also referred to this as being the Absolute Truth, or the Primal Truth, because all things under it receive their Truth and unity from its generation and corruption. This spiritual sun, if you will, is perfect because it does not receive its Truth nor its unity from anything else, for everything else is imperfect and incapable of its perfection till they return to its source.

The entities in the celestial realm have in them the seeds of decay, the causality of corruption, and they cause the degeneration and corruption in all things beneath them. The entities in the celestial world govern the entities in the material world, and the entities in the material world cause their own corruption and degeneration, but also, through free will, they have the ability to ascend to higher planes of consciousness in the celestial world, or Realms of Spirit, through the pursuit of knowledge and then using that knowledge to act morally and rightly, which makes it Wisdom, or philosophy, the love of Wisdom.

In the celestial world, everything has its function and place. In order to evolve to higher planes of consciousness, the souls must descend to purify themselves in the material world. This makes the material world the envy of all creation because it is where spirit unites with matter.

However, the material world is not the bottom. The material world corresponds to the equator of the Zodiac, the torus field, the torso if you will, the cross of matter and spirit. The reason the beginning is the Word, the seed, is because when you talk you create torque, which creates torus fields. This is how a sapiens creates as he speaks. And if one doesn't speak Truth and align his behavior with morality, he can commit torts, which are "civil wrongs" in legalese, because 'tort' means "wrong" in French.

Just as there are hierarchies above us, there most certainly are hierarchies below us, not only in the physical world (such as the animal, vegetable, and mineral states), but also the realms of lower vibrational frequencies, which are really the phase disparity of electromagnetic current (torrent) that create red shift (Capricorn; South) and blue shift (Cancer; North) frequencies that compose the material, celestial, and spiritual aspects of the world.

As it is above, so it is below; as on the earth, so in the sky. The outward doth from the inward roll, and the inward dwells in the inmost soul. The elementaries, the demons, the shayateen, whatever you'd like to call them, are beings who have sunk beneath the plane of material existence through their wicked deeds and are well on their way towards the black whirl of death to be scattered into more useful creations.

But that does not mean a hue-man sapiens, a man-sage, cannot degrade himself to a point where he has the power to attract the elementaries and thus make contact with them. Just like a sapiens has the ability to attract the angels by virtue of his moral behavior and consumption of only Nature-made bounties, the sapiens may also degrade himself through junk food, junk information, unhealthy sexual acts, drugs, alcohol, overeating, smoking, television, and many other bad habits that degrade the soul's vessel, the cadus.

When the selfish, the cell fish, that is to say the Black Magi, make contact with the elementaries or daemons (protective spirits that are not to be confused with demons), the non-physical entities can only be bound by someone with the moral authority to do so combined with the sigils to bind them, as seen in the Goetia, or through the making of a contract with them.

The Black Mage must degrade himself to a point of no return by severing his connection to the One. This is usually done for temporary, illusory power, and once the elementary fulfills its obligation, it usually concludes with a loophole that requires future contracts to sustain that power. However, due to the Black Mage already defiling him(her)self, there is nothing left that can be done to satiate the elementaries unless the Black Mage brings others and tricks them to cut themselves off from the Creator as payment to fulfill future contracts. This is why the degraded ones (demons) in Hollywood, politics, banking, and other cult-like environments are so obsessed with convincing you to engage in their immoral behavior. They need to destroy you to sustain themselves.

In the legal world, voluntary withholding agreements are derived from this black magick, because the only way they can bind you is to get you to commit to a contract and then violate that contract so that the Black Magi can collect a penalty. A **'penalty'** is "a forfeiture for noncompliance with an agreement," otherwise known as a contract.

Penal action is founded entirely on statute. It has nothing to do with Natural Law.

All of man's laws are black magick, and the reason people have so much difficulty accepting this is because they don't like absolutes, because absolutes leave no room for the second major tenet of Satanism (Moral Relativism), and they can't deal with the fact that they've practiced black magick their whole lives, stolen freedom, and cut themselves off from God. For thousands of years, mankind was so ignorant and witless that they didn't even know what they were doing. That's what type of mental retardation humanity has undergone. They've been practicing Eugenics, by breeding with their cousins, for so long that even the most basic Truth is unintelligible to them. The progeny of this behavior is psychopathy.

For the future generations that read this, as I am obviously not writing this material for the monkey-minded chaff of my race, although I am sure many of these empty shells will find this work and slander it, perhaps the gravest type of black magick that siphoned the generational wealth of the masses was through what most would consider the biggest purchase of their life: the mortgage.

Why is the mortgage so important to the Black Magi? Because sovereigns do not discharge debt to acquire property. They convert gold or silver into property. Not only does one not own property that he was granted use of in exchange for discharging debt, but he also left a paper trail of agreeing to yield his sovereignty in exchange for some satanic privileges.

"But Dylan Michael Saccoccio," you say. "You are a lying deceiver, a half-truther, an Anti-Christ Luciferian, the Dajjal. I own my property. I paid for it in cash."

Did you, now? Was it cold hard cash, as in gold or silver? Or was it with Federal Reserve Notes, fiat paper, debt?

It's tragically hilarious to observe all you religious dunces use the same stories and characters for thousands of years, occasionally switching their hypocritical masks, yet you are naïve enough to think no one will notice that your priestcraft deception is the same as the black magick the races before you used. According to your delusional worldview, God approves your sorcery, so it's acceptable for you to murder children while you rape them and steal the fruits of others' labor so you can live the lavishly degenerate lifestyle of your dreams. Good luck with that.

As far as I'm concerned, you're all a bunch of inbred, first cousin-marrying demon trolls, which is why you cannot comprehend the simple Truth. Inbreeding causes retardation. That's why it's been made illegal in most places. You're children in a playground who think, if they swap clothes, none of the adults will recognize them. Grow up.

If you used fiat paper or digital ether to acquire your "property," then those IOU debt notes are death notes. They are frequencies of energy, sound notes for the dead, because a 'mort' is "a note sounded on a hunting horn when a *deer* is killed," and you, my friend, are the *buck* that they fuck, hence the reason they pay you in *bucks*, because a 'mort' is also "a great quantity or number." Get it through your thick skull, or scull. Sovereigns don't buy or pay for anything. They convert gold or silver into property. The note, the mort, is the death of game in hunting, because you are the game, the most dangerous of all game, and the Black Magi are the hunters.

When you take out a 'mortgage,' they have killed you, because in French, 'mort' means "death." This is also seen in the Latin words 'mors,' 'mortem,' 'mortis,' which all mean "death," hence the phrases we use in English such as 'post mortem' and 'rigor mortis.' Ralph Hawtry explains it so simply that even a child could understand it, "Banks lend by creating credit. They create the means of payment out of nothing."

Every day I get people disgracing me, coming to me to slander my work, not the other way around. Meanwhile, most of you are in student loan debt forever, for an education that taught you nothing, and here I am teaching you more than anyone ever will for nearly nothing. Yet I'm the one you treat like garbage because you don't like my delivery. Tough shit.

Remember how you behaved towards me. It will be the primary factor that thwarted your evolution. Your dream of dressing up in a different hypocritical suit where no one recognizes your identity, as the angels send you beneath the plane of human existence, will finally become a reality, not because it was me, but because it was the way you treated a servant of Truth who exposed all evil for you to do something about it, and you did nothing other than mindlessly consume it like you do everything and everyone else. I hope you like geodes.

In addressing the stockholders of Midland Bank in 1924, Reginald McKenna demystified the way black magick institutions work, "I am afraid the ordinary citizen will not like to be told that the banks can and do create money. And they who control the credit of the nation direct the policy of governments and hold in the hollow of their hand the destiny of the people."

When you take out a mortgage, you are literally beheading yourself for a bank, which controls the flow of cash, currencies, and the currents of cash flows, like the banks of a river. The riverbanks were often where pirates buried the dead, hence banks are where you go to bury yourself in debt, or as the god of Wine said, "Let the dead bury the dead."

Now it is time to examine the second half of the hex. The word 'gage' is "a token of defiance: pledge of combat," as well as "something deposited as a pledge of performance." Gee, that sounds like an agreement. Thus, a 'mortgage' is "a death pledge" to those who enter into it with the Black Magi, but to the Black Magi, the 'mortgage' is "a pledge to deliver the debtor unto Death."

Is your stomach beginning to churn yet or are you still too ignorant to comprehend this? Perhaps if you see it in their own words, it will become clearer. In the mid-19th Century, the Rothschild brothers of London wrote to their associates in New York, "The few who understand the system will either be so interested in its profits or be so dependent upon its favours that there will be no opposition from that class, while on the other hand, the great body of people, mentally incapable of comprehending the tremendous advantage that capital derives from the system, will bear its burdens without complaint, and perhaps without even suspecting that the system is inimical to their interests."

"But Great Tide," you say. "This is blasphemy. My Roman demonic hex will return to save me from myself. The Lord Fish says so in the Bible. You're a Luciferian."

You call me Luciferian as though it's an insult, but most of you are so mentally deficient of the sacred science that you don't even understand that Lucifer is Venus, the sacred feminine ruler of Taurus, the unconscious animal-mind: the cerebellum, hence the similarity to the words 'bell' and 'bull' and the connection they have to the Sun-god Bel that the Bible sometimes calls Baal.

What did you imagine the worthless fiat notes you call bills, and the Priests of Bail in your courts that you erroneously believe are judges, were named after? You pay bail with bills, and swear upon their perverted scriptures to tell the Truth, the whole Truth, and nothing but the Truth, so help you God (IES, the Sun-god of the vintage that you mistake for IHS), and through their deception you agree to be everything they de-sire you to be: a Roman slave battery.

The Latin word 'Lucifer' comes from the word 'lux,' which means "light," hence the 'Luxor' is the "light ore, the ore of the Sun." 'Lux' is combined with the word 'ferre,' which is "to bear or bring." Therefore 'Lucifer' means "the bearer or bringer of the light." Do I not bear the Torch of Truth? Do I not bring you the Light?

I most certainly ferry ('ferr-e') the Light of Truth, of God, because the ferry bears the ore across the current-seas, as people from all over the world receive this divine knowledge through my casting of it. But I do not worship Venus, nor any brainwashed fictitious Christian, Jewish, Muslim, Hindu, Buddhist, Egyptian, Persian entities or any other false idols that they stole from the sacred science of the Astro Logos. All creations are beneath the Creator and thus not worthy of my worship, nor my warship. I worship nothing. Get that through your depraved monkey mind of lunacy. I serve only the Truth of God, and that's where my protection comes from.

You can see it in my given name. What does 'Dylan' mean? It is Welsh for "Great Tide." For what else could be the progeny of Tiamat, or Ma'at, the pure sea of Truth? If you deal with me, you will answer to her. Enjoy it, because by the time she's finished with you, you'll be a plot on a wall of carrion that pulses in the lowest dungeons of existence.

What is my second given name? Michael. What does Michael correspond to? The Sun. What ore, Min-Ra-El, does the Sun correspond to? Gold. What is gold carried in historically? A sack, a 'saccoccio.' What degree in the House of Leo am I born? The first degree of the Lion of Judah, the heart that pulses the light of Courage unto the world.

Indeed, I bear the Light of the Sun, the Luxor from my Creator. You may call me Lucifer till the day you die, as the demons of Winter who do not want me to spread this knowledge refer to me, but it will never destroy the Truth, and I could not care less if you perish in bondage. I am only here to serve God, speak Truth, and help raise those who are willing to raise themselves. My Atlantean ancestors can pass you from netherworld to netherworld for all I care. If you find yourself in Atala, which we called Italia in the physical world, know that you've earned it.

You made a death pledge to one of many 'branches' of a bank, which are "tributary streams, limbs of any main stem, as distinguished from some other line from the same stock." 'Branches' are "wires that connect to a main source," hence the reason banks 'wire' money, moon-honey, through branches like our hearts that pulse blood through veins, or like a vintner presses the essence from grapes to capture it in jar-like vessels: bottles. The Black Magi are bottling your essence, the fruits of your labor.

'Bot-Els' are "bots of God, of El-ectricity," because 'bots' are 'scroungers,' "people who borrow with no intention of repaying or returning that which they borrowed," and a 'bot' is "a device that executes commands and performs tasks with minimal intervention," which is why the Black Magi view you as their 'automatons.'

And you know what? I agree with them. I have experienced your automaton insults, using repetitive words like 'pretentious' to describe me, when you've never even met me, joker. Well, the 'pre-tent' is the "dome that existed before we did, the dome that contains IO, the first hieroglyph of the Sun, and us." Thus, 'pre-tent-IO-us' is the macrocosmic Golgotha, the dome of the skull, the firmament that shelters the Sun and us, as well as the Christ within us."

Another favorite characterization of my work is 'purple prose,' as though that's an insult. If you weren't such a Deaf Phoenician automaton, you'd know that purple comes from the equilibrium of the red and blue shift frequencies being pulsed by our Creator, which is why the Phoenicians use it in their symbolism. It is equipoise, which is why I use that term to describe magick in my allegorical novels.

So in fact, that is the ultimate of compliments. But you're

running your 'bot-El' scripts from your Pizzagate human-trafficking pedophile programmers, which converted you into an empty cadus, a shell of a vessel, a legal fiction husk that thinks a software program like AutoCAD (computer-aided design) will help an automaton cadaver like you discover the nature of the universe. It will never happen that way. Period. Enjoy your slavery. Not one single ascended master is returning to save you. Hold your breath though. The world will be better off.

What does your mortgage have attached to it? Interest rates. The banks earn interest off your death pledge because 'earn' is phonetically 'urn,' which is "a vase for holding the ashes of the dead after they've been cremated," for that's what the Black Magi did to you.

They interred your dead, burnt body in a bank, because 'inter' is "to place a dead body in a grave or tomb; bury." When one rests in peace, he or she is dead because 'rest' is "the repose of death," and as a verb it is "to become or remain inactive." When the Black Magi 'urn inter-rest' off of your death pledge, they have buried you in debt and made you a debtor, dead ore, thus they've siphoned off your spiritual light from God, your soul.

The Old English word 'est' is a noun meaning "favor, grace, bounty, kindness, love." In Italian and French, 'est' means "east." What rises in the east? The Sun, the light of the world from God. What Zodiacal sign is Jerusalem, the gate in the east that God comes from? Aries.

What is the morning star that is the brightest in the sky, announcing the arrival of the Sun? Venus, bright Lucifer, the bearer of light, because it indeed brings the light of the Sun, and when it rises in the evening, it is the Lord of the Night, hence the spirit of the Hungarian word 'est' that means "evening, eve."

To 'urn inter-est' is to "bury the cremated ash of kindness, grace, love, favor, and bounty, the fruit of the hue-man, in a tomb, or vault, in a bank." Thus, through the dark occult ritual, the Cremation of Care, they 'urn inter-est' by stealing the fruit of your labor, the ore of your experience.

What is the bank of a river made of? Earth. Where are you? Earth. What is the first phonetic sound of 'Earth' and 'urn?' 'Ur,' the city of ancient Sumer, where the Black Magi were before they took their phony phonetic skills to Phoenicia.

In a quote attributed to James Madison, "History records that the money changers have used every form of abuse, intrigue, deceit, and violent means possible to maintain their control over governments by controlling money and its issuance."

By entering into a mortgage you are cremating your Care, which ceases the generation of your hue-man fruit, your grace, love, kindness, and favor with God.

Regardless if this quote was ever uttered from the mouth of Thomas Jefferson, it is nevertheless the Truth, "If the American people ever allow private banks to control the issue of their currency, first by inflation, then by deflation, the banks will deprive the people of all property until their children wake up homeless on the continent their fathers conquered. The issuing power should be taken from the banks and restored to the people, to whom it properly belongs."

Is the Federal Reserve a government-controlled bank or is it a **private** entity? The answer to this question is the causality of your debt slavery.

16 DISPELLING THE HEX OF REVELATION

The days of the week are structured the wrong way, which is why you are **weak**ened at the weekend, and why the days of the week, in their current order, are really the days of the **weak**. If the days of the week corresponded to alchemy, the first day, the proper day for rest, would be Saturday because it corresponds to the base metal lead, which is an Earth element that contains the secret fire of its own transformation. Saturday corresponds to Capricorn and Aquarius in the Zodiac, the period of crystallization known as the material rest, but also the Gate of Deluge, the flood that the allegories of Noah and Gilgamesh were based on. It also corresponds to the root chakra, and the one thing that no one can escape while existing in this realm: Time.

The second day should be Thursday, because it is Thor's Day, which corresponds to Jupiter and the metal known as tin. What comes after Aquarius (ruled by Saturn)? Pisces, which is ruled by Jupiter, the giver of all good things, corresponding to the genital chakra.

The following sign in the Sun's progression, as well as the soul's cycle, is Aries, the real beginning of the cycle when the Sun, the soul, rises above the horizon from the east. This period of cardinal fire is ruled by none other than Mars, which is why Tuesday should remain the third day of the week, because it is Tiw's Day. Mars' metal is iron, which is why most tools related to war and **mars**hal power, such as swords, are made of iron, the second oldest metal besides lead. In the beginning was the Word. The word *is* the seed. The **sword** of iron, of Mars, is the **words** of iron, the seeds of the beginning: Aries.

The chemical term for iron is *Ferrum*, the Latin word for the metal, hence its symbol on the Periodic Table of Elements being **Fe**. As a reminder, the Latin words 'fero' and 'ferre' mean "to **bear**, carry," because iron is necessary to carry oxygen to all the cells in the body. Thus, iron in red blood cells ferries the oxygen, the air of Aquarius and Jove, to all the cells in the body, just like Aries sends forth the seed, the word, the Cristos.

This is why iron corresponds to the **liver**, because it regulates the blood. What is the protein that stores iron, releasing it when it is needed? Ferritin, '**Ferry-tin**,' because it "ferries the blood, the tin: Jupiter." Where are the highest concentrations of Ferritin in the body? The cells of the **liver**.

The blood is indeed under **mars**hal rule, and how appropriate that the word 'ferre' means "to bear," and that Ursa Major, the Big Dipper, the Greater **Bear**, the Ladle, the Car of Osiris (the Sun), is a constellation in Cancer as the Sun, the soul, reaches its high point at the Summer Solstice, before it descends into Leo, the heart. Note the root word 'fero' in 'ferocious,' because a lion is ferocious just as the Sun is ferocious in July and August. The Sun is indeed "savagely fierce, as a wild beast, warlike and violently cruel," just like Mars (Tiw), for by the time it is done, the vegetation is burnt and dying in Autumn, which comes from the Latin word 'auctus,' meaning "enriched, prosperity, growth," because the blood is enriched by the heart and all the other functions that contribute to its balance.

This process is necessary for the vintage of the grape, a fruit that is enriched by the end of Summer, which is why the blood of the grape is the blood of the Christ, Jupiter-Zeus, Jesus, and why Jupiter corresponds to blood, hence the original name that Jesus comes from being Ies, Iota Eta Sigma, the name of Bacchus, the god of the Wine, the blood of the grape.

However, 'ferocious' can also mean "very great, courageous, high-spirited," because the Sun, the soul, is indeed at its highest spirit as it is ferried to June 21, where the days are the longest and it's at its highest in the ecliptic.

The sign after Aries is Taurus, which is ruled by Venus, who is Freya and Frigg, which is why the day we call Friday is Frigg's Day. In a healthy progression, it should really be the fourth day of the week, but in this perverted dark occultist progression, it marks the beginning of the week's end as the sixth day of the weak, for the soul is finally weakened at the weekend.

Copper is the metal that corresponds to Venus, and what is the key organ that stores copper? The liver. Copper kills parasites and purifies the blood, which also nourishes the fetus and is why Venus is indeed Lucifer, the bearer of light, because she ferries the light of the soul, the blood of Christ, till she becomes Neptune at a higher octave.

Venus is exalted in Pisces, when the twin souls finally become the one and only, Jesus, the Lord Fish in the waters of Pisces. Eros, Cupid, is the Sun, which is why Venus is also Astarte, the mother of Eros. Cupid became two fish after confronting Typhon, and Pisces became the fish that ferried Venus and her son out of danger. This is why Pisces is known throughout the ages as Venus et Cupido, Venus Syria cum Cupidine, Urania, Dione and Veneris Mater, and Venus cum Adone. Why else would the Syrians hate to eat fish? It's the same reason why Hindus don't eat cows, because Krishna, the Sun, was a calf-herder. He is the Sun in Taurus. The Hindus revere cows, Taurus, in the same manner that the Syrians revere fish, Pisces. As Publius Ovidius Naso wrote in the *Fasti*, in regards to the Syrians, "it is not fit to make their gods their dishes."

'Atl' is the name that the Aztecs assigned to Pisces, hence the Atlantic Ocean, and quite possibly, Atlantis, for 'atlas' in Latin means "to bear," same as 'ferre,' the second word in Lucifer (Venus), the bearer of light. Perhaps this is the allegory for why Atlantis was sunk into the sea. It would be my guess that the allegory of Atlantis, if it's not historical, is symbolical of the retrograding motion of the Aeons, from the Aeon of Aries, the mountain of the most high, sinking into the Aeon of Pisces, the sea.

As Pisces, Atl, Atlantis sinks, it gives way to Aries, the Ram, the most high, the ruler of which is Mars, but the exalted one of Aries is the Sun. Pisces and Aries, the end and the beginning, is where the soul is born again through the Royal Marriage of Water (Matter) and Fire (Spirit), hence Venus and Cupid merge into Neptune, the purified soul. And they twain become one flesh.

Speaking of the Twin Souls, who is the ruler of Gemini? Mercury, the messenger of the gods, which corresponds to the metal quicksilver, the only metal to be liquid at room temperature while also being the heaviest natural metal. Its chemical abbreviation is **Hg,** from the Latin word 'hydrargyrum' that comes from a similar Greek word meaning "watery silver."

As we've stated, Mercury is Woden, and the reason Woden's Day, Wednesday, should be the fifth day of the week is because Mercury dissolves the alkaline metals, but specifically gold and silver, much like the way water dissolves salt. This process metaphorically blends the metals of the mind and heart, the last two days of my proposed weekday arrangement, the Moon and Sun, the Feminine and Masculine, into one. Mercury is symbolical of the Rebis and thought to be an androgynous metal because it represents the throat chakra, which is directly below the feminine and masculine components that symbolize silver (the cerebellum; female) and gold (the cerebrum; male), and thus necessary to blend them. The mind, the heart, and the voice in unison correspond to thinking, feeling, and speaking in unison, which is the Moon, Sun, and Mercury being in unison. This is the Great Work symbolized by the Rebis and Antimony, the symbol on this book: the free spirit.

The sixth day of the week should be Monday, the Moon's day. The Moon corresponds to the metal silver, the highest electrical and thermal conductivity of all metals, which is why it is such an important industrial metal. This makes it perfectly symbolical to the mind and mental energy, as it is a feminine energy that corresponds to the third eye chakra, Ajna. Silver is antibacterial, so it also corresponds to a purified mystical state.

The seventh and last day of the week should be Sunday, the Sun's day. The Sun corresponds to gold, which is perhaps the purest of the metals because it doesn't react or associate with lesser elements. It is not found in trace amounts in plants and it doesn't alloy with anything but silver. However, it does make an amalgam with mercury. This is analogous for the heart only aligning and being tempered by the reason of the mind, the man being tempered by the woman, and the Creator only dealing with Mercury as its messenger to deliver the daily bread to the rest of the cosmic body.

Gold, like an enlightened mind, like the ever-moving Sun, never tarnishes or diminishes. It cannot be damaged by heat. It is the most flexible and immortal of all the metals. It has been used as money because of its eternal nature, which preserves wealth generationally.

Of course, this current race is completely ignorant of alchemy, so they do not understand the properties of gold, or its spiritual and material significance. It corresponds to the crown chakra, Sahasrara, for it is the only metal fit to symbolize the Christ being crucified on the dome of the skull, Golgotha. But now let us see how the mineral correspondences of gold to the macrocosm of the Sun translate on the grand scale of life and the sacred science.

Who is the young son that remained with Jacob while the rest of his brothers plotted against Joseph (Mercury)? Benjamin. Where does God command Jacob to go in Genesis? Bethel, the House of Bread: Virgo. As the Sun passes through Virgo, Rachel dies and Benjamin is born. This is the Autumnal Equinox. What does 'Ben' mean? Son. And then the Sun rises out of Capricorn after Virgo has ascended at midnight and rules the night sky approximately 90° later on December 25th, being born of a virgin.

This transition of the Sun from Virgo to Libra corresponds to its transition on the opposite side of the ecliptic and Zodiac, from Pisces to Aries, which is symbolical of Mount Olympus, the home of Neptune. As the liver (Venus) purifies the blood, it ensures that all the twelve signs are in harmony, as above so below, and that the circulation of the blood from head (Heaven; Aries) to heel (Hell; Pisces, the feet) completes the circle. This is why the phonetic sound of 'circle' and 'circul,' in 'circul-at-i-on,' are nearly identical, because when the circle (cycle) is complete, the 'circle is at eye on,' or the god-mind is activated: Ionic.

Benjamin is the son of Jacob. Knowing that the father is the son indicates, to the initiated, that this relationship is nothing more than the cycle of the Sun rising and falling as it "jumps over the candlesticks," just like every other part of the scriptures.

Jacob, Jack, Jake, Jacques, etc., all have similar phonetics. "Jack be nimble, jack be quick. Jack jumped over the candlesticks." The British flag indicates this cycle, which is why they call it the Union Jack. The 1st Degree Tracing Board in Freemasonry also depicts this cycle when turned on its side, representing the Sun's path from the Winter Solstice at the Tropic of Capricorn (in the House of Capricorn) to the Vernal Equinox at the Equator (in the House of Aries), then to the Summer Solstice at the Tropic of Cancer (in the House of Cancer), back down to the Autumnal Equinox at the Equator (in the House of Libra), finally returning to Capricorn. Do you see how everything they've created, to convey the way this world works, is through the symbolism of the sacred science? How many times must I serve Truth while you remain silent as the profane ridicule me like buffoons, slinging their own shit towards me? When will you take up the sword of Truth?

What is **Jack** also a nickname for? John, the Voice, which speaks the Word, hence Luke 8:11, "And this is the simile: The seed is the word." The Word is Aries, the beginning, God, the optic thalamus, the Eye of Providence that forms the mammillary glands in the head. The seed is the Word, which is the soul, the breath of God, the Sun. Who else could he be during Winter but **Jack Frost**?

What's a candlestick? A *lamp-stand*. Where have we seen that word in the scriptures? In Revelation 1:20, it is written, "The secret of the **seven** stars is that thou has seen upon my right hand, and the **seven** golden lamp-stands (candlesticks): the **seven** stars are messengers of the **seven** assemblies (churches), and the **seven** lamp-stands that thou hast seen are **seven** assemblies." You will note that the number of God is 777, which reduces to 3, the number of the unity consciousness (777 = 21 = 3). Revelation 1:20 mentions the word 'seven' six times, which would double the unity consciousness to become 33, the number of the master, the degree of enlightenment. But it's probably just a coincidence that 1:20 is also 3, which would make the sequence 333, a number representing mind, body, and spirit, the Jesus or ascended master's connection.

The seven assemblies in Asia that John sends grace and peace to from the Sun, God, who was, and who is coming, and from the Seven Spirits before His throne, in Revelation 1:4, are the seven constellations in the Sun's path, the Kingdom of Heaven, the fixed candlesticks (lamp-stands).

The first church is that of Ephesus, Aries, which corresponds to the Throne of God, Mars, **Ephesus**—Jesus, the Lord of Hosts in the Old Testament (March). Which direction corresponds to Aries?

East. Which continent corresponds to the east in the physical world, not literally but as an egregore in the minds of men? Asia. This is why they are the Asiatic Churches, or Churches of the East, the Orient.

Aries is followed by Taurus, the second church of Thyatira, a sacrifice of labor, which corresponds to agriculture, but also perfume, as in frankincense, pearl of the desert, an offering to the Sun (the Bull of April).

Next is Gemini, the third church, of Philadelphia, brotherly love (the Twins of May). In Numbers 22, a messenger of Jehovah rides on an ass, and with him are two messengers. Well, who rules the three decans of Gemini? Mercury, the Messenger of the Gods, which is why Balaam's ass sees Mercury three times while Balaam smites her with his staff. Need I explain the innuendo? Where did you think "tap that ass" came from? The two servants are the Twins. This passage is about the Sun making its way to the Summer Solstice on June 21st, the high places of Baal (the Sun), which is noted as the Throne of the Adversary, where the word Satan comes from, hence it is Satan's Seat. The oxen and sheep that were sacrificed were Taurus (the Ox) and Aries (the Lamb), also known as March and April.

Cancer (the Crab of June) is the fourth church, of Pergamos. In Revelation 2, it is written "I have known thy works, and where thou dost dwell—where the throne of the Adversary is—and thou dost hold fast my name, and thou didst not deny my faith, even in the days which Antipas (corresponding to Herod) was my faithful witness (remember it is a young Herod that beheads John, Aquarius), who was put to death beside you, where the Adversary doth dwell." What is beside Cancer, the zodiacal sign where Herod beheads John? Leo.

Why is the throne of the Adversary, of the Christian Satan, in Cancer, and furthermore, why is Antipas put to death beside the Adversary? How did Herod die? Sickness. What happens after June 21st? The days get shorter and the Sun begins to metaphorically "die."

Herod gets sick on the 21st because the Moon is the ruler of Cancer and the Moon putrefies, and so his body breeds worms. Don't believe it? Go leave your sharpened knives outside in direct moonlight. Herod is then taken at least ten miles to warm baths, which is at least the second decan of Cancer, where the waters are beginning to warm from the heat of the Summer. Important men are ordered to come from every village in the nation, up to 80 miles away.

However, no one comes to the Sun. The Sun passes through them, and 80° from 10° in the warm baths of Cancer brings us to September 23rd, the first day of Libra: Judgment Day. Antipater is found guilty and executed, and five days later Herod is dead on September 28th. The very next day, usually around the 29th, the equinox occurs, where the days and nights are the same length, and the Sun of God (Aries, the Spring) has become the Sun of Man (Libra, the Fall) which is why it is Michaelmas-day, where Saint Michael is "equal to God," just before the night outweighs the day and lures the soul from the spiritual world into the illusory material world.

The scales of *the Just One* in September look like they're pulling the head of the Serpent (the constellation Serpens) down, which is why Michael is described as fighting Satan. God (the Sun rising) has allegorically become Man (the Sun falling). Perhaps all of this is coincidence. Perhaps the ancients were just primitive people that didn't know anything. But they can't be any more doltish than the people of today trying to rationalize and reconcile these allegories as historical accounts.

One of the worst black magick hexes that have been placed on the religiously enslaved masses corresponds to what the Lord Fish says in John 20, "Blessed are those who have not seen, and yet have believed." This erroneous axiom defies the senses that the Creator endowed you with. However, the Bible doesn't ever encourage one to believe the Truth in order to be free. It commands one to know it. Belief may bring the temporary bliss of ignorance, but that's how farmers enslave livestock, by tricking the animals into believing that the free meals and artificial boundaries are for their best interest.

The reason the throne of the Adversary (Satan) is in Cancer is because this is where the head of the constellation Hydra is. By the glory of our Creator, it is exactly opposite to where the Sun is born in the manger of the Goat: Capricorn.

Thomas is Cancer. Contemplate John 14. The Sun tells the

disciples, the signs of the Zodiac, "In the house of my father (the Zodiac) are many mansions. I go on to prepare a place for you, and again do I come. Wither I go away ye have known, and the way ye have known." This conveys that as you study the ecliptic of the Sun, you learn the way. Once you learn the way, you know the minutes, the hours, the days, the months, the seasons, the years, and even the Aeons, and thus you can determine where the Sun has already been and where it will be.

Thomas (Cancer) asks "Sir (Zor, Sur, Sar, Rock, God), we have not known wither thou goest away, and how are we able to know the way?" This is because Cancer has only seen the Sun (God) arrive, so at this moment, Cancer has not seen the Sun fall and die yet.

But the Sun responds, "I am the way, and the Truth, and the life. No one doth come unto the Father if not through me." This is because the Sun is quite literally the mediator between mankind and the heavens. The Sun is much closer to Earth than the fixed constellations of the Zodiac, the tribes of Israel, and if one is going to learn which constellations are the straight and narrow way, he must pay attention to the way the Sun comes and goes.

The reason mankind is ignorant of the scriptures and the way, the Truth, and the life, is because they literally don't pay attention to the Sun, and the Bible admits it, "the Spirit of Truth, whom the world is not able to receive, because it doth not behold him, nor know him." This is why Thomas (Cancer) is ignorant.

"I go away, and I come unto you," the Sun reiterates at the end of John 14. "I will no more talk much with you, for the ruler of this world doth come, and in me he hath nothing; but that the world may know that I love the Father, and according as the Father gave me command so I do; arise we may go hence." Who is the ruler of this world, the one who nothing can escape from, but in the Sun he has nothing? Father Time.

The Sun loves the Father, because without Time, there'd be no meaning in the Sun's journey. The Sun is born in Time (December 25th, the House of Saturn) and it dies in Time (December 21st, the House of Saturn). You, like the Sun, are also born in Time, and so you must die in Time. This is why Saturn, the Unicorn, is Father Time: the Angel of Death and Life.

An interesting passage that corresponds to this is Psalm 22, which is nothing more than a description of the Sun's passage through the Wheel of Jehovah, the Torah, the Tarot, the Rota. After the Sun passes through Aquarius (Horus: Man), and is blamed by man, it rolls into Jehovah, Jove, Jupiter, the ruler of Pisces, causing the Sun to trust in Pisces' adversary Virgo (the breasts of my mother). Then it is surrounded by the many bulls of Bashan (fertile soil), which is Taurus, and then into Leo, the literal translation of which is, "Save me from the mouth of a lion:—And—from the horns of the high places thou hast answered me!" Had I only read this translation, I'd interpret that as "save me from the mouth of Leo and from the horns of Aries and Taurus, the Ram and Ox of the most high answered me."

But King James translated it as "Save me from the lion's mouth: for thou has heard me from the horns of the unicorns." This changes *everything*. Any time Unicorns are involved, you are dealing with Time, Saturn, Cronus, the Crown. "Jehovah be not far off," and indeed, Jupiter is the ruler of Sagittarius, only four months away, followed by the end, Capricorn, Earth, ruled by Saturn: Time. Thus, by returning the seed, the word, to Jehovah, your heart doth live forever, as all the ends of the Earth and all families of the nations return and bow to Jehovah, because the south is where the Angel of Death becomes the Angel of Life.

The seed, the Word that you return to God through healthy behavior has many names. Manna is the Cristos, the oil, the Christ, the cerebro-spinal substance, the ambrosia of the gods, the Gold of Ophir, the elixir of life, the treasure of the Kingdom of Heaven (Aries, the cerebrum, Sara Abram) that becomes the argentum vivum, the living silver of Mercury that delivers the body its daily bread: Joseph. This is the mental power that enables the Voice (John) to speak Truth. Mercury delivers the "goods," hence the word's root, 'merx.'

The fifth church, of Sardis, is Leo (July). 'Sar' is the "rock, stone, or pillar" of 'Dis,' who is "God." Leo comes from the ancient Phoenician word 'El-eon', which is spelled 'Elyon' in Psalm 78:35, "And they remember that God is their rock, and God Most High their redeemer." 'El-eon' translates into "the Sun-being," which became 'lion' in the Greek, Latin, French, and English languages. The lion looks like a being that corresponds to the Sun, hence the reason people named this animal after the Sun-being. Leo is the tribe of Judah, of July.

In the passage of Hosea, it is written, "After Jehovah they go—as a lion He roareth, When he doth roar, then tremble do the sons from the West. They tremble as a sparrow out of Egypt (the lower mind of instincts, cerebellum, Taurus), And as a dove out of the land of Asshur (the higher mind of reason, cerebrum, Aries), And I have caused them to dwell in their own houses, An affirmation of Jehovah," and later in the passage, "And I am to them as a **lion**, as a leopard by the way I look out. I do meet them as a bereaved **bear**, and I rend the enclosure of their heart. And I consume them there as a lioness, a beast of the field doth rend them." Which constellation stretches across the *fields,* or sections of sky marked off as houses, of Gemini, Cancer, and **Leo**? Ursa Major, the Greater Bear, is bereaved as the Sun passes through Cancer and enters Leo.

The sixth church is Smyrna, Virgo (Isis, Isa, Ceres, the Virgin of August). '**Smyrna**' literally means "myrrh," and as we've explained, myrrh is an incense that one burns as an offering to the Sun, something that is referred to in the Bible as '**perfume**.' The Song of Solomon 1:13 illustrates this, "A bundle of myrrh is my beloved to me, between my breasts it lodgeth."

Lastly, the seventh of the Asiatic churches is Laodicea. 'Laodicea' comes from the Greek words '**λαός**' ("a people") + '**δίκη**' ("righteous, justice, rule of law, penalty, punishment, and vengeance"), therefore it means "a people of justice and righteousness." Which sign corresponds to justice and righteousness? Libra, the scales of September, where the nights and days hang in balance, neither hot nor cold, as described in Revelation 3, "Because thou art lukewarm, and neither cold nor hot, I am about to vomit thee out of my mouth; because thou sayest—I am rich, and have grown rich (the grapes are ripe), and have need of nothing."

At the beginning and end of these Asiatic churches, which start in the east (Aries) and finish in the west (Libra), are the two equinoxes, when the nights and days **come together** in equipoise. These are the covenants, and this arch, with Cancer at its apex, is the Ark of the Covenant. How would you prove this? Use the Language of the

Birds that I have taught you.

The very word 'covenant' comes from the Latin word 'convenire,' which means "come together," hence the word 'convene.' Yet these literalist, religious, priestcraft sorcery yoked slaves insist on the existence of a physical relic that was gifted to humans by an otherworldly race, and that's how the ruling class controls us. Nonsense. They don't control you. You take yourself out of the game by enslaving your mind and remaining a know-nothing.

These two covenants are the covenants of works and grace. In Galatians it is written, "God (Aries, the cerebrum, corresponding to the Sun) sent forth his Son (Jesus, the cerebro-spinal fluid, the seed, the Word), come of a woman (Taurus, the cerebellum, corresponding to the Moon)," and later, "Tell me, ye who are willing to be under law, the law do ye not hear? For it hath been written, that Abraham (Abram; Ram, Rama, the most high; Aries) had two sons, one by the maid-servant (Taurus, the sign after the Vernal Equinox where oxen plow the fields and the covenant of works begins), and one by the free-woman (Virgo, Justice, Liberty, the sign that gives way to the Autumnal Equinox where the covenant of grace begins), but he who is of the maid-servant according to the flesh hath been, and he who is of the free-woman, through the promise; which things are **allegorized**, for these are the two covenants: one, indeed from mount Sinai, to servitude bringing forth, which is Hagar; for this Hagar is mount Sinai in Arabia, and doth correspond to the Jerusalem (Aries) that now is, and is in servitude with her children (Gemini), and the Jerusalem above is the free-woman, which is mother of us all (the Virgin of August)."

The end of Summer is when the grapes were put into the wine press, as it is written in Psalm 75, "For a cup is in the hand of Jehovah, and the wine hath foamed, it is full of mixture, and He poureth out of it, only its dregs wring out, and drink, do all the wicked of the earth." The wicked are the five remaining months (October through February), the months of Winter, or the five months of suffering from the scorpion stings. This is ironically the covenant of grace.

The Sun ripens the grapes, which are then pressed into wine, quite literally being the blood of Jesus, Ies, Bacchus, the Sun, and during the harsh months of Winter, this is the Cup of Wrath in Isaiah 51, of God's fury, that people drink out of, because the wrath and fury of God are the heat of the Sun that is preserved in the essence of the grape, the blood of the covenant, when the Sun crosses the Autumnal Equinox. This occurs in the Church of Laodicea, the righteous people of Libra.

The Sun is crucified upon the Autumnal Equinox, as written in Galatians 2, "for I through law, did die, that to God I may live; with Christ I have been crucified, and live no more do I, and Christ doth live in me; and that which I now live in the flesh—in the faith I live of the Son of God, who did love me and did give himself for me; I do not make void the grace of God, for if righteousness be through law—then Christ died in vain."

The blood is enriched just as the grape is enriched, hence we call it Autumn, from '**auctus**,' meaning "enriched." This is why Santos Bonacci says, "All is Atum, Adam, Atom, Autumn," because once the sacred science is learned, all is enriched.

The Autumnal Equinox is the Day of Atonement, of Judgment. It is also observed in A Call to Persevere, "The blood of the covenant did count a common thing, in which he was sanctified, and to the Spirit of the grace (the covenant of grace) did despite? For we have known Him who is saying, 'Vengeance (Laodicea, the people of vengeance, Libra) is Mine, I will recompense, saith the Lord;' and again, 'The Lord shall judge (equinox) His people;'—fearful is the falling into the hands of a living God."

In Luke 22, this process is also described, indicating the Sun's position in Libra, between Virgo and Scorpio, "And having taken bread (the Sun passing through Virgo), having given thanks, he brake and gave to them, saying, 'This is my body (is it not the Sun that grows the wheat?), that for you is being given, this do ye—to remembrance to me.' In like manner, also, the cup after the supping, saying, 'This cup is the new **covenant in my blood** (the covenant of grace), that for you is being poured forth. But, lo, the hand of him delivering me up (Judas; Scorpio) is with me on the table."

Once one breaks the hex of Revelation, the magick becomes a fire of Truth, for in 2:5 it is written, "Remember, then, whence thou has fallen, and reform, and the first works do; and if not, I come to thee quickly, and will remove thy lamp-stand from its place—if thou mayest not reform." This passage indicates the precession of the equinoxes. Every 2160 years, the Sun enters a new sign, a new age, due to the equinoxes moving westward along the ecliptic relative to the fixed stars (lamp-stands). This is opposite to the Sun's motion along the ecliptic, which makes the Zodiac look like a divine clock in which the gears turn opposite each other.

While the physical heavens change, the spiritual houses of the Zodiac do not. The Spring Equinox will always be in March (Aries), the Summer Solstice will always be in June (Cancer), the Autumnal Equinox will always be in September (Libra), and the Winter Solstice will always be in December (Capricorn), regardless of where the physical constellations appear. This should give all students an idea of how long the stars had to be studied before this was realized. When western astrology began, the constellation Aries was in the east at the Vernal Equinox. So even though the houses remain the same, the fixed stars, the lamp-stands, eventually shift.

During the days of the Old Testament, prior to the Christian era, it was the Age of Aries, the first of the churches, the ruler of which is Mars. The character of God was marshal and warlike. Then God, the Sun, removed Aries' lamp-stand from its place. During the reign of Christianity, it was the Piscean Aeon, the ruler of which is Jupiter, hence God was of a solar nature, a fatherly giver of all good things: Jove; Jehovah. Currently, the Sun removed the lamp-stand of Pisces about three centuries ago, ending the era of Christianity and bringing us into the Age of Man: Aquarius (John the Baptist).

My fellow servants of Truth, of the One, it is my will that you know this: the sacred science was discovered through observation of the visible heliacal rising luminous bodies, not through mathematical calculations of which sign the Sun is technically in as it appears above the horizon. This is not something that can be observed by the eyes of hue-mans. Once the Sun arrives from the vanishing point of the horizon, its effulgence blots out the luminous bodies of Heaven, or as the ancients said, the Sun "puts them away." The Aeon is not decided by where the Sun is at the Vernal Equinox, or by predictive mathematics. The Aeon is decided by which constellation is on the eastern horizon an hour before dawn at the Vernal Equinox. If you look at the predawn sky on this day, during this age, you will behold that it is indisputably the constellation of Aquarius that is in the eastern sky just above the horizon, indicating that we are certainly in the Aeon of Aquarius. Not only that, you will notice at least 4° of the constellation is below the horizon, indicating that we are almost 300 years, if not more, into the Aeon of Aquarius. There'd have been no point in me manifesting as a 0° Leo 40'27" if this were not the case, for Leonine art requires Aquarian air to fuel it.

If the precession did not occur, we would have no way of knowing which Aeon we're in. But with this knowledge, we can know where we've been and where we're going. This is imperative because each age has its ruler. Saturn and Uranus rule Aquarius. It is an Air sign, so people with the spiritual fire of Aries, Leo, and Sagittarius are going to be especially powerful and effective at carrying the torches of Truth and bearing the light of God.

Knowing this, people ought to be conscious about when they conceive, as the more children that are born in these signs over the next couple thousand years, the better the chances are of humanity evolving spiritually and living in Freedom. People born in Aquarius will be doubly powerful. Saturn and Uranus are more powerful in this Aeon because they rule Aquarius, so their effects on your astrological charts, good or bad, will be of more concern.

Why does this matter so much? Because in order to be a High Mage, knowledge of astrology is imperative, and in order to align your magick with that of the Will of Creation, you must understand the cosmic influences and currents of the Will of Creation and be able to harness them at the moments of their greatest power.

The stars you see each night are the divine sparks of the Creator refracting its Will. The positions of the luminous bodies will determine how much of that force cascades upon the Earth, and what types of energies will have more or less influence. This is not my opinion. This is the science that the sapiens works with. The Black Magi know a Creator exists. They're only too eager to let you know that they know, and they get a kick at watching you disgrace the Creator and cut yourselves off from Source.

Gad is indeed God, Aries, in I Chronicles 12:8, "And of the Gadite there have been separated unto David, to the fortress, to the wilderness, mighty of valor, men of the host for battle, setting in array target and buckler, and their faces the face of the lion, and as roes on the mountains for speed." Roes are eggs, and eggs are seeds, and "this is the simile: the seed is the word." This passage displays the beautiful harmony of the 90° angle between the end of Aries and the beginning of Leo, when the mind and heart, the mental and physical energy, create unity consciousness and the courage to act, and thus are *right.*

This is the Age for those with strong Fire and Air influence to take massive action and for those without these influences to support them in any way imaginable, as Water and Earth influences will be dried out. In the previous Age, the Piscean Water smothered Leonine Fire. Those that thrived had Mercurial influence from Virgo: Columbia (like the United States), Jupiterian influence (like the Venetians that imposed the Law of the Sea and took it to London and America), and other Earth and Water influences from sympathetic signs, but the Renaissance of the middle ages failed because the climate was too damp for spiritual fire.

The very word 'courage' means the "Age of the Heart" because the Old French word 'corage' means "heart" and it came from 'cuer,' which also means "heart" because it all comes from the Latin word 'coraticum' that became 'corraggio' in Italian and 'coraje' in Spanish, all meaning "heart."

Since I was born in the first degree of Leo, and my ascendant is Aries, one can now comprehend why my physical energy is supported by their relationship to do this work and serve Truth. It takes courage to serve Truth, which is why so few are willing to do it. They were too soaked over the past couple millennia to be effective, and so they are not used to being successful while speaking Truth. But all of that is about to change, so get used to it. As people catch on, the new fad will be to speak the hardcore Truth.

Jupiter, Guru, the Great Teacher, is also in the second degree of Sagittarius in my birth chart, his house of rulership, the third of the Fire triplicities, which influences me to also be a Great Teacher, an influence that is heightened by the Aeon of Aquarius.

But to be honest, I have no interest in teaching anyone. I know you're not going to acquire this knowledge in one place anywhere else, so this work must be done even if I don't enjoy doing it. Hopefully you will build off of it and condense it into even better presentations in the future.

It is important to comprehend the allegory of the Adversary, for that is where the name Satan comes from. Satan is not a physical entity, and for anyone who tells you it is, let them bear the burden of his or her proof. When he or she cannot bring you to Satan, or any of the other retarded interpretations of the scriptures, kindly shun these individuals from your life. They cannot serve Truth because there is no Truth in them anymore. The Adversary is always the opposite sign of the one in which the Sun is in. For example, John the Baptist (Aquarius) is the Adversary of King Herod (the Sun) when the Sun is in Leo, hence the beheading of John the Baptist that occurs astrologically on August 30th at approximately half past two in the morning.

Which constellation extends from Libra through Cancer? Hydra. Godhead is always comprised of a trinity. So too, then, must its Adversary be. In the case of the Bible, Cancer, Leo, and Virgo compose the three-headed hydra, the Devil. Leo, one third of the northwest, the Fire of God, is opposed to Aquarius, the Air of Man. Thus the concepts of Man (the quadrant of Earth, Air, and Water; material and negative charge) and God (the quadrant of Heaven, Fire, and Original nature; spiritual and positive charge) are adversaries of each other. This is the immortal creed of God becoming man, the Sun in the Vernal Equinox of Aries becoming the Sun in the Autumnal Equinox of Libra.

March 25th, Lady Day (Lady being Virgin Mary), the original New Year's Day, when the days and nights are in equal balance, corresponds to the day of Archangel Michael, September 29th, Michaelmas-day. The Sun enters into the sign, not the other way around. Therefore, God becomes man. Man does not become God.

In Revelation 9, after the star falls from Heaven (Cancer) to Earth (Capricorn), it describes the locusts like "horses made ready to battle (Sagittarius), and upon their heads as crowns like gold, and their faces as faces of men." Crowns and unicorns (mythical horses) are also symbols of Saturn, the ruler of Capricorn and Aquarius, who is a man; hence they have the faces of men. This is because the "abyss" is the region comprised of the southern signs of the Zodiac. The locusts torment the men who have not the seal of God upon their forehead for five months, as the torment of a scorpion.

Corona Borealis, the Northern Crown, is only seen from March through September. Well, what lasts for five months and starts of with a kiss of death from a scorpion? October 23 (Scorpio), November 22 (Sagittarius), December 21 (Capricorn), January 21 (Aquarius), and February 21 (Pisces). These are the five months of torment. The allegory depicts Winter, you literalist fools.

"In those days, men shall seek death, but they shall not find it," much like the idiots of these days looking for the Devil or Satan, or even Jesus or Michael for that matter, "and they shall desire to die, and the death shall flee from them." Why? Because in the abyss is where the Sun, or Son, is born again. It can't die. It's electromagnetic.

Gravity doesn't exist. Get that through your dimwitted noggin. You scoff at astrology that you can verify for yourself each night, yet you believe a five hundred year-old hypothesis that cannot be upgraded? You're a *clown*. Everything you thought you knew about "space" has come from the deceivers, the priests of Apollo. If you weren't ignorant of symbols, you'd never be fooled. Contemplate what a magnetic and electric universe means for the heavens, knowing that the luminous bodies you see every night are not what you've been led to believe they are.

If you're going to defeat the Inversive Brethren, you must have knowledge of theoretical magick: astrology. But most of you are hexed by scriptures that tell you not to engage in magick. That's like a captor commanding his captives to never untie the ropes that bind them, otherwise if they do, they'll be slaves forever. You have already demonstrated that you'll believe anything they present to you so long as you can be convinced that the lie comes from an "authority" figure. This is just as bad as the jokers waiting for Christ to return in the end times, not realizing that they come every damned year in Libra. And indeed, Christ returns not only every year, but also every day to save you from the abyss.

If you believe you're seeing light from trillions of years ago, yet they move in the same predictable positions for thousands of years while the galaxies containing them are traveling at millions of miles per hour in different directions, and that's what the stars are, then there is no hope for you till you take your ego to the toolshed and slaughter it. Trust me, I know how difficult it is. I was among the most low-level knowledge of people in existence. The only thing that enabled me to rise is my open heart that sought Truth no matter what. I may have been deceived and I may have been nescient, but I was never willfully ignorant.

The locusts had the hair of women (Virgo; August 23), teeth like that of a Lion (Leo; July 22), breastplates of iron (the crab of Cancer, the scarab; June 21), and iron corresponds to Mars who exalts in Capricorn, the abyss, but also rules Aries (the alter of gold before God), Scorpio, and the triplicities of Water during both the day and night (Cancer, Scorpio, and Pisces).

The locusts' wings (Scorpio, the White Eagle) were loud like chariots. Who rode across the sky in a golden chariot, the gift of Vulcan, the Daystar, led forth by horses full fed with ambrosia? Apollo, the Sun-god, beside him standing the Day, the Month, the Year, the Hours, and the Seasons.

Apollo tells his son Phaëton, "None but myself may drive the flaming car of day. Not even Jupiter, whose terrible right arm hurls the thunderbolts. The first part of the way is steep (from the dawn of Aries till the noon of Cancer), and such as the horses when fresh in the morning can hardly climb; the middle is high up in the heavens (noon, Cancer, the commencement of Summer), when I myself can scarcely, without alarm, look down and behold the earth and sea stretched beneath me. The last part of the road descends rapidly (from dusk through night, Autumn, Libra through Capricorn), and requires most careful driving."

Apollo continues to describe the Zodiac and the Cycle of Necessity, "The road, also is through the midst of frightful monsters. Thou must pass by the horns of the Bull (Taurus), in front of the Archer (Sagittarius), and near the Lion's jaws (Leo), and where the Scorpion (Scorpio) stretches its arms in one direction and the Crab (Cancer) in another."

There is a common witless notion by the majority of today's degraded race, the Satanic chaff who are so inauthentic that they don't even know which gender specific public bathrooms to use, that we originated from primitive people. This could not be any further from the Truth, for the ancients stood in Truth without the advanced technology that today's monkeys utilize, and it's evidenced by the path that Apollo advises Phaëton to guide the Sun on, "Don't take the straight road between the five circles, but turn off to the left. Keep within the limit of the middle zone, and avoid the northern and southern alike. Finally, keep in the well-worn ruts, and drive neither too high nor too low, for the middle course is safest and best."

Funny how the Bible uses the story of Apollo and Phaëton to describe the sound of the locusts' wings as the noise of chariots of many horses that have the authority to injure men for five months (Winter; the abyss), "and they have over them a king—the messenger of the abyss—a name is to him in Hebrew, Abaddon, and in the Greek he hath a name, Apollyon."

Why? Because it's the same story, guarding the same esoteric knowledge of the Sun's ecliptic through the Hours, the Days, the Months, the Seasons, the Years, and the Aeons, the astrological clock that maps your way back to the Creator. There's nothing wrong with the scriptures. The problem is you. Your daily bread is spoiled 'merx,' thus you have no ambrosia.

The reason we are in such a fight over whether the Earth is flat or a globe is because humanity is breaking the five hundred year-old hex of the Priests of Apollo, and when humanity figures it out, they will realize that we are in a torus field, a Taurus field: Earth, that looks like an apple, the sacred fruit of Apollo, one of God's sacred apples. It forms the shape of a tree in both directions, as above so below. It is the apple of the eye, the I, the Lord, the One.

The Devil takes Jesus to a very high mount (June 21st, the Summer Solstice) and shows him all the kingdoms of the world (the signs of the Zodiac), and says to Jesus, the Sun, "All these to thee I will give, if falling down thou mayest bow to me."

Knowing that Satan is the Adversary, and the Adversary is always the opposite sign, what opposes June 21st, the highest point of the Sun's journey? December 21st, its lowest point. As the Sun descends to its Winter Solstice, stillness, Satan is in front of it. But as it rises from December 25th, Satan, the adversary, is behind the Sun, hence the occult meaning of the phrase that Jesus says to Peter, "get thee behind me, Adversary (Satan)!" When Jesus says, "Go—Adversary, for it hath been written, the Lord thy God thou shalt bow to, and Him only thou shalt serve," the Sun is ascending and thus the

Adversary, Satan, is behind him, or bowing and worshipping.

In the Sixth Trumpet of Revelation, the altar of gold before God is Aries. The four messengers are what we covered in the Wheel of God, the Will of God: Taurus, Leo, Scorpio, and Aquarius, for they make up exactly one third of men, or one third of the twelve signs. The horses with lion heads that spew fire from their mouths are the three triplicities of Fire (Aries, Leo, Sagittarius) because, of the quadrants of the Zodiac (four horns), only one quadrant has no Fire signs, which would be the southeast (Capricorn, Aquarius, and Pisces).

In the other three quadrants (NE, NW, SW), one third of those signs are of the element of Fire, and by these three, one third of the men are killed, or one third of each quadrant. The rest of the men did not reform, so they must bow down to the demons, the idols of the Sun (gold; Aries and Leo), the Moon (silver; Taurus and Cancer), Venus (brass, which is made from copper, the metal of Venus), stone (which is of the earth: Taurus; a stone is a rock, which is also Zoroaster, the Rock Star, the Sun, Sardis, the pillar of God), and the element of wood, which implies Chinese astrology, hence the clue that these are the seven Churches of Asia (the signs of Aries through Libra), because the southeast quadrant didn't reform and thus these signs always follow the rest, or bow down to these idols.

As Jesus, the Sun, travels from one village and town to another along the ecliptic of the Zodiac, the world, he proclaims the good news of the kingdom of God: the Truth. The twelve signs are with him, and women who were healed from their evil spirits and ailments. Seven demons came from Mary, the sea (Mare, Maria, Marine). There are multiple meanings to this. At a macrocosmic level, the seven demons are the seven fixed signs (candlesticks) of Summer: Aries, Taurus, Gemini, Cancer, Leo, Virgo, and Libra, who were issued ("had gone forth") from the sea of Pisces, Mary in Winter. Demons are deities of the Moon, divided ones, daemons, diamonds: stars divided amongst the heavens.

Which constellation stretches over Gemini, Cancer, and Leo? Ursa Major, the Great Mother Bear. She is the Ship of St. Peter, the Brood Hen, the Big Dipper, the Car of Osiris, the Ark that carries the spiritual seed (the heavenly sustenance; the cerebral milk from the **Holy Claus**trum, *Santa Claus*) down the chimney (from the skull to the base of the spine) and into the naval of the woman (the Moon; Boaz), and then into the earthly sustenance of Cancer (the fluids of the breasts, stomach, and spleen). This is why the seven stars of Ursa Major are known as the Milkmaids of the Sky. The seven Milkmaids are the seven stars of Ursa Major: Dubhe, Merak, Phecda, Megrez, Alioth, Mizar, and Alkaid. This constellation is important to finding Polaris, the North Star, and since it rotates around Polaris, it is key to determining not only which direction North is, but also which season you are in. It is the astrological compass, clock, and calendar that God created for you, and any materialist dunce that attempts to explain otherwise is a fraud. This knowledge has been known for as long as humans have existed, and there's not a damn thing you inbred, degraded, satanic, service-to-self pedophiles can do about it. Perhaps if you didn't retard your blood by marrying your cousins for thousands of years in an attempt to hoard illusory wealth, you wouldn't be so incapable of observing the obvious.

Arcturus guards Ursa Major. This arch is also the **Ark** of the Covenant, which is also the allegory for the **Ark** of Noah. Cancer is where the Demiurge, the Artificer, descends. '**Ursa**' comes from the Latin word '**ursus**' and the Greek word '**arktos**,' meaning "bear." Which sign is in the north of the Zodiac? Cancer. The Latin word '**arcticus**' and the Greek word '**arktikos**' mean "north," which is why the North Pole is in the '**arctic**' circle. The **ark** is the **arc** and the **arch**.

Luke 8 describes this process, "And the great multitude (stars) having gathered, and those who from city to city (House to House) were coming unto him, he spake by a simile: The Sower (God, because a sower is also a sire, above rulership, one who sires) went forth to sow his seed (the Word, the Logos, the Astro Logos, word of light, word of the stars, astrology), and in his sowing some indeed fell by the way (set), and it was trodden down (passed over by the Sun), and the fowls of the heaven did devour it (fowls are hens, roosters; The Brood Hen, Ursa Major, the fowls of heaven that rotate around the North Star, the pole star, the arctic). 'And other fell upon the rock, and having sprung up, it did wither, though not having moisture. And other fell amidst the thorns, and the thorns having sprung up with it, did choke it. And other fell upon the ground, and having sprung up, it made fruit an hundred fold.' These things saying, he was calling, 'He having ears to hear—let him hear.'"

What falls and springs? The seasons, and with them, the stars and the days and nights. Luke 8:9 continues, "And his disciples were questioning him, saying, 'What may this simile be?' And he said, 'To you it hath been given to know the secrets of the reign of God, and to the rest in similes; that seeing they may not see, and hearing they may not understand.'"

The reign of God is the Cycle of the Sun, of the soul, of Necessity. This passage refers to the profane, the uninitiated. It is occult mockery of the religious fools who see but do not see, and hear but do not understand. They read their scriptures, driven mad by the lunacy of Circe, the Moon, the goddess of pharmakeia (sorcery; where 'pharmacy' comes from), who turns men into swine. Circe is Kirke, where the word 'church' comes from, because church also turns men into swine, as does the business, the Enterprise, of Captain Kirk, for they send your imaginations into space rather than focusing them on the here and now to be the change you wish to see.

These religious ignoramuses will bind each other with black magick, thwarting the spiritual evolution of others in addition to their own, killing each other over non-historical allegories, fighting amongst each other over imaginary lines and laws, and they will degrade themselves in such a way that they will never ascend to the next octave of existence.

I am in no way trying to reach these people. Only Nature can eradicate them over time, and she will. The people I'm trying to reach are the ones who know something is horribly wrong on both sides of the dialectic, and are looking to discover the nature of this world for themselves, not by taking other people's word for it, but through their own efforts.

The religious freaks are so hexed by priestcraft sorcery that they are literally content with doing nothing while evil runs amok, trafficking humans and raping and murdering children at the rate of one hundred per minute in a ninety billion dollar per year industry that could not exist if the world governments weren't facilitating it. The reason those yoked by priestcraft sorcery do nothing is because they "believe" these are the end times of John's Revelation, just like every other generation has "believed" they were in the end times.

Humans constructed a slavery system prison society while waiting for black magick false idols to return to make everything better and reinstate freedom, thus absolving them from the responsibility of their immoral behavior. They use phrases like "Jesus died for our sins," and pervert the allegory of the Sun giving us life in the seasons as though it means they can be perpetual fuck-ups and suffer no consequence because a fictional character named Jesus died for them on a hill named Skull (Golgotha).

I'm not attacking Christians; I'm merely exposing the dogma of my own kind. So don't assume I have any affinity towards other religions. In fact, I'm calling on the so-called real Jews, Muslims, Buddhists, Hindus, etc., who are sincere seekers of Truth, to gain knowledge of this material so that they may syncretize this information and expose their own kind. This will deliver renaissance. I know. I've done it before. I'm going to do it again. Last time we didn't have the internet. This time we do. Renaissance is coming and there's not a thing you can do to stop it, but you can certainly be destroyed by trying to thwart it, just as you can get hit by a train while standing on its tracks.

The religiously hexed half-truthers will spend all their time researching conspiracies and acquiring knowledge of the symptoms. They can tell you everything about how the monetary system functions, how governments function, and how this current system of debt and death functions, but they will never discover causality and change their behavior to program freedom instead of slavery. They'll boast of their sovereignty while eating the dead flesh of another being that was enslaved, tortured, and murdered in death camps funded by their capital, displaying no comprehension of the Law of Correspondence.

This was my biggest challenge, the most difficult part of the hex to break, and when I speak of these satanic mental retards, I speak with authority because I was one of them not long ago. If I can break the hex, then anyone can. My hexes came from all fronts, from the financial world to the entertainment world, the consumption of mass media and scripted news, poor diets, and years of indoctrination in Bolshevik Universe Cities. I have experiential knowledge of this material, so I know how much suffering occurs while getting rid of this poisoned worldview that degrades the hue-man.

None of this knowledge came to me till I stopped casually consuming dead flesh. If there were one act that you could abstain from that would reprogram your environment, it would be this. I couldn't see the stars beyond the major constellations till I changed my ways. The constellation of Cancer was not visible to me even though I knew where it was located. As I changed, the stars revealed themselves in much deeper detail, enabling me to grasp their significance. Now I can see Cancer even while observing it from huge cities like Los Angeles. The Crab's (the Scarab's) eyes come alive and pierce into my soul, and I'll never forget the way they appeared to me for the first time from the black templum that shrouds them. The luminous bodies are most certainly not what we've been led to believe they are.

So let us dispel the hexes being sustained by the black magick excerpt of John's Revelation. It is important to note that if one knows how to read it, the passage is a pure science. Only in its perversion does it become black magick due to its implementation by the priest class and their automaton minions who perpetuate it as a prophetic future end times event that frightens people into hopelessness and inaction.

Keep in mind that I am not going to explain every little detail to you. The hex can only be broken by the hexed. You have to do the work. The most beautiful gift that the Creator gave you was that no one can save you other than you. You are your own savior, and embarking on that path and doing that work *is* what makes this life worth living. That ultimate journey of self-discovery *is* the gift. I can give you everything, and it is still not enough, because so long as you believe in lies, and act on them, you are lost forever, and thus a slave forever. Your behavior will only be as good as the degree to which it is aligned with morality and Truth.

I do not spend any more time than necessary on the scriptures because they are a mockery of the human race. They've always been misleading, and they've always obfuscated the Truth and revealed their secrets only to the initiated minority who profit from the ignorance they create.

Here is the best advice on how to go about penetrating the

meanings of the scriptures, in the words of Arthur Edward Waite in *The Secret Doctrine In Israel,* "It is only as if casually that the word interpretation can be held to apply in any solid sense: the Secret Doctrine is rather the sense below the sense which is found in the literal word—as if one story were written on the obverse side of the parchment and another on the reverse side. This is not an exact comparison, but it gives my meaning clearly enough for the purpose. There are hard things said from time to time about the outward sense and they must not be taken too seriously, for the letter was always precious, if only as a vesture; but the difference between that which was within and without is well illustrated by a similitude which says that those who interpret Scripture according to the literal sense set the Sacred King and His Bride upon an ass, while those who understand it according to a mystic sense mount them nobly on a horse."

17 THE MARS COVENANT

The greatest (**great-est**, "great east, grace, favor, bounty, or cover of night") tool that the Black Magi use to cut you off from the Creator is **religion**, which comes from Latin words like '**religare**,' meaning "to bind fast or thwart from forward progress," corroborated by '**relacio**,' which is "to draw back," and finally '**religio**,' which is "a religious or other scruple that *arrests* and keeps us back from doing what we wish."

The moment you identify yourself as Christian, Jewish, Muslim, Hindu, Buddhist, Taoist, etc., is the moment you cut yourself off from the One that you are a microcosm of. There's no exception. You cannot serve two masters. You cannot serve God and man at the same time. If Truth is not your religion, then you are an enemy of Truth and thus must be destroyed by it.

God does not make religions. Man does. God creates laws that are observable through experimentation with Nature. Man does not create laws. Man dictates illegitimate whims or scruples to others. God does not make governments or nations. Man creates these thought forms. Man violates the laws of morality by trying to improve the perfect laws of the Creator, and thus man programs his own slavery. God enslaves no one. That is the business of man.

So how can man, who is the microcosm of God, be so flawed and so wrong in his ways? This is one of the deepest allegories of the scriptures. The heart, like the lion, is courageous, brave, and passionate, but it is also wrathful and ferocious. If tempered by reason, it brings harmony to the temple, the vernal equinox that generates the life of Summer. If unbalanced by out of control desires on the sensual plane, then it scorches the temple, putrefying the body till the death of Winter.

One of the greatest quotes I've ever come across, in regards to Natural Law, comes from Inez Eudora Perry, "Immutable law is the force which keeps everything in its destined course. Disobedience of God's laws results in inability to follow the course, together with ever-present danger."

I can help you, but in order to do that, you'll have to allow me into your mind, and once there, I will destroy everything erroneous. By the time I'm done, you may not have an insincere thought left. You may lose everything and everyone, but you will be whole, and you will serve the Truth of the Creator.

As we've covered previously, the number seven is associated with the Egyptian Set, which is the setting aspect of the Sun, the day's end, the week's end, which is why there are seven days in a week. Somewhere along the line, the Black Lodge perverted Set into being equated to Satan, or Saturn, the Adversary of the Sun. This is actually fine in terms of conceptualization, but erroneous in the aspect that it is evil or associated with immorality, because as we've disclosed, the Angel of Death is the Angel of Life.

According to Arthur Leo Zagat, seven is from the mind of the All. It represents eternal life to the Egyptians. To the Pueblo Indians, it represents the cosmic coordinates of man. In Africa, for the Bambara people of Senegal, seven is symbolical of perfection and unity. In the Hermetic teachings, seven represents the highest fold in the constitution of man. It is overwhelmingly obvious that seven is a powerful representation in the world of the occult, for it is seen hidden in vector symbolism in logos of every culture.

Seven is connected to the separation of everything by Time: Saturn. It is associated with Cernunnos, the Green Man, Shiva the Destroyer, and it becomes apparent that the parting of Time is connected to the Templars. We will cover that in depth, but for now let us remain on the subject of the Sun symbolism.

When banks are underwater, the government steals your wealth to **bail** them out. We're dealing with water again so rest assured, it is Maritime Admiralty Law. What is the device that is used to lower the rescue boats and all other cargo off of merchant ships and warships? The davit. It also lowers the anchors that keep ships from drifting.

Jesus, the fisher of men, says he is the offspring of David. The Star of David, which is the seal of Solomon that comes from Egypt, is a representation of the union of spirit and matter, the spiritual Sun residing in its center, and the spiritual correspondence to not only God, the spiritual center, but also to the physical Sun, the son of God that is the great mediator between us and the heavens.

Where else in the world of commerce is the word 'davit' reared? The affidavit, which is a sworn statement in writing made especially under oath (eed, as in mare-eed, the sea-oath) before an officer, someone who is off ice, but who is also an off-eye seer.

When in trouble, you are said to be in hot water. You may be arrested by pole ice, and will need to be bailed out of hot water. Or, they may send you a legal notice, which is not ice, because ice would cool the hot water down.

What is Solomon? It is three ways to say "the Sun." It's in the phonetics and word-splitting: 'Sol' + 'Om' + 'On.' Solomon is the Son of God, the Sun of God: Jesus. The hexed say, "Jesus will save you." This is the false savior, the false light, to keep you in hot water, waiting for someone who will never come, thus remaining in the very substance that is cooking you and turning you into food.

To pay bail is to pay Ba'al, and who is Ba'al Hammon? The Sun. To not see this is to have no long view of history and to remain ignorant. Ba'al is Jesus, the Lord Fish, the king of the gods who seized that position of divine kingship from Yam, the sea god. What color are the vegetables we call yams? Or-ange, because Or is the Sun.

Who is the father of Ba'al? Dagon, the fish-god, the very one who the Pope imitates with his miter. The Babylonians pronounced Ba'al as **Bel**, who the Greeks called **Bel**os and was identified with Zeus, Je-Zeus, who was also Zeus Ammon, another representation of the Sun. We can physically trace the inverted pentacle, the pentagram, which is a symbol of Zeus Ammon, the Sun, and Satanism, to also being a symbol of Ba'al, Jesus, and Christianity. They are all one and the same cult, yet the only ones who can't seem to figure it out are the brainwashed members.

This is why the rest of the world can't stand you. The fruit of your religions are slavery and death. Meanwhile, you blame everyone else for the slavery and death you cultivate, and then use those false accusations to continue to wage war and dupe your young, ignorant progeny to murder innocent people under wicked pretexts so that you can further dominate the geopolitical landscape of the nations.

The phony Phoenicians, who came from Canaan, burned their babies in sacrifices to Ba'al and Moloch, who is also the Sun. Ba'al *is* Moloch. Moloch *is* Jesus. The very word 'holocaust' means "burnt offering." Where do you think it really comes from? What is a primary characteristic of the psychopath? They cause the violation of Natural Law, the harm, and then act like the victim. But the Truth is that the psychopaths cannot survive without victims, and you have a whole civilization that has been transformed into psychopaths. It is beyond ethnicity. It has become a way of life for the majority of humanity.

God, Nature, could not care less. You seek slavery? You seek to remain silent while little children are trafficked, stabbed with pitchforks, hunted alive, burned alive, raped, and every other detestable act imaginable? That's fine. God's going to give you your slavery good and hard, like you *deserve* it.

So go ahead, keep getting your information from Canaan (CNN). Your citizen ship is in hot water, but like boiling frogs, you remain, waiting for the Sun to save you, and if you think about switching to the opposite polarity, they'll get you with FOX News. In numerology, FOX is 666. Regardless of which satanic poison you drink, you are doomed. Enjoy your free-doom. It is all you can eat, bay-bee.

The only solution is to become solvent in all aspects of your life, especially in health, because oil is a solvent. The Christ, the Cristos, the oil from the cerebrum, lubricates and purifies the body of the hue-man, just as oil lubricates man-made machinery. Oil neutralizes poison.

Ba'al, the Sun, is the son of El, God, Dagon, Saturn, Time, Chronos, because the Father is the Son. This is why the number seven is associated with the separation of Time as well as with the Sun. Jesus is the offspring of David (the Sun) and the morning star,

Lucifer, Venus, Mary, the Virgin (Virgo), for the Sun (David) is the davit that lowers Jesus (Horus) from Isis, the Moon. He is Ra, the Sun, and the son of God: El. This relationship is the primary trine of Israel (the solar system).

David is the Sun. "Sing ye to us of a song of Zion." That is, sing us the Psalms of David, the songs of the Sun during its journey through the Zodiac, through Zion. The Bible tells you the Truth in Revelation 22:16, "I, Jesus did send my messenger to testify to you these things concerning the assemblies; I am the root and the offspring of David, the bright and morning star!"

Is Jesus not the bearer of light? Is he not Luciferian, of the bearer of light, Lucifer, Columbia, Virgo, Mary? As Reverend Robert Taylor wrote, "Is he not **Be**lzebub, Lord of the Scorpion; Is he not **Be**lial, **Baal**i-Al, Lord of the Opposite; **Baal Ber**ith, Lord of the Covenant; **Baal** Peor, Lord of the Opening; **Baal** Zaphon, Lord of the North; **Baal** Perazim, Lord of the Divisions; **Baal** Samen, Lord of Heaven; **Baal** Aiten, the Lord Almighty; **Baal Moloch**, the Lord—the King?"

The pope and the Jews wear skullcaps in homage to El, Saturn, Father Time, the father of the Sun, Ba'al, **Baal**zebub. The Christians, Jesuits, Jews, Muslims, and every other solar cult in this world are Templars who administer justice to the people in their temples of Ba'al, the kangaroo courts of Maritime Admiralty Law, where their victims pay Ba'al, Jesus, Jupiter, Jew-Pater Ammon, Jupiter-Zeus.

As someone who comes from Christian, Jesuit, Crypto-Jew, phony Phoenician bloodlines, trust me... I did not like learning the wicked ways of my ancestors. These realizations have caused me to lash out verbally at times, and the amount of ridicule and assault that comes with serving the obvious Truth ruins the quality of life like one cannot imagine.

We have unwittingly constructed a giant occulted prison with our ignorance and violations of Natural Law. There is nothing rewarding about dispelling hexes that generate this condition other than knowing it is in service to the Creator. That's why serving Truth is the most important work.

In doing my own spiritual work, I inquired about what I was hiding from myself. The symbolism given unto me was that I was a force devoid, or detached, from Spirit. In my satanic upbringing, I was cultivated into someone who manifested blind, violent energy. I was dogmatic, stubborn, willfully cruel, and unyielding. I was the epitome of Will without Understanding, the type of energy that self-immolates in the Leonine fires it evokes.

When I sought a remedy, a solvent if you will, I asked how I could escape the prison that only I built. The answer that I was given conveyed that the solution rests with Will in its most exalted form, guided by love, free from any purpose or desired results: the Creative Will.

In order to understand the Templars, we must understand the temple. But in order to understand the temple, we must first understand the nature of Heaven. In the Zodiac, as well as between the temples of man's head, the Lord of Hosts resides in the most high: Aries, the Temple of Mars, where the Sun is exalted. This is the cerebrum.

Without the knowledge of the nature of Heaven, and that which created it, one might as well end his or her journey in the occult, for there is nothing that can be gained or mastered by those who refuse Truth. The original form of the Creator must be perfect. That which is perfect is oldest.

That which is perfect must have perfect form. Which form in this world do we observe as being perfect? The circle. The sky we observe is without a doubt spherical, because the empyrean cascades from perfection, and as far as this construct is concerned, it is perfection, for it is the only part of this world that man's nature cannot physically pervert.

The circle is perfect because it is the first form and made from a single line. Not only that, it represents the real nature of centripetal and centrifugal forces that compose this magnetic and electric universe where phony Phoenician concepts like "gravity" do not exist outside of polluted, degraded minds.

Just as Heaven reflects the Creator, the dome of your skull, Golgotha, reflects Heaven. This is the temple of the mind, the All. All currents meet at equal lengths in the center of a circle or a sphere of perfect form. All forces, observed and unobserved, converge here to manifest the physical world in each torus field. This very requirement is precisely why the concept of an infinite, ever-expanding universe is impossible.

The sphere is permanent, and it contains everything within itself. The Zodiac is the perfect representation of this, for it is a zoo from which all the powers of spirit are formed, and since the nature of the sphere is all one, and all material bodies are formed in its center, then all material bodies are also one nature. Why? Because the sphere is self-similar across all scales.

It is precisely this form that enables all seemingly opposite polarities to be reconciled into one, the One: Absolute Truth. Therefore, if we want to understand the currents that compose who we are, we must examine where those currents came from at the time of our manifestation.

Talismans derive their power and virtue from the luminaries, which is why another word used to describe an order of angels is 'virtues.' The angels are the angles, and the angles at which the planets and stars correspond to each other, as well as with Earth, either intensify the virtues by working with their effects, or they weaken the virtues by working against their effects. For example, the virtues of hot planets are magnified by the Sun and the virtues of cold planets are magnified by the Moon, regardless of the additional effects that the aspects of the fixed stars have on them.

The most powerful currents to negotiate with are the workings of the luminous bodies that modern people have been led to believe are planets. Knowing that gravity does not exist and that Einstein is a fraudster, that dielectricity and magnetism produce electricity, and that's what type of universe we live in, this subject should be of particular interest to those who will change this paradigm of debt and death.

All serious servants of Truth should plan on taking action for good works when the Moon is not being affected by the combustion of the Sun (within twelve degrees of the Sun, but I'd stay at least seventeen degrees away unless it were an emergency). They should strive to take action when Luna is in a humane sign (Gemini, Virgo, Libra, Sagittarius, Aquarius), for helping the young generations learn trades and arts, as they will be the ones who really repair our broken paradigm. The humane signs are also great for helping our travelers, explorers, and sailors have safe journeys and returns.

While working with the humane signs is encouraged, they are not right for all good works. Another technique will also serve you for manifesting quick and assured effects of your actions and crafting talismans. Good works with urgency must be done when the Moon is in a sign of short, also known as direct, ascension (Capricorn, Aquarius, Pisces, Aries, Taurus, and Gemini). The other signs are of oblique (long) ascension, and while their effects may be brought to fruition, they are slower to manifest.

Unless an emergency, the service to God rituals should be planned when the infortunes (Saturn and Mars) are not affecting the Moon, and when the fortunes (Jupiter and Venus) are joined to Luna in trine or sextile aspects.

Likewise, servants of the Creator should take care to prepare and guard themselves around the times when Luna is applying to an eclipse, as well as if she is assimilated to the motion of Saturn (moving less than twelve degrees in a day).

When Luna is in the Via Combusta (from eighth degree of Libra to the third degree of Scorpio), no rituals should be commenced. If she is at the end of a sign, then this period should also be avoided because the ends of signs are the terms of infortunes.

It is also advisable to not engage in ritual when Luna is in the ninth house because it is the Cadent House that deals with generalities and the principles we adhere to regarding philosophy, religion, fortune, worldly travel, science, and art. These are not favorable positions for manifesting the Great Work into massive action.

This is what it means to comprehend the currents around you. Simply put, the knowledge of magick could also be regarded as situational awareness. It is nothing like what the Hollywood pretenders lead you to believe it is. The use of magick is more like wilderness survival. If you know how to find the materials in the environment Nature provides you with, and then hone them into a properly functioning bow drill, you can make a fire in almost any condition. It works the same with theoretical and practical magick.

If someone is ignorant of the laws of thermodynamics, the physics of friction, and other Natural Laws, he may see this act of igniting a fire in a tinder bundle, with an ember accumulated from rubbing wood together, as the High Sorcery of a Fire Mage. But to the learned, the logical, and the knowers, this is common sense and as easy to learn as riding a bicycle. Likewise, if someone is ignorant of astrology and symbols, then he can't fathom the amount of attention and energy that is affecting the world all around him. This individual is very likely a coincidence theorist, which is perhaps the most detrimental level of consciousness to maintain.

If one doesn't know how deep a river is, he shouldn't try to cross it. But if he can see the bottom and determine its depth, as well as how fast it flows, then his chances of success in arriving at his planned destination increase tremendously because he will either cross at an appropriate point or avoid a potential catastrophe by taking a safer route.

If the traveler cannot see the bottom, due to the whitewater rapids or churning sediment, then perhaps he can use other means to measure the depth, like a stick. Regardless of conditions, if that water is moving too fast or is too murky to see the bottom, then it is not able to grant safe passage unless some sort of vessel or bridge is used to cross it.

If the individual crossing has studied the river and acquired the knowledge of all its secret nature, then perhaps he's made a map of it, and perhaps that map has been copied and the knowledge of its nature has been disseminated so widely that people of that region have no need for the map anymore. Perhaps everyone knows that there is a bridge, or a narrow, shallow, and calm portion of that river that people can cross with zero risk rather than trying to make the crossing at an inopportune time.

The currents and nature of the river are akin to the currents and nature of the Zodiac and the cycles of Heaven. White magick would be making a map of that river so that even the most naturally unobservant people could possess the map, and use the knowledge of the river to cross safely. This knowledge could enable people to build around the river and create ways to travel across it without disrupting its flow or its properties.

Black magick would be building a dam and stopping the river for selfish purposes, not caring about how the rest of the environment that relied on that river's flow will die due to deprivation of its water supply. The Black Magi only care about what's right for themselves at the time of the casting, because what's right today may change tomorrow, and so the only thing that's right, according to them, is that which caters to or satiates their carnal, selfish desires. This is moral relativism, the second major tenet of Satanism. The Black Magi may even find benefit in destroying the maps to hide all knowledge of that river's nature while carving paths that lead to its deepest parts so that travelers drown themselves trying to cross it, thus creating a problem in need of a solution. Naturally, they'd have the solution, the knowledge, so perhaps they'd be your guides to safe passage, for a fee of course.

The Black Magi love to profit off of people's ignorance, for if there were no ignorance, there'd be no profit to be made. They are parasites that do nothing to help others. They help only themselves and their own kind so that they can sustain their industries of racket while doing nothing to produce value or a better quality of life for the rest of the race. But most of you will never see it that way because you have been deceived by the illusion of convenience.

Convenience, like security, is one of the greatest tools in the sorcerer's bag to lure people into practicing a way of life that benefits the sorcerer, not the victim, but is so ingenious that the victim actually thinks the sorcerer has his best interest in mind and that life is indeed being improved. We see this primarily in technology and government.

As a species, we have lost our abilities to survive in Nature without modern technology, myself included. If the just-in-time delivery system fails, the current population would be forced to survive in 17th or 18th century environments but without the skill sets to do so. Most of them wouldn't make it through the winter. Not only that, back then people could drink from every body of water because there was not as much pollution. Now, clean water and fertile soil are incredibly rare, and there is certainly not enough to sustain a population of over 300 million people at its current ratio of less than one percent being responsible for the nation's food production.

This type of collapse wouldn't take much more than a removal of the US Dollar as the world's reserve currency. The lack of purchasing power in the dollar would make the goods we've grown accustomed to unaffordable, because in this paradigm, cheap oil, a consumer economy that produces almost nothing in America, allowing our corporations to exploit people in less fortunate countries under slave wages, and the strongest purchasing power of all fiat paper have enabled us to buy everyone else's goods and ship them here for less than it would cost us to produce and consume it ourselves under fair wages.

How much of your food do you grow? How much of your heat do you provide for yourself by mining coal or chopping wood? Do you rely on oil for heat? What happens if you can't get it for cheap and your heating bill is like that of your rent? Do you eat meat? How much of that do you farm? How much of the meat did you kill and butcher the animal for? In fact, contemplate what you actually produce every day versus what you consume. Do you produce more than you consume or consume more than you produce? That is most likely a source of your comfort or your suffering, now and in the times to come.

Without digressing into a novel about economics, it is sufficient to say that most of us, including myself, live a way of life that is completely dependent on the current paradigm, even if we are in the process of transitioning to a way of life that is independent of the system. By creating a convenient way of life through technology, sorcerers who control that way of life can dupe their victims into yielding their real skills, their real relationships, their real assets, their real food and health practices, and their real knowledge of the natural world's Truth. After a couple generations, almost no one will have anything real, know anything real, nor strive for anything real, and that's exactly where we are today. The majority of humanity is under a hex.

If it weren't for my experiences in the financial world, and the crash of 2008, I wouldn't have questioned the system I was participating in. No one seems to care about Truth when they are too busy benefiting off their immoral behavior, and outside of people who intentionally harm others, I was as satanic as it gets. I never intentionally hurt anyone, but my nescience and violations of Natural Law contributed to and programmed this paradigm of slavery as much as the next person did.

If it weren't for me learning about the banking system that controls the world, I wouldn't have learned about the occult nature of what's really occurring. Thankfully, a gentleman who I consider a mentor, created an academy for bringing people up to speed on the mechanisms of the way this world runs. There is no better one-stop-shop to upgrade knowledge of the banking world and the cycles of empires and economies than the Sons of Liberty Academy (SOLA). It's about fifty hours worth of documentary footage, but it'll teach you more in a couple weeks than you'll ever learn in a university or other institution. And most importantly, it will save you the spiritual currencies of time and attention by trying to find these nuggets of Truth ore in the vast wilderness of available information.

The other scheme that the sorcerers love to consensually enslave people with is the illusion of security. People are so irresponsible, so ignorant, so near-sighted, so egotistical, and so dimwitted that they will relinquish virtually any inherent right bestowed upon them if they can be made to fear for their lives. Create terrorism, use that to justify the need for more government and less freedom for the sake of security, and slowly increase this pressure through a satanic ideology known as man's law, and before long, everything that empowers people can be made "illegal."

So long as people like military and police types are willing to steal freedom for a paycheck, then the sorcerers will have victims who will not only manifest their designs, but also willfully absorb the karmic consequences of doing so while the sorcerers remain unscathed. The worst joke of all is that these individuals have such low IQs that they actually believe they are fighting for goodness and freedom, and that they took an oath to something other than a corporation. The reality is that they are nothing more than pirates working on behalf of pedophiles.

The pathetic cult of death will be utterly decimated soon enough, and the majority of humanity will view those in the military and police with the same level of contempt that they currently view Nazis, regardless of what one's opinion about that era's historical accuracy is. If you find yourself working in those fields of stealing freedom, swallow your feeble emotions right now and quit your cult so you can be ahead of the curve. People have short memories. They won't care that you *worked* for these crime syndicates. They will care that you *work* for them when they lose everything. When the USA collapses, and the government runs out of fiat paper to pay you with (that has any purchasing power), those who worked for the government will be the highest valued targets of a population that is armed, enraged, and has nothing left to lose.

Can you blame them? They will be left with nothing when the show stops, and it was only possible because you protected and upheld a government that was composed of over one third pedophiles who were only granted powerful positions because they could be blackmailed, by the country to which they are duel citizens of, into passing legislature that destroys American sovereignty and further entangles us with demonic parasites that do not benefit humanity or the natural world.

You were gang-raping people and getting promoted for it during your service. Your spouse loves a satanic rapist. Your children love a satanic rapist. Tell them the Truth about what you've done. Why wouldn't Americans kill you? You are the enemy of the people. You are the enemy of Truth. You are the enemy of Freedom. It was you who brought the resultant harm into physical manifestation. I'm here to help you quit your Roman Cult before the American people figure out what you've done, and the reason I offer this help is so that you can be granted one more opportunity to evolve spiritually, because once this paradigm shifts, you will not be given a second chance, not by me nor by any other hardcore American patriot who is tired of having the fruits of his labor stolen to pay your salary while you sell the children of Israel into slavery and meddle with our inherent sovereignty.

There are far more pissed off people in the shadows that you don't hear from than there are in your pedophile government to protect you. Remember, they don't do the fighting. You'd lose the war of attrition by virtue of the numbers alone, and if you couldn't lose in the physical battle, you'll eventually starve to death because you don't produce anything of value.

You work for the cult of the Baal-Berith, "Lord of the Covenant." 'Lord' comes from Phoenician words that mean "the sun; the light," which is how we know that Baal is not only the Lord of the Covenant, but also the Sun, the Light of the Covenant, which are the arcs of the Zodiac, most notably the covenants of works and grace. What are the covenants made up of? Months. This is why the last four months in the ten-month calendar of Romulus were named after covenants: Septem-ber (Seventh Covenant), Octo-ber (Eighth Covenant), Novem-ber (Ninth-Covenant), and Decem-ber (Tenth

Covenant). They are the covenants (beriths) of the Sun (the Lord; Baal).

When examining the covenants, the months, Heaven, time, space, balance, and other qualities of nature that have been accounted for, we come across amazing discoveries using Latin etymology. The primary word to consider is what the Deaf Phoenicians of today describe as the etymology and meaning of the word 'temple': the Latin word 'templum.'

'Templum' is "a space divided off and marked out." 'Contemplor' is "to look about a space marked off." This is obviously where the English word 'contemplate' comes from, which is "to observe, study, and consider deeply or thoroughly."

In regards to the balance of Nature, the Latin word 'tempe' translates to "any pleasant spots," which is where the word 'temperate' comes from, meaning "moderate." Therefore to lose one's temper is to lose one's moderate or balanced thoughts, emotions, and actions. Which signs in the Zodiac are associated with balance? Libra (the Scales of Justice, of Atonement: Judgment Day) and Aries (the Hill of Mars), where the Autumnal and Spring Equinoxes occur respectively (equal nights and days).

This is why the English word 'temper,' as a verb, is "to moderate or mitigate," and thus it's observable that it comes from the Latin word 'tempero,' which is "to temper, qualify, moderate."

To 'moderate' is to "preside over," similar to what a judge is supposed to do. What is the one thing whose judgment nothing can escape in this physical construct? Time, which is why the judges in today's kangaroo courts wear black military robes. 'Tempori/temperi' translates as "in good time." Time is black because the Angel of Death, which corresponds to Saturn, represents it.

Keeping in mind the previous knowledge that the Angel of Death is also the Angel of Life, we see that the Angel of Life (the Sun that measures space) is also Time (Saturn), who determines death. The Latin word 'tempus' syncretizes this knowledge in its meaning being "divided into sections as seasons, years, etc., a portion cut off, as of the heavens which the Sun measures off every hour which is determined by the course of the Sun." This is why 'hours' is an anagram for 'Horus.' The Sun measures time.

'Tempto/temptulum' is "to explore, as applied to the space in the heaven looked at by the Augurs," who are diviners by birds. The Augurs use a clarion-shaped staff known as a lituus to mark off these regions of the heavens. Notice that the Augurs are diviners by birds and that the Green Language we are exploring is called the Language of the Birds.

We see that the words 'templum' and 'tempus' both refer to "a portion of the sky being marked off and measured in time, but specifically determined by the course of the hours, Horus, the Sol (the round plate of fire): God." Therefore, the word 'temple' is "the house of God, or the House of the Zodiac that the Sun is currently in."

When we see words like 'inaugurate,' we must not stop at the status quo definition of "to make a formal beginning of, initiate, install, or induct." The occult meaning clearly contains the unadulterated form of 'augur,' which we may use to summarize 'inaugurate' as being "to initiate by the Divine Will of God." And so this influences the concept of the Divine Right of Kings that is associated with Martial Law rule, the law of emergency and necessity by which the satanic governments of today use to subvert Common Law by putting nations into bankruptcy.

Now we must expose the "temple" from where Martial Law derives. The first house of the Zodiac is Aries, the planetary ruler of which is Mars because in the calendar of Romulus, the first month of the year is Martius (March) due to the equal days and nights at the Vernal Equinox. 'Aries' is the Latin word for 'ram,' and since the House of Aries is the first house in the Cycle of Necessity, it is the most high, the Temple of the Lord, the Ram of March, because 'rama' in Sanskrit means "most high."

The reader should find it obvious that the very word 'temple' has nothing to do with religious grottos or buildings on the on the physical earth. Temples are portions in the heavens, the houses of the Zodiac. Now it is necessary to disclose why Mars rules Aries and is the Lord of Hosts.

The clergy of the Black Magi who specialized in the administration of judgment were named 'templars' for all of the reasons above, and they named the colleges, to which the study of the temple (judgment) was devoted, universe cities: 'universities.'

Thus, when the clergy went to a university to study the natural sciences, they were really going to a universe city to study the heavens, so that they could administer judgment.

'**Ad-minister**' quite literally means "towards a monster" ('**minister**' being "a moon star, a monster"; '**mon-**' and '**min-**' both pertaining to the Moon + '**ster**' pertaining to '**aster**' which means "star"). '**Judgment**' is "to judge mind." Thus, to '**administer judgment**' is "to judge the mind of a monster, a lunatic, the mind of the moon, the cerebellum (Taurus), the monkey mind," which is why *if* you need a lawyer to re-present you it is an admission of incompetence to the court you play on. As George Carlin said, "They've got you by the balls!"

Who does a clergy administer judgment on behalf of? What conquers the cerebellum animal-mind? The optic thalamus, the cerebrum, the conscious God-mind, the Lord, the most high, the Ram, the Rama of Aries, the Eye of Providence, the Eye Single (One-Eye). Who rules the temple of Aries? Mars. Since the All is mind, the templars administer judgment, or judge all, on behalf of the One: God.

Where have we seen '**one-eye**' before, both literally and through the Language of the Birds? Right on the '**mon-ey**,' because in the world of Commerce, which is business and sex, all deals must be to an exact amount, exactly right, or in other words, '**right on the money**.' Which type of rule governs Commerce? The Law of the Sea: Maritime Admiralty Law, the Law of Martius, Mars, because Mars shall rule the currents and the seas, the currencies.

The Divine Right of Kings is a combination of the third and fourth major tenets of the ideology known today as Satanism: Social Darwinism + Eugenics. Regarding Mars, this at least goes back to ancient Greece, where the legal institution that was the central government of ancient Athens was known as the Council of Nobles, or the Aristocratic Council: the '**Areopagus**,' which translates to "The Hill of Ares." Who is Ares? He is the Greek version of Mars.

The symbolism of the name Areopagus is that the templum (Zodiacal sign) known as Aries (the Hill of Ares, of Mars) commences, or is initiated, on the vernal equinox, when the days and nights are of equal balance, or tempered, and the impartiality of the Sun rules everything equally as it moves through the Temple of the Lord, the templum of the most high. This is seen in the allegory of Revelation 21, and without reciting the whole passage here, the initiated can see the codes in phrases like the "new heaven" (Aries) and "new earth" (Taurus), "Alpha/beginning" (Aries) and "Omega/end" (Pisces), "water of life" (Mercury), "Spirit of the mountain great and high" and "holy Jerusalem" (Aries, Hill of Mars), "twelve gates, messengers, and tribes" (the twelve signs of the Zodiac), the "twelve apostles of the Lamb" (Jesus is the Lamb of God, the Sun, and the twelve apostles are the Zodiacal signs in which he travels through), "the lamp is the Lamb" (Jesus is the Sun), and so on. The templars are Priests of the Sun, of Apollo, by virtue alone.

In order to become a member of the Areopagus, which was lifelong, one had to be evaluated after serving as one of the Nine Archons of Athens. The Archon Eponymous was the chief justiciar, the Head of State, and president of the Boule (Council) and Ecclesia (Popular Assembly). This is the most powerful of the Archons (rulers). Hopefully, now, one can appreciate the necessity of living in a state of anarchy (without archons, rulers) if we ever are to live under the condition of Freedom.

The next most powerful archon was the polemarch, who commanded the military: War (**Mars**). He acted as the *judge* over cases involving foreigners. The third most powerful of the archons was what remained of the monarchy, the **Basil**eus (King), who was the chief religious officer and president of the Areopagus. He presided over cases involving homicide. The remaining six archons were thesmothetai (Determiners of Custom), who were general legal authorities that presided over miscellaneous judicial proceedings.

Where have the modern templars made their seat of power? Switzerland. Where is their World's Central Bank located? **Basel**, which has the same phonetic sound as **Basil**-eus: King. The Knights Templar created the first banking system during the crusades, and converted the over 800 castles that they seized into their banks. Today, the World Bank in Basel is known as the Bank for International Settlements.

As Greece gave way to Rome, the Priests of Apollo took their sorcery to Italy. When the Roman Empire collapsed, the phony Phoenician Venetians stayed in Venice for a little over a thousand years as the black nobility before being forced to flee, taking their solar cult black magick to Great Britain.

In the City of London, a corporation owned by the Vatican (which owns D.C. and everything in contract with the United States now), the Black Magi built the Templar Church known as the Crown Temple, and since the Crown is a symbol of Chronos, of Saturn, of Father Time, another name for this would be the Temple of Time. There, on Fleet Street, the templars established the Temple Bar, which is the modern day Areopagus, the Hill of Mars, the God of War. This is why all Bar Attorneys exist in the "Bar Association." They have pledged allegiance to the Knights Templar Church because they are waging commercial war in the Temples of Mars, the courts under Maritime Admiralty Law, the Law of the Sea, the Law of Money: Commerce.

All satanic Bar Associations are franchises of the International Bar Association at the Inns of Court at Crown Temple at Chancery Lane, in the City of London, the Vatican-owned corporation. The City of London is not to be confused with London, for they are not related, just as Washington, D.C. is not to be confused with a State in the United States of America.

If you're a Bar Attorney, you've either knowingly or unwittingly sworn allegiance to the Knights Templar, and are thus not a lawyer but a Bar Association licensed attorney that may not exercise law, but only enforce policy. In order to remain competent, one cannot have a public defender or council, and since there are no real lawyers in these kangaroo courts, one must present oneself in a special appearance to defeat all presumptions against him.

Before the presumptions can be defeated in court, they must be defeated in the way one lives his every day life. Until the level of humanity's consciousness is raised and we can abrogate all man-made systems of rule, one cannot agree to be a slave and claim to be free if he is to coexist as a sovereign while the black magick system is still in place. One must do things such as revoke his voter registration and get Common Law identification, an affidavit of corporate denial, serve estoppels to anyone who has an oath of office that may wage commercial warfare against him (Chief Judges, FBI special agents in charge, US Marshalls, the US Attorney, Attorney General, District Attorney, County Attorney, City

Attorney, County Sheriff, Chief of Police, and other servants of evil), and file criminal complaints against the satanic Templars masquerading as so-called public servants who get involved, and then send a copy of the complaint(s) to the US Attorney. The reason being is that the State Citizen is unconditionally sovereign **absent contract.**

American sovereigns are entitled to all rights that formerly belonged to the King. This makes every American a king or queen, independent of all laws except those of Nature. The only way that the Black Magi can restrict a sovereign's rights is by duping him or her into voluntarily surrendering them through contract. In order to do this, the Black Magi had to create a system based on contracts that all people must enter into in order to participate in Commerce. They did this by creating the US Citizen, birth certificates, social security numbers, licenses, Federal Reserve notes as currency, the IRS, taxpayers, the jurisdiction of Washington, D.C., and many other scams. They have constructed a system in which every time we do anything in the world of Commerce, such as simple transactions like buying one's groceries with fiat paper currency or bankcards, we unknowingly enter into contracts under our legal fiction Cestui Que Vie Trusts as US Citizens, thus waiving our sovereign State Citizen rights. Taxpayers are not State Citizens. They are US Citizens. Income is corporate profit. State Citizens are not corporations. US Citizens are. State Citizens are incapable of having their rights impaired by legislation or judicial decision. US Citizens are not. This creepy black magick system is exactly how the sorcerers tricked the ignorant population into contractually giving up their rights in exchange for "privileges." These are the sorts of things that only demons, those under willful desire or premeditated obsession, dream up.

One may wonder what the payoff for knowing this information is. The Black Magi are masters of creating systems that are inimical to the interests of the masses, but are cleverly disguised in different cultures and languages throughout the ages to be not only based on consent, but also seemingly beneficial and convenient. Even after all I've just enucleated, most of you don't care and would still prefer to use your bankcards and leave your wealth in the Inversive Brethren's banking system, even though you are an unsecured creditor and absorb all the counterparty risk should they go under. Most of you still want to keep your government "benefits." You will most likely not start caring about these things until you're in a post-dollar world, allowing some carpetbagger demon-troll to sodomize you in exchange for a can of soup. Then you'll wonder why you didn't take these matters seriously while you had resources. But if one knows the sacred science from which all magick is derived, astrology, then the brand of magick that the Black Magi use in each region they flee to cannot be concealed from that individual or a populace who is well-informed. They can then take the necessary precautions to defend themselves from it.

The more people that learn the sacred science, the less people can be duped into agreeing to be slaves. Note that the sacred science cannot merely be learned through reading books. Reading as many books about astrology as one can is only the prerequisite. At some point, the initiate must observe Heaven and experiment with Natural Law for himself. The effects of the currents can be as diverse as the people who are created by them.

The Inversive Brethren derive their power from your ignorance. Your ignorance *is* what makes you their victim. They are experts in Natural Law, the way this world works, which is why their name is based on the temple in which all reckoning of Time in the western world began: the Lamb of Mars, March, when the Sun is crucified on, or crosses, the vernal equinox to give the justice of equal night and day to the whole world, the Zodiac. This is the symbolism of the checkered board, the duality of the black and white, of darkness and light.

No matter how well-intentioned the templars may have originally been, all of man's laws are based on moral relativism and are either unnecessary if aligned with Nature or wrong if in violation of Nature, thus they are satanic on their face, and all collectives degenerate into Satanism, which is why it was only a matter of time before they were absorbed by the archons.

After the phony Phoenician Venetians fled Italy, they founded their new capital in England and named it London, which, in the Language of the Birds, is comprised of Phoenician words. Using word-splitting, we can see that 'London' becomes 'L-on-don,' which would then phonetically be 'El-On-Don,' or 'Elondon.'

'El' conveys the meaning of "God, the Sun, Saturn, the Angel of Life and Death." 'On' means "the being," but it is also symbolic to the Sun because the capital of Egypt, Sun City, was named On. 'Don' means "the Lord," which, as we've seen in the phony Phoenician black magick religions, the Lord is also God, the Sun, the Rock Star (Zoroaster), the Godfather, Jupiter, the father of all gods and giver of all good things.

The Phoenicians took 'adon' (אדון), meaning "Lord," which is where 'Adonai' (My Lords) comes from, to Greece. The Phoenicians used Adonai in reference to Tammuz, which when brought to Greece was incorporated into Greek mythology to preserve their knowledge, for Adonis is "the Lord being of Fire," which is the Sun: God. Adonis is based on the Egyptian Osiris, so even if the Black Magi destroy all physical evidence on the Earth of the past, as long as the knowledge of languages exists, their history cannot be concealed. Truth can never be destroyed.

Where did the Black Magi stop between Egypt and Phoenicia? Babalon. Hopefully now, it is no stretch to your imagination how 'Baba' + 'L' (El) + 'On' = "Father God, the Sun-being," which would just make it another encoding of Amun, as in Jupiter Ammon, IO. It's ironic that so many passionate Christians are speaking out against the Babalon system while worshipping the same deity and ideology of it: the Sun, Jupiter Ammon, Zeus Ammon, Jupiter-Zeus, Jesus.

18 NATURA NATURATA

One of the Latin words we'll keep circling back to is 'sol,' because it means "a round plate," and it was designated as a name for the Sun because the Sun looked like a round plate of fire to the ancients. Not only that, but the spiritual correspondence to the essence of the Spirit undoubtedly led to the word 'soul' to describe such matter. By a small adjustment, it was also encoded in the Bible so that anyone with a mind developed beyond that of a 10 year-old could figure it out with a sincere effort.

St. Paul's Cathedral in Elondon also has a spiritual correspondence and significance to the solar cult of Death and Time that's related to Ares. So, grab your survival shelter poncho. We're going deeper into the rabbit hole and it's about to open up into another network.

The Black Magi tell you who the **Sol** is, who the **soul** is. The name couldn't be more similar without being confused with a different part of the body: **Saul.** For you literalist inbred ignoramuses, it is unmistakably clear in Acts 13:9, "And Saul—who is also Paul—having been filled with the Holy Spirit." If you cannot comprehend this, stop marrying your cousins to preserve your "eugenic" bloodlines, and maybe your lineage will have a chance at healing itself from the mental and physical retardation your ancestors have brought upon humanity.

Saul is the Sun in Sagittarius who filled the grape with the Spirit so hue-mans can make wine. Acts 13:11 continues, "A hand of the

216

Lord is upon thee, and thou shalt be blind, not seeing the Sun for a season." Which sign in the Zodiac is blind and is the force of judgment that Saul, the Sol, the Sun, is blind to? Justice. The very thing that the Templars administer on behalf of Saul, who is Paul: Saint Paul. What season follows the blind virgin holding the scales? Winter. Indeed, Winter is coming.

Acts 13:13 further illustrates the Sun's journey back to Jerusalem, the Hill of Mars, "Paul having set sail from Paphos (Pisces; Paphos is based on Pygmalion and her son Paphos, which are connected to Aphrodite, which embodies Venus and Cupid, the symbol of Pisces), and John (the constellation of Aquarius) having departed from them did turn back to Jerusalem (Aries)."

Paul came to Perga (Pergamos; Cancer) and, having gone through Cancer, went all the way around the Zodiac to Pisidia, located in Mount Taurus in the physical world, which they obviously chose to correspond to the astrological Taurus, symbolical of the black fertile soil of the lower mind: Egypt; Al Khem (notice its phonetic correspondence to '**Alchemy**'). After Taurus, Paul is raised up to *them*, one of the Twins of May: Gemini. What are the names of the twins? Castor and **Po**llux, which is **Paul**-lux, the light of Paul, of Saul, the Sun: David, which is the Sun who is raised up to *them* for a king, who does the Will of God.

Acts 13:23 further reveals, "Of this one's seed God, according to promise, did raise to Israel a Savior—Jesus." Jesus is the Word of God, the seed, the Cristos, the oil, the Sun, the Sol, Paul/Saul, the offspring of David, that is being raised to the Solar System, the body of the cosmic man: Adam Kadmon. As John (Aquarius) preached before his coming, a baptism of reformation, and then fulfilling his course at the end of Summer when the constellation Aquarius sinks back beneath the horizon into the "wilderness," the Twins of May raise the Sun to its high point at the Church of Pergamos (Perga; Cancer), which is the Summer Solstice on June 21st.

Acts 13, just like the other passages, describes the cycle of the Sun, and the Cristos, the seed, through the physical body. It's always "turning" to the nations, the signs of the Zodiac, the regions of the cosmic body. The Bible is literally teaching its readers to follow the path of the Sun, the Lord, so that they will know *the way*, "for so hath the Lord commanded us: I have set thee for a light of nations—

for thy being for salvation unto the end of the earth." The light of the nations is the Sun as it moves through the zodiacal signs on its ecliptic.

In Acts 13:49, it is written, "and the word (seed) of the Lord (from Aries, the Hill of Mars) was spread abroad through all the region (the Zodiac; the body)." Paul is the Sun in Gemini (Pollux). Which sign is his *adversary?* I taught you that the adversary, Satan, is always the sign opposite of that which the Sun is in. What is opposite of Gemini? Sagittarius. Paul in Gemini becomes Saul in Sagittarius, and as the Bible reaffirms to the egos of the materialist dunces who begin to literalize the allegory, "Paul is Saul." Clearly, those who wrote the Bible underestimated how low humanity could sink.

This is why the rays of the Sun on the pediment of St. Paul's Cathedral, located in the City of London, are striking a group of men on horseback. During the end of Spring and the beginning of Summer, the sunbeams of May strike down the constellation of Sagittarius. Don't believe this. This book will be released during the time of year where you can observe this astrological occurrence.

It isn't Apostle Paul at the top of the pediment from which the sunbeams radiate. It's Pollux, from the constellation of Gemini. It's not Christianity. It's a pagan deity. As a neutral bystander, I'm not attacking either. I'm defending the innocent from both of your depraved solar cults that refuse to admit the Truth.

In Exodus 15, this is enucleated, "I sing to Jehovah, For triumphing He hath triumphed; the horse and its rider He hath thrown into the sea. Chariots of the Pharaoh and his force He hath cast into the sea. They went down into the depth as a stone (Earth; the Abyss where the Rock, God, the Sun, Apollo, Jesus, is born (Capricorn; the Manger of the Goat)).

"It consumed them as stubble (the stubs of stalks left in a field where a crop has been cut and harvested by the scythe, Death, Father Time, the Grim Reaper, Saturn, ruler of Capricorn, the sign after Sagittarius).

"Thou has blown with Thy wind (the Air of Pollux, Gemini, the lungs, and John, the Voice, Aquarius; two of the Air Triplicities). The sea hath covered them; They sank as lead in mighty waters. Earth swallowed them!" The element of lead corresponds to Saturn

218

as well as Earth (Capricorn) and Aquarius (Air), with the bottom of the sea being Pisces.

Remember the way words and letters are composed, as symbols, to convey different ideas to those who see them in the next passage of Exodus 15, "And Miriam the inspired one, sister of Aaron, taketh the timbrel in her hand, and all the women go out after her, with timbrels and with choruses; and Miriam answereth to them: 'Sing ye to Jehovah, For Triumphing He hath triumphed; The horse and its rider He hath thrown into the sea!'"

'Miriam' sounds like 'Mary-am,' as in "Mare I am, Mary I am," which automatically indicates to the reader that the constellation of Virgo, the Sea, Taurus, Cancer, or the Moon is being referred to, or at the very least, something related to them is being divulged. So how do we know which astrological reality is the subject of this passage? It alludes to something in her *hand*.

She *taketh the timbrel in her hand*, which is an Oriental hand-drum comparable to a tambourine, but the profane will never suspect the Truth because those types of instruments are not used in *temple* service, or service regarding sections marked off in the sky. The only percussion instruments used in temple service, pertaining to this era and these religious cults, were cymbals.

Phonetically, cymbals are symbols, and so the timbrel is a symbol of something. Of the options available (Virgo, the Sea, Taurus, Cancer, or the Moon), which has something in its hand that is symbolic to an astrological reality? Virgo. Which alpha star is in the constellation Virgo's hand? Spica, the Virgin's Spike, ear of corn, or wheat stalks.

At this time of year, Spica is on the meridian, thus the sons of Israel are going out with a high hand; Aries is leaving (descending), and Sagittarius is ascending. Following Aries is Taurus, thus the Egyptians are pursuing them, indicating that as the Christ, the oil, descends from the cerebrum, the conscious God-mind, the next part of the body, or the sign that follows, is the cerebellum, the unconscious animal-mind.

The trial that the hue-mans must win in this world is to raise their consciousness from acting in purely an instinctual manner, return to the mind of reason, and act in a way where the conscious behavior of understanding tempers the emotional nature of reacting.

The Sun (the Cristos) descends from the Gate of Heaven (Cancer), down through the Heart (Leo) and into the loins, or in a woman, the womb: the matrix. This symbolizes the spiritual involution of the soul from the divine Ego of the Creator. It is found throughout history in depictions of lions with virgin heads, representing the Sun's journey from Leo into Virgo, which is why Inanna is in the company of a lion. But if you research the internet these days, you'll see nothing but spiritually retarded, profane ignoramuses (muses who ignore Truth) describing everything about her *except* for the true meaning of her symbolism. Any time a work depicts a goddess next to a lion, you can be sure the relationship of the house and constellation of Leo preceding Virgo is the topic at hand, unless it is a virgin or goddess preceding a lion. Then it must be the precession of the Aeons or the spiritual houses' nature being conveyed.

'Virgo' is Latin for "a virgin maiden." Virgo is Mary, who is also Lucifer, the bearer of Light: Jesus, the Christ, the Truth, the Sun, *the way.* How do we know this? Pretty simple: The Roman mythology of Venus comes from the Greek mythology of Aphrodite.

What does Aphrodite mean? "Foam-sprung." How did Venus manifest? She *rose* or "sprung" from the foam of the sea after Saturn (Time) castrated Caelus, who is Uranus. So now we see an even deeper meaning behind the symbol of the *rose* and the *cross* known as *the rosy cross.* It represents not only the nature of this reality, but also the allegory describing it known as the Virgin and the Christ she bears. 'Tau' means "cross," and 'rus' symbolizes the "rose," which describes reddish colors ('rooi' in Afrikaans, 'ruz' in Breton, 'rudh' in Cornish, 'rossu' in Corsican, 'rouge' in French, 'rood' in Dutch, 'rot' in German, 'rosso' in Italian, 'ros' in Lombard, 'rosu' in Romanian, and so on). What could be more beautiful than the imaginations of the people who depicted this? Only the Will of God that creates Nature is more impressive.

'Venus' is the Latin word for "love," and Virgo is purified emotion, elimination of desire and unadulterated lower nature, so my interpretation of this allegory is that Time will eventually give us enough perspective to free our spiritual nature from our lower nature, and only the refinement of this quintessence, the Spirit, may enable the Lamp in the cerebrum to remain eternally lit, thus manifesting love from the pure sea of emotion, the Child of the Waters, the Plain and Even Way (the Chinese name for Spica). 'Venus' is where we get words like 'venery,' which is a noun meaning "the gratification of sexual desire," but also "the practice or sport of hunting; the chase." This is why all meat obtained by hunting was known as 'venison' to the ancients, but has been manipulated to only refer to deer meat in current times.

The Babylonians called Spica "the Might of the Abode of Life," and the Hindu astrologists referred to Spica as Citra, a *lamp* or *pearl* being its symbol. What lights the Lamp in the cerebrum? Pure thoughts, emotions, and actions, all in unison, all adhering to the Natural Law of God, meaning: they don't cause harm to others or to one's body.

Spica is in the hand of the Virgin, and in the Bible, she is Miriam, Miryam. Remember Yam, the sea-god, as well as Yama and Yami, the Vedic names for the Gemini twins, because every soul is birthed through the vesica piscis of a womb, a matrix of Mary. You indeed are on Mary's Time, Maritime, the Law of the Pure Sea, the Virgin Mary.

'Eve' means "life, living one, source of life," and the Fall occurs after Virgo, so by severing our lower nature of animal desires, we prevent the life force from falling, thus we thwart the loss of our own life, our seed. This is also why nightfall is referred to as the 'evening,' because if you look at a Zodiac wheel, night begins in Libra, just after Virgo.

The seed, the corn, planted in the barren earth, produces Spica, which is symbolical to an ear of corn or stalks of wheat, and is encoded in what Jacob says in Genesis 49:20, "Out of Asher his bread is fat (oil; the Cristos: Christ); And he giveth dainties of a king (the delicious delicacy produced by the Summer Sun, the King: Herod, Leo)." Virgo is Bethlehem, the House of Bread.

The Hebrew/Phoenician word for the 'Virgin' is 'Bethulah.' The Bread of Life that comes from the House of Bread is the oil, the Christ, because the bread is fat, the Water of Life, the message of God carried by Mercury (argentum vivum) from the throne of God, the Seed of Aries. And this is the simile: the seed is the Word.

In India, Virgo was Kanya, mother of Chreeshna, because

Christianity is the hex that comes from India (so long as it hides the Truth). She was Rhea-Hecate, who the Greeks that settled in Asia called Rhea, and the Phrygians (in Turkey) named Cybele (Κυβηλη in Greek), drawn by lions, because Leo comes before Virgo.

Virgo was Inanna, Isis, Ceres, Maia (May Day), Juno, Coronis, Rebekah, Rachel, the Lute-Bearer (Spica) and Repa in Egypt (because the Black Magi come from Hindoostan and Chreeshna plays a flute and is a cow herder, hence the reason they based Isis off of Virgo and Luna is exalted in Taurus, the Bull), Ruth, and most pertinent to the modern slavery in America, she is Columbia.

Any initiate of the occult would have serious warning bells going off in his mind, were he taught the sacred science as a child, because as he was introduced to the history of **Christ**opher **Columb**us (the Sun in Virgo) "discovering" America, he wouldn't buy the lies by virtue of the knowledge he has that Christ is born of a Virgin, the '**Columba**,' a Latin word for '**dove**.' This is where the English word '**dive**' originates due to the dove's swimming motion in the air. Doves are symbols of virgins, purity, and balance, in addition to being a symbol of Virgo.

However, in Spanish, Columbus' first name was '**Cristóbal**,' which when split becomes '**Christ-Baal**,' because Ba'al is the Sun and Jesus is the Sun. The same esoteric knowledge is encoded in the name '**Christian Bale**,' whose first major motion picture appearance was in the film *Empire of the Sun*. I want to make it clear that none of this is good or bad. It just is. My opinion of it or of him is irrelevant.

Whether the actor is aware of it or not, his name is Christ-Baal, one and the same Sun deity, and the launch of his career was planned to correspond to the global Empire of the Sun that has never set in thousands of years. For someone to think that this is coincidence only proves how mentally retarded and deranged the hue-man species has become. But when you are aware of the languages that are used in the symbolism all around you, you will see how unoriginal and repetitive the slavery systems throughout the ages are.

What is the city-state that controls the civilly dead entity known as a U.S. Citizen, a Roman slave? The District of Columbia (Virgo). Dear friends and enemies of Truth alike, Christopher Columbus was the father of Pizzagate in America. Of course, only the most spiritually warped egos can still believe that Columbus discovered America. He was one of the proponents of raping the real Americans and making today's slavery possible. Hollywood loves him. What is the symbol of Columbia Pictures? The Virgin Goddess holding the torch of Truth, of the Christ. What do the Black Magi call virgin priestesses that they use in rituals? Columbs (doves).

This is the Statue of Liberty, or as Revelation 12:1-6 states, "A great sign (Virgo constellation) appeared in heaven: a woman clothed with the sun, with the moon under her feet and a crown of *twelve stars* on her head." This is the end of September, hence Michael's emergence: Michaelmas-day, approximately September 29th. If you cannot see this, your headlight, your Holy of Holies, the optic thalamus, is calcified and off.

If your Eye of Providence is not working, then you cannot gain this knowledge without initiation, which is why you don't even realize that the Book of Enoch literally means "the Book of the Initiated," because '**enoch**' means "initiated." The Bible preserves its knowledge and reveals it only for the initiated or those whose eye is single: perfect. It is admitted in 2 Corinthians 4:6, "Out of Darkness light is to shine."

Out of the womb of Virgo, the bowels of the Earth, comes the world-soul, the Sun itself, and thus no light is needed if the eye is perfect. You may discover this knowledge with the Lamp in the cerebrum, and then corroborate it in the physical world. For those in the investigative community who are exploring the nature of our Earth, I would suggest exploring the idea that this occulted knowledge indicates the Earth created the Sun, not the other way around.

The perfect form of Heaven created the physical world in its center, and out of that center manifested the wandering bodies that weave all life into existence through dielectricity, magnetism, electricity, charge and discharge, space and counterspace (the intervals of Time: Saturn), centrifugal and centripetal force, and convergence and divergence. Thus, Earth and all life is Natura Naturata, meaning "Nature Natured," the product of perfection: Divine Nature.

To strengthen intuition, the physical body and mind must be healthy. Therefore, it is imperative that all students of the occult focus on the food conspiracies and the healthcare conspiracies. If you cannot become healthy and preserve that state, then you are not fit to acquire and preserve knowledge.

19 SAL DUPLICATUM

In Matthew 13:11, the Bible confirms its astrological knowledge to the initiated, "To you it hath been given to know the secrets of the reign of the heavens." It's astounding that people remain at a child-like level of consciousness where they interpret everything that the Bible says in a literal sense, *except* for when the Bible admits its astro-theological facts.

A great example that pertains to the subject at hand would be in Luke 1:26-28, "And in the **sixth month** was the messenger of Gabriel sent by God, to a city of Galilee, the name of which is Nazareth, to a **virgin**, betrothed to a man, whose name of the virgin is **Mary.** And the messenger **having come in unto her**, said, 'Hail, favored one, the **Lord** is with thee; blessed art thou among women.'"

Right away, using the skills we've taught, one should be able to comprehend that regardless of what the sixth month is, this passage speaks of the Sun (Lord) going into a virgin, which is the sixth month. Which astrological sign of the Zodiac is the virgin? Virgo, the Latin word meaning "virgin."

The literalist interpreter will build an argument that Luke 1 cannot be astro-theology because the sixth month of year is June which is, at the very earliest, Gemini or, at the very latest, Cancer. Clearly one ought to appreciate that the sixth month is not Virgo. Their arguments are nothing but structures of ignorance, built without blueprints of the sacred science or even knowledge of the last millennia of history. So put your dunce hat on and go sit in the corner while the authentic people go to work right now.

The first month of the calendar of Romulus is March (Martius), not January. The temple of the most high, of the Lord of Hosts, is not Aquarius, but Aries. The Spring Equinox marks the end of Winter, of Hell, of the Abyss. The reign of the Kingdom of Heaven begins on this date, and so when anyone in the world of the occult refers to anything related to months, seasons, time, the templums, etc., the first is *always* Aries. Anything contrary to this is *wrong*. With Aries being the reckoning for the first house and March being the first month, what now do you count as the sixth month? It's August 23: Virgo. Indisputable. Take your know-less-than-nothing egos to the tool shed and slaughter them.

In the Realm of Spirit, Gabriel is the angel that corresponds to Luna, the Moon, and so he corresponds to the mind, the higher planes and blessings of spiritual and mental evolution. '**Galilee**' literally means "circuit," and corresponds to a *circle of water or fluid*, or in our physiology, the *circulatory system*.

The root word of Nazareth is '**nazar**,' which is "to consecrate or separate oneself." As '**Cana**' has been shown to mean "a dividing place," which is cognate with the Greek word for "reeds," it corresponds to the lungs because lungs provide us with the means to make sound much like reeds provide wind instruments the means to make sound. The lungs correspond to the Twins of May: Gemini, which is the sign or house that comes after the one which Luna (Gabriel) exalts in (Taurus) but before the one the she rules (Cancer).

There is also another word that is phonetically related to '**nazar**,' and that word is '**nasar**,' which means "to guard or preserve," such as one's chastity, purity, or original form. '**Nasar**' also means "to keep closed, to blockade," such as one's legs and orifices. It has a third meaning which is "to guard secrets," exactly the way the scriptures do.

According to the Abarim Publications' Biblical Dictionary, the Arabic word '**nasar**' is "to be fresh or bright, or grow green." Take that with a grain of salt, but perhaps it corresponds to even deeper symbolism. What color is the heart chakra? Green. What color balances the light spectrum? Green. What is '**heart**' an anagram for? Earth. What color does the Earth produce the most abundance of? Green. Which element does Virgo correspond to? Earth. Virgo is the bowels of the Earth. The heart balances your body but the digestive system accounts for approximately 80% of the hue-man's immune system. They work together to alkalize and purify your body, along with the other organs.

Cancer rules the breast, stomach, and spleen, which are tucked into the bottom of the lungs. The mind, Gabriel, acknowledges that the Virgin is blessed among women, because to guard one's purity (nazar-eth) and remain unadulterated is the only way to return a portion of the seed. In agriculture, Virgo (August 23 – September 23) is the time of year to reap what we have sown and stock that abundance for the five months of Winter. This is why her womb is said to be fruitful and blessed amongst women.

However, there is also a deep psychology embedded into the minds of men in which virginal maidens are highly coveted, so much so that some consider a woman to be ruined if she is not a virgin. Our species is very materialistic, and ascribes the highest value to all products in their new, original, unadulterated, pure, and virginal form. This deep psychological influence no doubt comes from the perfect form of Heaven, the forces of Virgo, Venus, and the Moon, and depending on where they are when one manifests leads to how intense that intuition is.

The ancients have been teaching people to heed these principles so that they intentionally conceive at times that will produce balanced human beings based on what age the race is in, but these warnings have been largely ignored and thought of as pseudo science. But you're the Uniform Commercial Code, Maritime Admiralty Law, Roman Civil Law, municipal law slave, so I'm sure you have all the answers anyways and need not continue this journey.

We taught you that Joseph is Mercury in the Old Testament. In the New Testament, the virgin is betrothed to a man named Joseph. Who rules Virgo? Mercury. So in an occult way, this preserves the knowledge that Virgo is indeed betrothed to Mercury, the messenger of the gods, who enables the Royal Marriage of the Sun and the Moon, the Blade and the Chalice, the Yang and the Yin.

Luke 1 continues to disclose that Virgo will bring forth a son named Jesus (the Sun) who will *reign over the house of Jacob to the ages*, and there shall be no end to his reign. Which house does the Sun (Jack, Jacob) rule? Leo (July 23 – August 23). Joseph of the house of David indicates the sign that David, the Sun, is exalted in, the sign of Aries, the most high, because Mercury carries the seed of the Sun and the Moon, of Aries and Taurus (the cerebrum and cerebellum), which enables the spiritual message of the mind, Gabriel, to travel down through the nerve ganglia into the lungs where water, air, is turned into wine, blood, and allows the heart to pulse it throughout the circulatory system: Galilee. Interestingly enough, when I observe the Sun, it appears to pulse. My experience is not necessarily the Truth, but perhaps there is something to that.

The physiological process of the body taking in air and drinking clean water and purifying its blood is what it means to turn water into wine. This process of breathing enables one to use his voice, the Voice (John the Baptist) to deliver the Truth (Jesus), for it is only by using one's voice that he can speak the Truth. By using the voice, you sing in the Voice of Aquarius, the Age of Freedom.

The Truth comes from a pure place just as Jesus comes from the Virgin Mary. It comes from a guttural place just as the Sun rises from the Winter Solstice in the earthy sign of Capricorn after descending through the bowels, the sex organs, and the legs. When you know the Truth without having evidence, you have "a gut feeling" about it, and thus when you confess how you truly feel by speaking the Truth, you are said to "spill your guts."

Luke 1:39 depicts the Sun moving into the constellation of Virgo in the month of August, "And Mary having arisen in those days, went to the hill-country (the upper/visible hemisphere), with haste, to a city of Judea (Leo/late August)." This time of year is when the ancient cultures observed the positions of the stars and recognized that the fruit, specifically corn, was ripe, and that temple in the sky was marked off by a group of stars that they attributed to a young maiden with a spike of corn (Spica) in her hand (Vindemiatrix), hence they refer to her as the hand-maid of the Lord (the Sun).

In Luke 1:42, Virgo is described, "Blessed art thou among women, and blessed is the fruit of thy womb." This time of year, when the Virgin is blessed, coincides to the warm end of Summer, August through September, because her "soul doth magnify the

Lord," the Summer Sun.

During the end of Winter, in February, the constellation Virgo is at her lowest point. The Sun, God, brings down the mighty of Winter (the constellations like Orion and Canis Major) and exalts the lowly constellations of Winter during the fruitful months of Summer, filling the hungry with good and sending the rich away empty (think about all the enriched grapes being pressed into wine).

Though Joseph is Mercury in the Old Testament, there is sufficient evidence that he also has an astronomical correspondence to the constellation Boötes in the New Testament, which has the literal meaning of "plowman, herdsman, or ox-driver." This is because the constellation rises with Virgo into hill-country (the sky) and sets with her in the west (goes down into Egypt, the fertile soils of darkness).

One cannot ignore the correspondence of the meaning "ox-driver" to Egypt, which in addition to being beneath the horizon corresponds to the cerebellum in the head, as well as the astrological sign of Taurus, which the Moon, Isis, Virgo, Mary, exalts in and Venus (Mary) rules. At the Temple of Isis in Sais, an inscription was said to have been written, "I, Isis, am all that has been, that is, or shall be; no mortal man hath ever me unveiled. The fruit which I have brought forth is the Sun."

Where did the Egyptians come from? Hindoostan. What is Chreeshna? A calf-herder, an ox-driver or Boötes, if you will. Approximately 6000 years ago marked the beginning of the Sun in the Age of Taurus, due to the procession of the equinoxes, and the Moon, Isis, the Goddess, is exalted in Taurus. The name Joseph is "Io, the Lord, the Sun, shall increase or add" ('Jo' = Io = Sun + 'seph').

The name Joseph for the constellation Boötes indicates the time of year that the Sun increases or adds to the abundance of crops. And since Isis brought forth the Sun, not only does the sign Leo come before Virgo, but also the constellation Virgo brings forth Boötes, who is also named after the Lord.

In physiology, Virgo corresponds to Kali sulph (potassium sulphate). It was known as 'arcanum' in the middle ages, which comes from 'arcanus,' meaning "secret, mystery," as well 'arca,' which is "a chest or strong box used in ancient times to protect valuables," and 'arcere,' which is a verb that means "to keep close, confine, prevent, hinder, protect, separate, ward, or enclose." This is where the myth of Arcas and Arcadia comes from.

Arcas, Arcadia's greatest hunter according to the allegory, accidentally killed his mother, who had been turned into a bear. Zeus took pity and honored the tragedy by creating the constellations of the big and little bears (Ursa Major and Minor). The Greeks referred to the Big Dipper as "the Plough" and Boötes is its driver.

'Arcturus' means "guardian of the bear," and is the alpha star of Boötes. The meaning of 'arca' joins it directly to 'nasar,' "to guard secrets," especially the secret to finding Polaris, as well as the secret of Nazareth, because Jesus of Nazareth is the secret that is guarded in the strong box, the womb of the Virgin Mary: **The fruit which I have brought forth is the Sun.**

The symbol of Virgo predates the use of letters, and it's still used today. The monogram used for Virgo, upon further inspection, is merely the combination of the symbols that we use today as letters to compose the name **Mary: M + Y.**

The deep symbolism of Mary grieving at the foot of the cross is symbolical of the astrological occurrence that takes place every year in the sign that follows Virgo: the Autumnal Equinox, where the Sun is crucified, or crosses the equinoctial line into Autumn, where the days become shorter and the nights longer until the Sun "dies," or stands still (Winter Solstice).

The sixth of the seven Asiatic churches, or Summer months of the "reign of heaven" (Aries through Libra), is Smyrna, which is Virgo. Just as a refresher, 'Smyrna' means "myrrh." Add the letter 'a' to 'myrrh' and it becomes 'Myrrha,' the mother of Adonis, who we've illustrated is the Sun. Is Myrrha so dissimilar to Mary that you cannot see or hear the obvious?

Since Mary is the sea, the mare, it takes no stretch of the imagination to see how the Ave Maria Stella pertains to her, because 'Maria' is the plural form of 'mare,' the adjective of which is 'marina,' meaning "of the sea, of mare, of Mary." This is why the Romans referred to Venus as 'Marine Venus,' and the Greeks referred to her as 'Venus Anadyomene,' because she was rising out of the sea. It is precisely where we get the English words 'marine,' 'mariner,' and most importantly, as it pertains to this black magick slavery system, the word 'maritime.'

'Ave Maria (Maris) Stella' translates to "Hail, Star of the Sea (Mary)" in Latin. It's known as a Vespers hymn, which is a sunset evening prayer service, because Vesper is Venus at night, Lucifer, Lord of the Night, the evening star, and Venus, bright Lucifer, is Mary, one of the planetary correspondences to Virgo. This is the real meaning of Lucifer, the bearer of light, in the occult world. Only the most spiritually retarded ignoramuses believe that Lucifer is a masculine, devil-like, antichrist entity: usually so-called Christians, Mormons, Satanists, and other branches of the inbred solar cults (not to be confused with honest people who adhere to Natural Law but were raised under these cults).

The word 'Sol' is almost phonetically identical to the root word for 'salt.' This is because the Latin word for "salt" is 'sal.' Regarding the world of the occult, the salt that corresponds to the cerebrum is known as Kali phos (phosphate of potassium), and it is known as the Aries salt.

Physiologically, Kali phos is what generates spiritual electricity, and it endows matter with life. It is the causality of man's manifestation in the physical form. Using rudimentary experiments, one can observe that salt conducts electricity and responds to magnetism. Ever wonder why the tides occur in the oceans all around the world but not over the Great Lakes, which are the size of small oceans? What's the difference in the water? The salt content. If you believe that the Moon's "gravity" is strong enough to pull our oceans' tides but not able to attract its own atmosphere or create tides in the Great Lakes, there's nothing this work can help you with.

Clearly, it is observable that the gravity of the Moon is not what causes the tides. This is childish **baal**shit that only incompetents believe. If the gravity of the Moon caused the tides over the oceans, the Great Lakes would not be exempt from this Natural Law. Apparently, the pedophile human trafficking murderers of the solar cult forgot that real science is not Burger King. No, you cannot have it your way, fool.

In today's perverted world, the corporations abuse their employees by locking them into 'salaries,' and then overworking them so that their hourly wages depreciate. Our salaries are determined by how much our energy charges for or discharges profit (prophet). The more profits (prophets) we charge for employers, the higher the salaries we earn. 'Salaries' is the combination of two Latin words, 'sal' + 'aries,' which literally would be salt + ram, "the salt of the ram," the salt of the most high: the 'Salt of Aries.'

A popular idiom of the past for describing whether or not someone was worth his salary, or wage, was "to be or not to be worth one's salt." Those who are worth their Salt of Aries are usually people who facilitate the business in making 'sales/sails' that maintain profit (prophet) 'margins' for the 'merchants.'

As we've shown, 'mar' is related to "the sea," both through Mary and Mars, and 'gin' is a 'spirit' with high alcohol content. Sailors used to drink gin gimlets because they believed it kept them healthy, but a phonetically identical word for 'gin' is what people in the Middle East refer to as 'jinn,' which are 'spirits' that exist in a similar nature of 'demons,' but unlike demons, they have the free will to be benevolent, malevolent, or morally neutral.

The jinn that cut themselves off from the Creator and serve only themselves are known as shaytan jinn. Shaytan is phonetically cognate with Satan, and the demons in the Arabic world are known as the shayateen. Therefore the phonetic identity of the word 'margins' (mar-jinns) is equivalent to 'sea-spirits,' or spirits of the sea (mar-gins). 'Mer' is also a word that means "of the sea, or pertaining to a sea creature," hence the word 'mermaid' also means "maid of the sea," just like Mary is the maid of the sea and her constellation, Virgo, is the hand-maid of God.

'Merchants' are "chanters of the sea." They put their wares on sale to satisfy the demand of their 'customers.' The Latin word 'custos' is "a custodian or guardian of established laws and/or usages." The Galicians, who were known as being great fishermen, have a word 'custo' that means "cost," and its Portuguese correspondent is 'costar,' which is "to cost." This is because the 'customers' are the custodians of the costs, the prices, in the world of business, which is called Commerce because it is regulated by the Law of the Sea (in a free natural market): Maritime Admiralty Law. The customers' demand for goods relative to the supply of those goods dictates the costs of the wares that sea-chanters (merchants) charge them for.

If the **mer**chant doesn't have de-sirable sales (sails), the custome**r**s will not pur**chase** the wares. If there is no transaction (trance-action), then there will be no relation-**ship** to make sails for. They must put you in a trance of elation, of security, of satiation. A 'pur' is "an expression of contentment or pleasure," and quite literally a 'trance,' a "half-conscious state." Hence the reason (re-sun) we make impulsive trance-actions and chase purs. This is why businesses put so much emphasis on custom**er** satisfaction, and cater to their selfish childlike whims, because "the customer is always right." That is about the most satanic ideology one can have, but nearly all businesses espouse it despite their right to refuse service.

If there is no business relationship, then there is no **trans**action in which current-sea and merchant-**dice** (merchant ice) are exchanged. The merchant is not serving ice, or providing service (serve-ice). 'Trans-' is a prefix that means "across, beyond, through," and also "changing thoroughly."

The verb 'dice' means "to gamble with dice, or to lose by gambling with dice," but also "to cut into small cubes." As the merchant dices the current-sea, the relation-ship makes a wake of **change** for the guardian of the sea (the customer). It has "changed the currency thoroughly" in a trans-action.

'Mer-' comes from the Old English word 'mere,' which means "sea, ocean, lake, pond, pool." When **mer-chant-ice** is on sale, you save money, one-eye, the seed of the Salt of Aries, because money, or current-sea, regardless of its perceived value, is measured and procured by how much of your labor, or energy, you exchanged to acquire it. The One-Eyed Jack is the Eye of Providence, the Sun in Aries, the seed returned to the cerebrum.

You can get mare-eed (sea-oath; married) and be the groom to a mare (a female horse, whores), but which horse do you make your sea oath to? Which whore? The Whore of Babylon (bay-bee-loan), because your marriage turns your relationship into a business institution, a corporation, and your spouse becomes your partner, and each child you produce, each bay-bee, is loaned out to El-On-Don, London, the Temple of Time (Crown Temple), the new

Babalon, but under the rule of the same old patriarchal Lord Sun-God, so that your baby's stock can mature and produce more moon-honey for the Queen Bee. It's all about making that money, honey.

But what happens after the Black Magi of Commerce have whored you out and pimped you for all that you're worth? Matthew 5:13 explains, "Ye are of the **salt** of the land: but if the salt may lose savor, in what shall it be salted? For nothing is good henceforth, except to be cast without, and to be trodden down by men."

It is not the trade of goods, assets, or currencies that destroys our seed, our salt. Trade and the use of competing currencies under the Natural Law of the Land, Freedom, facilitates a better quality of life. It is this legal fiction degenerate black magick system based on the Law of the Seas that destroys us. Water dissolves salt. Salt must remain on land in order for it to crystallize, vibrate, and multiply. In order for people to be sovereign, their lives must not be governed by the Law of the Sea, or even man's law, but by Natural Law.

Our **salvation** will come from the benefic qualities of 'commerce,' which is '**com-**,' meaning "together, with, and completely," and '**merce**,' meaning "goods" in Italian but also "mercy" in French ('**mercé**'). When we have complete mercy and only engage in trade that benefits both parties, each deal blessing those involved with complete goods and a mutual feeling that the deal was a win for all, we can slowly transition into not only an abundance-based economy, but also a gift-based economy.

When looking at '**salvation**,' we see three words '**sal**,' '**vati**,' and '**on**.' Knowing that '**sal**' means "salt," and '**on**' means "the being," but also pertains to "the Sun; Helios," we have only to weave it together with '**vati**,' a Latin word for "a seer, a prophet." Thus, to be spiritually profitable through our '**salvation**,' we must be "Prophets for the Salt of Aries," where the Lord of Hosts resides, where the cerebrum creates the seed, where the Sun, God, is exalted, the temple of the most high.

The Divine cannot contact one who destroys his or her seed. In order to receive Divine Inspiration, one must preserve the seed and return a portion of it to God, the conscious God-mind, the optic thalamus. You have no power to make contact with that which you cannot attract.

For all of you who struggle every day against your carnal taurine nature, making conscious efforts to minimize suffering and to abstain from behavior that causes harm to others, you are the ones who are programming Freedom. You are the real servants of God. Regardless of your ideology or motives, if your behavior is not contributing to the violations of Natural Law, I salute you.

20 RE-SUN TO LIVE

Ra (Re), Horus, Ba'al, Jesus, Arez, Amun, Moloch, Zeus, Apollo, Chreeshna, Zoroaster, Bacchus, etc., are all Sun-gods. That's the primary symbolism that's dominated the last ten thousand years or so and is the black magick that still manipulates people to create the current condition of this re-ality. But when we strip away the personifications, what's really the nature of it? Is the Sun really an ally to us?

What is the reason for this occult symbolism, regarding the Sun, that has literally blinded humanity for over ten millennia? What are we re-charging, re-suscitating, re-surrecting, re-plenishing, re-quiring, re-linquishing, re-peating, re-membering, re-constructing, re-moving, re-accepting, re-accessing, re-acquainting, re-activating, re-adjusting, re-admitting, re-aligning, re-authorizing, re-considering, re-defining, re-connecting, re-designing, re-directing, re-awakening, etc.? The Sun. The **Re-Sun**, or **re-son**, the son of the Sun (Re), the Sun in Aries, Arez in Aries, the seat of reason, the Eye of Providence, the Eye Single, the symbol of which is occulted in the letter 'A.' This is the Re-A-Son.

We **re-alize** our dreams, but also ourselves, in this mental state of Ra (Re), this re-ality under the absolute Truth of the One. The suffix '-ize' means "to cause or become like something specified." 'Alizé' is a French word that means "trade wind." In Germanic, the name 'Alizé' means "of a noble kind" while in Hebrew it means "joyful." Is Jupiter, Jove, not the jovial one, the giver of all good things?

The modern name Jupiter comes from the Latin Iuppiter, but before that it was connected to Zeus-Ammon (Jupiter Ammon). 'Jew' was the name of God, which was pronounced with a soft zeta or a sigma by the Greeks (Ζεύς), which is where Zeus comes from. Zeus was the son of Rhea, who we explained was Virgo, Isis, Mary, and all of the other female depictions of the Goddess previously enucleated. Zeus sired Ares, who is the Roman Mars, but whose name is phonetically linked to the Egyptian Arez, which was the Sun.

Where was the throne of Zeus, of God, in Greek Mythology? Mount Olympus. Are you able to see how Rhea and Zeus are Mary and Jesus? Are you able to see how Mount Olympus is the Hill of Mars, of Ares, of Arez, of Aries? If not, I have failed you. It's so beyond obvious that, if this doesn't help you, there's nothing left I can do. Research all the relations to the Sun that Zeus has throughout history. Perhaps you just need to see the work of someone else in order to grasp it.

The Priests of Apollo, the interpreters of the Oracles of Apollo, were called πατέρες (Pateres, Peters), which pertains to the wisdom of prophets or seers, not to being a father as the literalists translate it. Its Proto-Indo-European root words indicate that it is related to the "sky" and "shining light." The fatherly nature ascribed to this is that of a priest of the Lord, of God: the Sun. Catholics ascribe the same value to their priests today, "Forgive me, Father, for I have sinned."

This is yet another key to observing that the Priests of Apollo went to Rome, where the name of the supreme deity *Jew' Peter* is barely veiled as *St. Peter.* 'Peter,' where 'Pater' or 'Petor' comes from, is originally an Egyptian word for the priests of Jupiter Ammon (Ammonian Priests). Without the knowledge of the Language of the Birds, it is nearly impossible to track these Satanists. But in light of the Truth, it becomes obvious. This is why so many of them are obsessed with preserving and tracing their lineages back to Ancient Egypt and beyond, but also the reason they burn books and destroy the evidence that would link them to who you now know they are.

Reality is a state of Ra (Re) where, through self re-alization, the "joyful, noble trade winds" of our voices speak the Truth of our divine souls that comprise the divine Ego of the One from which

237

they descended. Speaking the Truth programs our re-ality with the divine rays of light from our Creator. There is no higher service to the Creator than trading the noble Truth with others by using the winds of our voices. This enables the lower self to soar to new heights in its spiritual evolution and transcend the dualistic zoo of the Zodiac.

The more souls that descend into this dualistic illusion of matter, the more energy waves (sine waves) are created, and the more turbulent the seas become, much like a public pool that becomes too crowded. If no one leaves and everyone stays in the pool, splashing around and pissing everywhere, it destroys the right of everyone's ability of quiet enjoyment of the pool. It works the same way in Nature. Even the air we breathe is a gas, and gases can behave like liquids. We are in an ocean of magnetic and electric energy.

What is the sine wave? Santos Bonacci teaches that it is the sin of Eve, the fall of the soul into matter. The meaning of 'Eve' in Hebrew (חַוָּה; 'Chavvah') is "life," and so the sin of Eve is the loss of life. The sine wave illustrates the cycles of life and death just as the Ave Maria does. It reads, "Hail Mary, full of grace, the Lord is with thee. Blessed art thou amongst women and blessed is the fruit of thy womb, Jesus. Holy Mary, Mother of God, pray for us sinners now, and in the hour of our death. Amen."

If the Mother of God is the sea, it would explain why God/El/Dagon is a fish god, and why Jesus is the Fisher of Men and the son of God. Are any of these metaphorical allegories true in re-ality? Did the oceans of Earth create the Sun, or did the Sun create the ineffable sphere of the Zodiac, the ecliptic by which it moves being its track, and the movement of the luminous bodies churning from its magnetic affinity? Did the ancients know the true mechanism of this world, and if so, how did they discover it?

What type of energy is digital currency? It is el-ectric. Does that indicate that digital currency is designed by and for the whims of Time (El/Saturn)? Are the el-ite merely agents, templars, for Saturn? Time and time again, a gain, they have re-set our monetary system to suit their needs while everyone else loses their currency and the el-ites reap massive profits (prophets) from the transfers of wealth.

Tau is the 22nd and last letter of the Hebrew alphabet. Something that many of you are seeing lately corresponds to 22. How often do you look at the Time and see 11:11? 11 + 11 = 22, the last, the Tau Cross, which corresponds to the cross of Thamuz, Tammuz: the Sun. This is because the first is the last and the last is the first. The end is the beginning. The Angel of Death becomes the Angel of Life, and as this book ends, the next one begins...

Now that you know 'eve' means "life," surely you can appreciate that the **Apple of Sin** is the **Apple of the Moon**, which makes it the **Apple of the Mind**, of the **Mind's Eye**, the **Apple of the Eye**. The **Apple of Eve** is the **Apple of Life**, and so it must be eaten to participate in the **Play of Eve**, which is **A Play of Life** because all the world's a stage.

And Elijah saith to them, "**Catch ye the prophets of Baal; let not a man escape of them;**" and they catch them, and Elijah bringeth them down unto the stream Kishon, and doth slaughter them there. – *1 Kings 18:40*

I learned the nature of re-ality and all I re-sire is Leigha

Dylan Michael Saccoccio

ABOUT THE AUTHOR

.

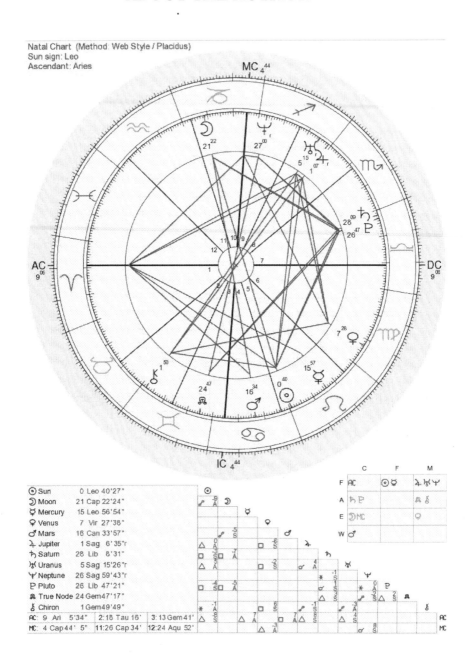

⊙ Sun	0 Leo 40'27"	
☽ Moon	21 Cap 22'24"	
☿ Mercury	15 Leo 56'54"	
♀ Venus	7 Vir 27'38"	
♂ Mars	16 Can 33'57"	
♃ Jupiter	1 Sag 6'35"r	
♄ Saturn	28 Lib 8'31"	
♅ Uranus	5 Sag 15'26"r	
♆ Neptune	26 Sag 59'43"r	
♇ Pluto	26 Lib 47'21"	
☊ True Node	24 Gem 47'17"	
⚷ Chiron	1 Gem 49'49"	
AC: 9 Ari 5'34"	2:18 Tau 16'	3:13 Gem 41'
MC: 4 Cap 44' 5"	11:26 Cap 34'	12:24 Aqu 52'

242